Thinking about behaviour change: an interdisciplinary dialogue

Edited by
Simon Christmas
Susan Michie
Robert West

Silverback Publishing

Copyright © Simon Christmas, Susan Michie and Robert West 2015

The rights of Dr Simon Christmas, Professor Susan Michie and Professor Robert West to be identified as the authors of this work have been asserted in accordance with the Copyright, Designs and Patents Act 1988.

This edition first published in Great Britain in 2015 by Silverback Publishing

All rights reserved. Apart from any use permitted under UK copyright law, this publication may only be reproduced, stored or transmitted, in any form, or by any means, with prior permission in writing of the publishers or, in the case of reprographic production, in accordance with the terms of licences issued by the Copyright Licensing Agency.

A CIP catalogue record for this book is available from the British Library.

Trade Paperback ISBN: 978-1-912141-03-6

Every effort has been made to fulfil requirements with regard to reproducing copyright material.

The author and publisher will be glad to rectify any omissions at the earliest opportunity.

www.silverbackpublishing.org

Table of Contents

Foreword 3

Introduction 7

Models and behaviour change: a dialogue 12

1. Use and usability: are theoretical models of behaviour change practical? 69

2. In defence of the 'non-model': modelling the prevention of teenage tobacco use in Africa 85

3. Model Conduct 95

4. Industrialising behaviour change 105

5. Explanatory and predictive behavioural modelling .. 115

6. The common language of story 127

7. Probability and normativity: reconciling the two 'shoulds' of modelling 135

8. On epistemological and ontological incommensurability in modelling behaviour change . 149

9. Interdisciplinarity in the study of behaviour change: experiences, promises and challenges 165

10. Changing professional behaviour with cognitive engineering 179

11. Economic models in interdisciplinary studies of behaviour change: helpful abstractions or spurious distractions? 193

12. A social practice perspective 207

13. Clearing the pathway to change: a new psychodynamic perspective 223

14. How can we use literature as a tool for understanding and changing behaviour in complex contexts? 237

15. The role of forecasting models in transport planning – an historical perspective 249

16. Explanatory models and conviction narratives 261

17. Models, stories and leaders 273

18. Behaviour change through political influence: the case of tobacco control 283

19. Modelling as a process of describing and creating change 295

20. Behave yourself: why behavioural modelling needs subjective disclosure 309

21. Becoming a force of nature: a new direction for health promotion and disease prevention 323

References 329

Foreword
Lord O'Donnell

Recently behaviour change has become fashionable. But how should we think about human behaviours and how to change them? Social scientists have theories about how and why we behave as we do. Neuroscientists increasingly are looking at how we make decisions. Many others, from engineers and architects to people working in the humanities, offer useful and different perspectives. So do those outside academia: the private sector, for example, has been and remains a big spender in this area, sometimes but not always to the benefit of the consumer All these disciplines and fields of expertise create insights into how to change behaviour but the real traction comes when you start combining the insights from across subject boundaries.

This book contains many such examples and should be required reading for all those interested in behaviour change, particularly policy analysts in all levels of Government.

In different ways, the varied analyses in this book present and/or interrogate a model of how humans behave. Economists probably have the simplest model: people solve a constrained optimisation problem spending their money to achieve maximum satisfaction; and markets are competitive so prices move to equate supply and demand. This is a very powerful model and has allowed economists to become a very strong professional force in policy advice. In the UK Treasury, for example, economists have long been the dominant professional group. When other professionals, or just people using common sense, question economists' models the response is often swift and analytical. Even if there is evidence that questions the behavioural assumptions used, economists may dismiss the need for accuracy by emphasising the "as if" approach: even if the consumer can't solve the problem, s/he acts "as if" s/he could.

Indeed economists in general have been very reluctant to leave behind behavioural assumptions that are clearly not backed up by the available evidence. Until recently, to posit behaviours that are not in line with the standard "rational" assumption has been to run the gauntlet at an economics seminar. (The story of how economists have resisted the attempts of other professions to challenge their model of behaviour is explained very clearly in *Misbehaving* by Richard Thaler.)

In the policy world we are interested primarily in what works. Ministers want to change behaviours to improve people's quality of life, to save taxpayers money and to improve their chances of re-election. To achieve this end we need a genuinely interdisciplinary approach – one that combines the many strengths of economics with the insights that of other disciplines. The growing amount of data available on decisions people make in a variety of situations provides great evidence for testing models and looking for anomalies. If, having consulted the philosophers, we feel that the individuals themselves would be better off if they changed their behaviour, we then need to think how best to achieve this result. The best solutions will be found using an interdisciplinary approach as laid out in this book.

In the UK we are fortunate enough to have 'behavioural insights teams' working in many government departments, including until recently in the Cabinet Office. These are demonstrating how a behavioural approach can improve public policy. One key aspect of their work is the use of testing. Quite often this approach has resulted in findings that were not expected. For example when trialling messages to get people to sign up for organ donation it was believed that adding a picture of smiling people would help: it didn't. Another example was the addition of the CEO's signature to a letter to clients who might be eligible for compensation, which resulted in lower response rates!

However much of Government remains stuck in a world based on assumptions about how people behave that are invalid. Ministers are reluctant to test ideas – or at best think a pilot is the answer. The reality is we do not know enough about how people behave to get policies right without proper testing. That is why I sincerely hope that Ministers and officials will read this book and work out how to apply these ideas in their day jobs.

Introduction

The belief which inspired this book is easy enough to state, much harder to act upon. It's the belief that, if we want to understand and change the behaviour of human beings – never forgetting that 'human beings' means you, me, us – we need to draw on insights from many different perspectives.

Were copyright not an issue, we might have chosen a cubist painting such as Picasso's *Girl with a Mandolin* for the cover of the book. The cubist seeks to present the truth of an object by painting it from an impossible perspective, adopting many standpoints at once. The challenge of understanding behaviour is analogous. Theoreticians, researchers and practitioners, disciplines and sub-disciplines, sciences, humanities and arts – all see the object of study from their own distinctive standpoints, all offer their own kinds of answer to questions such as why the girl is playing the mandolin in the first place, or what might make her play more often, or play different tunes, or play a different instrument, or stop altogether. In a dialogue between those many observers with their many perspectives, perhaps we will, like the cubist, bring to light truths that are lost in monologues.

Of course, it's one thing to collect many different takes on a topic, as we've sought to do in this volume. As editors, we make no claims to be Picasso. What we present here is not the final work, ready to hang, but a palette with paints squeezed out upon it, for you to add your own colours, mix your own tints, and paint your own pictures.

About the book

The origins of this book lie in an interdisciplinary event hosted by the University College London (UCL) Centre for Behaviour Change in June 2014. The topic of that event – itself prompted by a conversation at an earlier event – was 'Models of behaviour change: how useful are they?' You can watch the event at http://sbk.li/1i81.

Following the event, we wanted to keep the conversation going and to broaden it out to engage more perspectives. After interviewing a number of people from different disciplines about the questions raised, the idea of using the traditional genre of dialogue emerged as a way of capturing differing takes on the topic. You'll find the output from that work – *Models of behaviour change: a dialogue* – in **Part 1** of the book.

By now, we were rather enjoying the diversity of perspectives we were hearing and learning from. So we sent the Dialogue out to a wide range of people with different takes on behaviour change and invited them to write short responses. We encouraged our contributors to have fun, to take risks, and above all else to strive to promote conversation – not close it down. You'll find their excellent and thought-provoking responses in **Part 2** of the book.

None of our contributors saw each other's articles. Nevertheless, we've done our best to order the articles to follow some of the common threads that emerged: from the role(s) of models in understanding behaviour, via the challenges of working across disciplines and the distinctive contributions particular perspectives might bring, to reflections on the activity of modelling itself, and what it takes to be a modeller.

About the Centre for Behaviour Change

Behaviour is at the heart of most of the world's big problems: health and wellbeing, social cohesion, climate change... the list goes on.

No one academic discipline has all the answers to the challenge of how to change behaviour and tackle these global problems. But each has an important contribution to make: engineering, psychology, economics, built environment, computing, sociology....

UCL's Centre for Behaviour Change (http://sbk.li/1i91) brings together expertise across academic disciplines and promotes engagement between researchers and those in a position to apply evidence and theories of behaviour change to solving real-world problems - decision-makers, policymakers, managers and intervention developers across the public, charity and commercial sectors. The Centre holds events to promote thinking and debate, contributes to multidisciplinary research, offers consultancy and training, and fosters collaborations and partnerships to step up the quantity and quality of thinking and action on behaviour change.

And we are always open to new ideas....

Sign up to our mailing list (http://sbk.li/1i92) and follow us on twitter @UCLBehaveChange.

Acknowledgements

By definition, many hands were required to bring this project to fruition. We are immensely grateful to the many individuals who have contributed their voices: both those who were interviewed in developing the original Dialogue, and those who have contributed responses to broaden the conversation out.

Part 1

Models & behaviour change: a dialogue

Models and behaviour change: a dialogue

Simon Christmas

This dialogue was constructed at the invitation of the University College London (UCL) Centre for Behaviour Change, following an event with the title 'Models of behaviour change: how useful are they?' hosted by the Centre on 2nd June 2014.

Its content draws on the event itself, and on interviews with Jamie Brown (UCL), Nicola Christie (UCL), Anthony Finkelstein* (UCL), Heather Gainforth (UCL), Graham Hart (UCL), Kate Jeffery* (UCL), Mike Kelly (NICE when interviewed), Susan Michie (UCL), John Owens (King's College London), Alan Penn (UCL), Jeremy Watson (UCL) and Robert West* (UCL). Interviewees who were also speakers at the CBC event are marked with an asterisk.

The dialogue brings together three imaginary graduate students – Evie, Paola and Yusuf – who attended the Centre for Behaviour Change event and have now met up to discuss further some of the issues raised.

~ 1 ~

Yusuf It's great that we've been able to find this time to talk further about models: what they are, why we need them, and how useful they are in the context of behaviour change in particular. I know we all found the event hosted by the Centre for Behaviour Change thought-provoking. For my part, I came away with a real appetite to explore the issues raised more fully.

Paola Me too. And even if we don't come to firm conclusions, we can at least try to get some sharper questions. Because I suspect there will be points we don't agree on.

Evie I think you were looking at me then Paola! I know one thing all three of us agree on, though: that some of the most interesting stuff happens when we talk across disciplines like this.

We're all so used to communicating *within* our own disciplines, with people who share the same worldview and assumptions. When we talk *across* disciplines, we have to re-examine the things we normally take for granted, make explicit our assumptions, and work extra hard to be really clear about what we're saying. And in the process, we learn so much.

Paola Exactly. Provided we approach the conversation with an open mind, ready to listen and to be challenged – and also to offer our own challenges. That's what I love about talking to you two!

Yusuf We'll certainly need open minds for this topic, I think. Listening to the three speakers at the event, I realised both how often the word 'model' gets used in my own field, and how rarely I ever stop to think what a model really is. Before the session, I'd never really thought about how people in other disciplines might use the term.

Evie Or the fact that they might mean something different.

Yusuf Exactly. But before we get onto differences, I wondered if there were some basic points we could agree on. I had two suggestions.

First, it seems to me that all models are representations of something in the world.

Evie Not all representations are models, though.

Yusuf No, I'm not saying that. But all models are representations. Perhaps we should go further and say that there's an isomorphism between a model and the world. For instance, that's true even of the kind of models that architects build so that people can see what a building will look like.

Secondly, models always involve a degree of simplification or abstraction. They help us get a grip on a complex reality precisely because they leave out some aspects of that reality.

Evie That's linked to the idea of parsimony. You only put into the model things that really need to be in the model.

Paola I'm reminded of a map. A map that included all of the same features as the real world would be completely useless. In fact it wouldn't be a map: it would just be a duplicate reality.

Yusuf As the saying goes: the map is not the terrain. It's important never to forget that our models are just that – models, and not reality.

Evie That's very interesting, because it strikes me that there are at least two types of model, with different relationships to reality. In some cases, we're using models to understand things that already exist or happen in the world. I think the map is a good metaphor for this kind of model. In other cases, however, we're building a model of something we want to make exist or happen – in which case our model is more like a blueprint. I think these are quite different tasks.

Paola That's a really good point. It raises the question of purpose – what our models are for – and how that affects the way that we put them together. I wonder if the distinction you make, Evie, makes a difference to *how* you construct a model.

Yusuf I think there's another distinction we could make here. It seems to me that there is a *continuum* of types of model. At one end, we have models which are precisely specified, typically in the languages of mathematics and logic. At the other end of the continuum, we have less precisely specified models, which seek to express insights about how things work without doing so in formal terms.

Evie I have to say, my first reaction is that what you're describing there is not a continuum of types of model, but a continuum from good to bad, or from model to non-model. From my perspective, a model that isn't 'precisely specified', as you put it, isn't a model at all. You have to be able to describe a model in formal terms for it to qualify.

Yusuf Well, don't you think it depends on your purpose, like Paola said? After all, some models are not intended to be analytical. They are thinking tools, not analytical tools.

I accept there needs to be structure in a model. That's at the heart of the idea of isomorphism: the structure of the model reflects the structure of the real world. But

I'm not convinced that this structure has to be describable in formal terms.

The Wider Determinants of Health model, for example, has a very loosely specified structure – but people find it extremely helpful. MINDSPACE is another example that's proved very useful in some contexts. Models like these can be helpful in thinking through the kinds of factor that could be contributing to a given issue. It's a different purpose, so a different kind of model.

Evie I don't dispute the value of things like that. All I'm saying is that for me they don't qualify as models. They are checklists, or frameworks, or communication tools, maybe. They may well capture quite sophisticated insights. But I don't think we should allow the fact that they're represented graphically, with boxes and arrows, to kid us into thinking that they are models – at least not in the sense I'd like to reserve for the term. What do the boxes really mean? What do the arrows mean?

I think we risk losing an essential technical term if we stretch the use of 'model' in this way. Not to mention the risk that people start believing that frameworks and checklists like these have the same standing as formally specified models. Which they clearly don't.

I mean, we could go in the other direction and say that the term 'model' can be used of *any* representation. For example, is a Picasso painting of a face a model? The question is not about the importance and value of Picasso paintings. It's about whether we lose something by stretching the term 'model' until it means pretty much the same as 'representation'.

Paola It's interesting because, while you were talking, I was thinking of a third kind of model – one that is there to provoke new thinking. For example, you might use gravity as a model for the flow of populations around and between cities. Or you might use an agent-based model to demonstrate how complex behaviour can arise from simple rules. The purpose of models like these is not to explain but to provoke. They challenge us to think of alternative ways of explaining the phenomena we observe in the world around us.

Evie For me, those sound closer to metaphors than models. I mean, if I've understood you, you're not meant to treat them as literally true.

Paola Definitely not. It can cause problems if people start believing that a model of the kind I'm describing is literally true.

Yusuf Hmm. I thought I'd cracked it with my continuum! I suppose this is even more complicated than I thought.

Evie It seems to me that what we need is some kind of framework here – I guess maybe you'd call it a meta-model, Yusuf – of the different kinds of purpose models can serve, and the implications that has for the form they take.

Yusuf I agree. A meta-model sounds great. Although actually, I think of it in terms of developing a common language we can use across different disciplines to describe and talk about these different kinds of model.

Paola And some kind of consensus on what gets called a model at all.

~ 2 ~

Evie For the sake of today's conversation, I wonder if we can narrow the scope a bit – especially as what we're really interested in is the role of models in behaviour change.

For example, Yusuf mentioned that architects build models of buildings, or maquettes, so people can get a sense of what they're going to look like.

In a behaviour change context, however, I think what we're interested in is a particular class of models: models that seek to represent the dynamic behaviour of a system or set of systems. For example, that wouldn't include the architect's maquette; but it would include a computational model of the thermal behaviour of the building, which modelled how it absorbed heat, cooled down, and so forth.

Paola I'm not entirely sure on that one, Evie. Buildings may be static in one sense of the term: but they differ when perceived and experienced from different points of view. So I could argue that the maquette is also a dynamic representation, because it allows the viewer to interact dynamically with it and adopt these different points of view.

Yusuf I'm not sure about the distinction either, but for a different reason. The fact is that a lot of our models of health-related behaviour are actually regression models. These can be very precisely specified and very useful – but they're doing something different from a dynamic system model.

Paola Sorry, Yusuf, can you explain that one to me? I've always assumed that the numbers on models said something about how much different elements of a system influenced each other?

Yusuf That's a common mistake. In fact a regression model is a statement of co-variation, not influence. It's entirely constrained by the natural variation in the population. Something may be an important influence, but if it doesn't actually vary much in the population, then by definition its variation won't explain much of the variation in other elements of the system.

For example, in the past, GPs all got paid pretty much the same. If you'd done a regression analysis, you'd have found that variation in levels of pay explained little if any variation in GP behaviour – for the simple reason that there was no real variation in levels of pay. But that doesn't mean pay is not an important *influence*. In fact, if you pay GPs lots of money to do something, they will do it.

It's also important to remember that these are models of variation in populations, not models of what is actually going on in individuals. For instance, suppose you found that, in a given population, intentions to go to the gym explained 20% of variation in whether or not people actually go to the gym. That could be because intentions are having some influence on the behaviour of everyone in that population; or a great deal of influence on the behaviour of just some of the people; or anything in between!

Paola Thank you. That's helpful.

Evie I take your points. Maybe that wasn't the most helpful way to define the scope. But let me have another go: surely we're looking for models that enable us to make predictions regarding outcomes – at least probabilistically. Predictions that we can go out and test.

It seems to me that that is central to the whole endeavour of science. The way I see it, a model is a way of formulating in precise terms what you *think* is going on in a system, that allows you to say: if I'm right about this, I ought to see the following things happen as well. Then you can go out and see if they really do happen.

That's one of the reasons why I think it's so important that models are precisely specified. It's one thing to say that you think two things are connected in some way: another thing entirely to express the nature of that connection in a way that allows you to go out and test whether or not you are actually right.

Yusuf That feels like a very important point when we consider behaviour change in particular. What we want to be able to do is predict what will happen as a result of some intervention – or at least assign probabilities to different outcomes.

Evie Exactly. For example, that's at the heart of how models get used in cost-effectiveness studies. In an ideal world, of course, you'd have trial data: hard empirical data of what happens when the intervention in question is made. But if you don't have that, you can look at models of how key variables interact with each other to at least estimate how much bang you will get for your buck.

In some areas, we have robust models to do this kind of work. For example, we can build models that link data about sexual behaviour in at-risk populations to data about the incidence of HIV, and use these to predict the likely impact on incidence of a given

|||intervention – the earlier use of antiretrovirals, for example.

Paola I was struck by the formula for cigarette consumption price elasticity which was presented by a speaker at the event. The change in consumption is 0.4 times the change in the price. I suppose that's a simple example of what you're talking about.

Evie Exactly. The model allows you to make predictions, which you either go out and test or use to make interventions.

Yusuf And in fact, those things are quite closely related. Every time you make an intervention, it's another test of the model. Even when we've tested a model many times, and have a lot of confidence in it, there's always the possibility that something new will come up.

Paola The wobbly bridge!

Yusuf Pardon?

Paola When they built the Millennium Bridge, they were using well-established engineering models that allowed for all sorts of factors – including the fact that people tend to synchronise their steps as a suspension bridge bounces up and down. What no one realised – because no one had built a bridge quite like that before – was that people would also synchronise with the side-to-side movement of the bridge. The intervention –

the bridge – showed up something that was missing in the model.

Yusuf That's a great example.

Evie I like this idea a lot: that interventions are also tests of the model that informs them. And it works the other way round as well: you test a model by making an intervention and seeing what happens. The difference is not in what you do but in how confident you are about the model.

In a control system context, for instance, you have a high degree of confidence in the model, because the model is so well tested. So when the real world doesn't match the predictions of your model, you look for problems in the real world rather than in the model.

Paola Could you give us an example?

Evie Well, suppose you're running a brewery. You have a control system which takes the same inputs as the brewery itself, and models its internal states and outputs. Now suppose the brewery and the model start delivering very different outputs – for example, you start seeing very different temperatures or pressures in parts of the brewery. Because you've a high degree of confidence in the model, you look for problems in the real world: a faulty component, for instance, or maybe a bad batch of yeast.

Paola So I'm trying to translate this into the context of behaviour change. I have a model of how I think people behave, and based on that model I make an intervention. For example, I develop a training intervention to improve hazard perception in novice drivers. I pilot my training, and it doesn't work in the way the model predicted. What does that mean?

It could be that my model was wrong in some way – for example, it was missing some key variables.

Alternatively, it could be that the model was correct but I did something wrong in the design of the training intervention – for example, I had people do it on a computer when there needed to be a group discussion as well.

So how do I decide which it is in practice?

Evie That's a really good question. I'm not sure I have an easy answer.

It seems to me there's a lack of shared understanding and methodology around *how* models are tested – at least in the field of behaviour change. What kind of evidence is needed to say that the model needs to be refined, or extended, or developed? How do we gather and interpret that evidence in a systematic way?

For me, this links back to issues around specification. In behaviour change, for example, the basic challenge is to build an evidence base of how techniques affect behaviour. The techniques are the independent variable, if you like, and the behaviour is the dependent variable.

But as you say, Paola, you also have to take account of other variables, such as *how* the intervention is delivered. And then there's the setting, the cultural context, the population – these things can make a huge difference.

Finally, which model you've used in designing the intervention is itself a variable. Because the question that sometimes comes up is: where is the evidence that interventions based on Model X or Model Y work better? And the answer is: there isn't any! In fact, we don't even have the evidence that theory-based interventions as a whole work better than interventions based on, say, intuition and gut feel. And that's because we don't have any systematic way of gathering that evidence or of ensuring that the model has been applied well in the first place.

What we need is some kind of agreed taxonomy, a way of coding these different variables each time we make an intervention – not just the technique used and the behavioural outcome, but also the way in which the intervention is delivered; the setting, cultural context and population; and the model used. That way we can start to systematically track their relationships.

Yusuf The kind of taxonomy that's already been developed for, say, types of intervention.

Evie Yes.

Paola That's going to be quite challenging in the case of something like culture. I'm thinking about the parallel with taxonomy in biology. Any taxonomy you come up with will be incomplete by definition, because new species will evolve in the future. In biology that's not such a big problem, because evolution happens so slowly. But culture changes much more rapidly, constantly creating new forms in the way that evolution creates new species.

Evie Well, I didn't say it was going to be easy!

~ 3 ~

Yusuf I'd like to bring in another angle on this. We've been talking about the need to test our models whenever we make interventions. Theory, we might say, needs to be continuously tested by practice, otherwise it won't be right! But I think there's another side to this. Practice should be informed by theory, otherwise it won't build on the accumulated learning we have built up over past interventions. We ought to be making behaviour change interventions with clear theoretical foundations.

Paola And do you think that happens?

Yusuf You know how I'm going to answer that question! No, I don't. Not often enough, anyway.

It's as if we've set up these two worlds: the world of theory and the world of practice. When in fact, that distinction is an artificial one: theory and practice should be in a dialectical relationship, two aspects of a single endeavour.

Paola I have one thought as to why that split between theory and practice might exist.

I was thinking earlier when you were talking about the idea that interventions are testing out the models they are based on... It seems to me this idea might make some of the people who fund behaviour change interventions very uncomfortable. Because another way of putting the same point is that there is always an element of risk that an intervention won't work. I'm not sure risk is something that people are always comfortable with.

I think there's this fantasy that, by doing research, you can remove the risk. You find out what will work, then 'roll out the solution'. People want research to tell them what to do, when all it can really tell them is what to *try*.

Evie And what *not* to do. Often it can be quite clear about that!

Paola Agreed! Either way, there isn't that dialectic relationship, that two-way conversation.

Yusuf You could well be right. But at least in the scenario you're describing there's a one-way conversation.

What worries me even more is situations where people simply ignore the theory altogether. I have encountered people who reject the idea that models have any role to play in the design of behaviour change interventions. 'I've got years of experience working in this field: what can your models tell me?'

Paola The reality is, of course, that even someone who claims to be anti-theoretical has some kind of model in mind when they design an intervention. It may not be articulated, even to themselves. But unless you make assumptions about how things work and why people do what they do, you have no basis for making any intervention at all.

For example, one you often see is the unstated assumption that people respond to financial incentives in line with economic utility theory. If you challenge someone on this, they will tell you it's 'common sense': but call it what you like, it's still a theoretical commitment, a model. And in this case, one that happens to be wrong!

Yusuf I like this way of putting it. Rather than say that some interventions have a theoretical basis and others don't, it would be more accurate to say that *all* interventions have a theoretical basis: but in some cases, this basis is clearly articulated in the form of a model, and in others it is implicit.

What we should be doing is bringing these implicit models into the open so that we can subject them to proper scrutiny. Does the evidence support them? Will the interventions we're planning test them? Are they even internally consistent?

Paola Doing that can be very hard, because these implicit models are things we think *with*, not things we think *of*. They're like paradigms that sit in our head, structuring our interpretation of everything else.

And as long as they remain that way, they can be remarkably impervious to evidence. For example, there's a common view among architects that enclosure creates community. When they apply the principle and it fails – enclosure fails to create community – the response is sometimes: 'Right, well clearly we didn't enclose enough. Next time we need to enclose even more!' The possibility that enclosure *doesn't* create community is not even considered.

Yusuf It would be like the engineers who built the wobbly bridge refusing to consider the possibility that the fault lay in the model they had used.

Evie This is why the discipline of creating an explicit logic model is so fundamentally important when developing an intervention.

Yusuf Is that what I'd call a theory of change?

Evie I think so. There are different names, but the principle is the same: that you specify clearly how the intervention is expected to work, based on what you already know about how things link together in the world.

Building the logic model is a way of forcing yourself to make explicit any assumptions you have about how the intervention is going to work. It's a way of making yourself go back to the existing evidence: what grounds have you got for expecting things to happen in this way? And it's a great way of identifying gaps in your knowledge.

Yusuf Because, let's face it, when it comes to behaviour change there are usually plenty of those!

Evie Absolutely. So what we need to do is be clear about those gaps, clear about our own hypotheses, and clear about how this intervention is going to allow us to test them out. Which is another key function of the logic model: it provides the framework for evaluation.

Paola I really like this idea that one of the functions of a logic model is clarity about the things you *don't* know.

However, I can also see why people might resist doing that. It goes back to the point about risk I made earlier. If you're about to spend a pot of money on trying to change behaviour, and if your personal performance is measured on the success of the intervention – not to mention your professional pride – then it can be a bit alarming to be told that the planned intervention is in fact testing the hypotheses on which it is based!

For me, it's all about understanding what that phrase 'evidence-based' really means. When people talk about an evidence-based intervention, I sometimes get the feeling that what they really hanker after is an evidence-*determined* intervention. They want the evidence to tell them what to do, and remove all the risk.

Evie I think what we should really say is that interventions should be evidence-based *and* evidence-generating. Yes, in so far as we have evidence, the intervention should be based on that; and in so far as we *don't* have evidence, the intervention should be helping to fill the gaps.

Even if you're consciously setting out to innovate, this formula still applies. The whole point of innovating is to try something new – something for which, by definition, there isn't an evidence base. But that just increases the need for your intervention to be evidence-generating. Hence you still need an explicit logic model – a clear articulation of the way you *think* your innovation is going to work.

Yusuf That's very good. And obviously, when you talk about interventions, you're seeing the evaluation as *part* of that intervention. Whereas in practice it's often seen as something over and above.

Evie You're right, I do see the evaluation as an integral part of the intervention. And again, applying the discipline of articulating a logic model helps to ensure that it is.

~ 4 ~

Paola It strikes me that there's another distinction we could make here, one that we missed in our initial discussion of different types of model. It's a distinction between generic and specific models.

When you develop a logic model, that sets out the way in which a specific intervention is expected to bring about a specific change in behaviour in a specific context.

On the other hand, there are generic models, like COM-B or PRIME or the Theory of Planned Behaviour, which seek to articulate the relationships between a range of factors and behaviour in general across a wide range of contexts.

Which raises a question. Evie, you've set out a very clear case for why we need the specific logic models when we make interventions. But what are the generic models for? If I'm designing an intervention, why should I pay any attention to them?

Yusuf That's an interesting question. I think the answer lies in what's *behind* those generic models. I mean, they didn't just appear from nowhere. Those generic models capture an understanding of human behaviour that has been developed over a century or more of scientific investigation. They're far from perfect: but starting with them makes a lot more sense than just saying: 'This feels right to me.'

No one would do that in, say, physics. But for some reason, when it comes to human behaviour, we're not always very good at building on what we've already learned.

Paola There's the makings of an interesting response there to the kind of person you mentioned earlier who says: 'I've got years of experience: what can your models tell me?' The response would go: 'Yes, you have years of experience; but these models capture the accumulated years of experience of many different people.'

Yusuf I may try that next time. I'll tell you if it works! The principle is right though: generic models provide a way of accumulating our experience and learning.

Evie I think we could go a bit further than that. Generic models aren't just an output of the process of accumulating learning. They're also what makes that process possible. If you're going to accumulate learning across many different studies, you need to be able to review them systematically. If different studies use different models, then you have a problem: how do you compare them?

Yusuf This is an important issue. Because in practice, even when people *do* base interventions on existing models – generic models, as you've called them, Paola – they often fiddle around with them and alter bits to fit them to their own purposes. And that makes systematic review hard if not impossible.

Paola It strikes me there are two potentially competing agendas here. For the person who wants to bring about behaviour change, fiddling around with models to fit one's own purposes sounds like it might be a good idea. For the person who is trying to advance our understanding of human behaviour through systematic review, it's a huge problem. I wonder if this tension accounts for some of the difficulties – and if so, how it might be resolved.

Evie You may have a point. But I also think that the problem comes back to the poor specification of many of the generic models of behaviour that we have. Not all of them, but many. If a model is not well-specified, then you *have* to fiddle with it before you can use it for behaviour change purposes – because you need to produce a well-specified logic model for your own intervention.

Yusuf I'm not sure whether the challenge here is with the models themselves or how they are *reported.*

Evie Sometimes there's no way of knowing. But you're right, from a behaviour change perspective we need much clearer standards for reporting models. If you can't report your model in a way that allows other people to use it *without* having to fiddle with it, then it's of no use.

Yusuf As a teacher of mine used to say: 'If you can't say it, you haven't thought it.'

Evie Something like that. It's an area where I think one could learn a lot from looking across disciplines as well. How do different disciplines report their models? What can we learn from each other?

~ 5 ~

Yusuf Another issue I have is the sheer proliferation of behaviour models. There are so many of them. As you said, Evie, part of the job of a model is to create a common language that allows us to compare and systematically review many different studies. Instead, we're all talking different languages. It's like the Tower of Babel!

Paola Though we did say at the beginning of this conversation that you might need different models for different purposes....

Yusuf That's true, Paola. But the reality is that many models are just exercises in relabelling psychological principles that have been around for many years. It's hardly surprising if people who are designing interventions throw up their hands in despair and pick the first one that appeals to them – for instance, because it reflects their untested assumptions about the topic.

Evie Or else they take a pick-and-mix approach. It's like those sourcebooks that designers use: you flick through them looking for something that sparks your thinking. In so far as designing a behaviour change intervention is a creative act, I can see how that could be really important. But it doesn't help with building a science of behaviour change.

Yusuf And another thing: when people develop new models they're not clear enough about the ways in which they are building on previous models. Typically they will make reference to other models, but they don't provide real detail about how they have built on or developed those models. So it can be really hard to map the linkages, the overlaps, the differences.

For example, take a construct like 'self-efficacy'. Lots of models use this construct, and typically the authors will cite Bandura. But when you look more closely, different models are using the construct in different ways, without making that explicit. Some focus more on control, for instance, others more on self-confidence.

The result is a set of models which aren't commensurable. They don't make our common language richer, so that we can talk about and understand more; they just add new dialects, so we understand each other less well.

Paola Poor Yusuf! You're quite exercised about this one.

Evie And you're starting to sound a bit like me. Better specification of models!

Yusuf It's true, it frustrates me. It's crazy how often people come up with new models. And yes, Evie, it's partly about better specification. But I think we also have to look at the culture we operate in. Why do people generate models? How are they rewarded for doing so?

In my view, people should not be allowed to generate new models unless they can show they've done a thorough review of existing models in the area they're dealing with, and established the shortcomings of those existing models.

There should also then be an agreed framework for the reporting of the new model, including real clarity about its heritage: the other models it has drawn on, the ways in which constructs from those other models have been developed, and why.

But making this stick would call for changes in career incentives, institutions, professional mindsets. The journals would definitely need to get behind it. It would call for behaviour change, in fact!

~ 6 ~

Paola Meanwhile, right now, we need to find a way of helping people make better use of the models we do have. I was struck, Yusuf, by the sympathy you expressed for people who design interventions and are faced by this plethora of models.

So I wonder if we could provide clearer guidance to people about how to select and use models. After all, even if our models met these high standards of reporting, there would probably still be more than one of them. We would probably still need different models for different purposes.

Yusuf I'm certain we would. In fact, I think the idea of striving for a single, all-embracing model is probably incoherent.

Paola Why so?

Yusuf Because the essence of models is to simplify. You have to leave things out. And what you leave out depends on your purpose.

Paola A bit like the difference between a road atlas and an ordnance survey map. They leave out different things because they're designed for different purposes. A road atlas would not be much use for walking in the hills; but if you're driving across the country, the ordnance survey maps would be very unwieldy.

Yusuf Exactly. But an all-embracing model would be one that could be used for *any* purpose. Which means it wouldn't be able to leave anything out. It wouldn't be able to simplify.

Paola It would be the terrain, not the map! That's a really interesting argument. So however much we tidy up our existing models of behaviour, we're still likely to have more than one. Which brings me back to the question of guidance. Can we provide guidance to people on how to choose the right model when they are designing a specific behaviour change intervention?

Evie It's a great idea. I think a key aspect would be to help people understand the *limits* of different models. For example, the Theory of Planned Behaviour gets used to investigate behaviours that clearly *aren't* planned. In that case, the limits of the model ought to be obvious: it's in the title! But I guess that's an indication of how clearly stated the limits need to be, if even the name of the model isn't enough.

Yusuf I like the idea of guidance as well. Building on Evie's point, it would be good to be very clear about what kinds of things a model is *leaving out* in order to simplify. When you're selecting a model, it's important to make sure you're not leaving things out that are really important for your particular purposes.

Paola So we don't want people yomping across the hills with a road atlas.

Yusuf That's one way of putting it...

Paola Building on that, I think we should also remember that, for some people, the kind of intervention they can use is determined in advance. They either have a car or they have walking boots. They don't have a choice between them.

I think we sometimes come at the topic of behaviour change from the perspective of someone for whom any intervention is possible in principle. I suppose that could be the case for senior policy people developing a Government strategy – say on smoking reduction. But it's quite an unusual perspective. Most people approach behaviour change with an intervention already in mind. If your job is in a pharmaceutical company, for example, then you already know that what you need is a drug to help people quit. If you're part of a communications team, you know you need a different kind of approach.

So in practice, most people selecting a model need one with elements they can actually hope to influence. They're not in a position to step back and ask whether they should be trying an entirely different kind of intervention.

Yusuf That's a really interesting point, Paola. It's a reminder that, if we're going to develop guidance on how to select and use models, we need to do it from the perspective of the people who are actually out there selecting and using.

In my head, I keep coming back to this point about the need for a common language which we can use to describe models and talk about their strengths and limitations. When I first made that point, I had in mind a language we could use across different academic disciplines. But actually, we should probably drop the word 'academic': we need a language that can be shared by all the different communities of thought and practice who use, test and develop models.

~ 7 ~

Evie What we've outlined here is the basis for a very rational and considered approach to the selection and use of models. That feels like it's quite a long way from where we are at the moment, don't you think?

Yusuf It does. As things stand, I think people tend to stick to the models they're familiar with. As I've said, I can sympathise with that. But it leads to problems: the more comfortable we get with a model, the more likely we are to forget that that's all it is – a model, a simplification of a complex reality. We start mistaking the model for the real world.

Evie Paola's map metaphor is quite useful again here. Maps of the earth all involve a degree of distortion of reality, because they're projecting the surface of a sphere into two dimensions. We're all so familiar with the Mercator projection that we tend to forget it's not the reality. For example, we start believing that the areas of countries are as shown on the map. It's pretty shocking the first time you see the Peterson projection – a projection which preserves area – and realise just how misleading a map can be if you use it in a way it was not intended to be used.

Paola That's actually an example of another potential problem, Evie. Different projections can become laden with political significance – for example, a tendency to overplay the importance of countries nearer the poles, which appear larger than they really are on the Mercator projection, and downplay the importance of those near the equator, which appear smaller. That wasn't the intention of the projection, but it's a product of *uncritical use* of that projection.

Something similar applies in the case of models. We've agreed that models simplify reality by leaving things out that are not judged important for some specific purpose. It just so happens that that's also what political and cultural biases do: leave things out that are not judged important. That doesn't mean that models are biased. But like maps, if we start using them uncritically, if we become over-familiar with them, then we risk allowing them to become laden with bias.

Evie We should always be dating our models, never married to them!

Yusuf That's a great way of putting it. Because I don't think familiarity is the only issue. In my experience, people become very personally attached to particular models. The model becomes part of their identity. You have to be very careful how you tell someone that the evidence simply doesn't support the model they are using.

Paola I think there's another interesting dynamic that can come into play specifically among researchers. Evie, you made the point that models allow us to accumulate learning, by enabling us to compare and systematically review different studies. But it strikes me that there is also a potential trap in that.

For example, suppose the first person to do a study on interventions to tackle a particular issue uses the Theory of Planned Behaviour. The next person to do a study in the same area wants to be able to compare their results, so they use the Theory of Planned Behaviour as well. Each subsequent study has a strong incentive to stick with that model. But no one tests whether the model is actually applicable to the issue in question. For example, is the target behaviour actually *planned* behaviour at all? Did that first researcher choose the right model?

Evie That's so true. Whereas if we had the kind of guidance we've been discussing in place, that first researcher could be encouraged to explain and justify their choice of model; and subsequent researchers might be encouraged to review that choice critically, rather than simply going with the flow.

~ 8 ~

Paola I'd like to introduce a new question into our discussion. Does it make any difference if the thing we are modelling is human behaviour?

I mean, we've been using examples from a wide range of contexts and disciplines – bridges, breweries, maps. At the Centre for Behaviour Change event, the speakers discussed examples like a drinks vending machine and rat navigation. I'm just wondering if it makes any difference what we're studying.

Evie It's an interesting question. I can't see what difference it would make, though. In principle, modelling human behaviour is no different from modelling the behaviour of anything else. Ultimately what you're trying to do in every case is understand a causal network, and how certain things cause other things to happen.

So in the case of behaviour change, what you're ultimately trying to do is map interventions to behavioural outcomes as closely as possible, via various internal states of the system. The challenge is in principle the same.

Having said that, I recognise that human behaviour is significantly more complex than, say, a typical engineered system. But that just means we need even more care and discipline in how we go about modelling.

Yusuf I'm inclined to agree with you, Evie. Modelling human behaviour is no different in principle, but complexity is a huge challenge. I also think it may be worth distinguishing two different sources of that complexity.

First, there's complexity in the inputs to the system. Whenever you build a model, you're trying to home in on the differences that really make a difference – the key variables. The challenge with human behaviour is that things you thought weren't important have a habit of making a big difference.

For example, I remember hearing this story about a new product launch. The marketing team piloted the product in Scotland, where it was a huge success. They then went on to launch it across the country – and it failed spectacularly. When they tried to work out what had gone wrong, they came to the conclusion that it all came down to the small print on the advertising campaign they'd used in the original pilot. For legal reasons, they'd had to add the words: 'Only available in Scotland'. The success of the pilot came down to a feeling of national pride which the UK-wide launch lacked.

Evie I think the *kind* of intervention you're making also makes a difference here. If your intervention is putting a drug into a person, then the task of deciding which things to leave out of your model is much easier. Still not straightforward, but easier than if your intervention is, say, a piece of advertising.

Yusuf I agree. And then, on top of that, there's the second kind of complexity: complexity in the system itself. In behaviour change, we're rarely talking about a single, linear pathway between intervention and outcome. Instead, there is typically a multiplicity of possible pathways between the input and the output, many or maybe all of them non-linear.

Even at the level of the individual, behaviour is the product of multiple mechanisms operating in parallel and interacting with each other – rational, emotional, instinctive. And that's before we take into account the interaction between the individual and their social and physical context. Not to mention the differences between individuals.

For example, take a relatively simple intervention like a GP giving advice to a patient on losing weight. The relationship between this intervention and the subsequent behaviour of the person receiving the advice is extremely complex. There are multiple possible pathways between the advice being given and the patient actually acting on it.

Paola That's really interesting, Yusuf, and it's sparked off a couple of thoughts in my head. One relates to 'the interaction between the individual and their social context', as you put it – but perhaps we can come back to that one later.

The other thought was about the layering of different mechanisms even within an individual. It just occurred to me that at the heart of our approaches to modelling are these ideas of simplicity and parsimony; but the things we are trying to model are the products of evolution, which often produces redundancy and complexity. Take the human eye, for example: no engineer would build it that way, with the nerves on top of the receptors, but that's how it's ended up. So this thought just popped into my head: when we model human behaviour, is our desire for simplicity well-placed?

Evie I'll have to think about that one a bit, Paola. But I think there's a difference between wanting a model to be simple and wanting reality to be simple. For me, the value of simplicity in models is that it helps us start to get a handle on complexity. A simple model is at best partial, but it still gives us a platform from which to explore the complexity further. The problem comes when people want the real world to be simple as well. They latch on to simple models as 'the answer'. Maybe it links back to the points you were making earlier about risk.

Paola That's really helpful, Evie. I'm reminded of that quotation – I think it was Einstein who said it: 'Everything should be made as simple as possible, but not simpler.' The difficult bit is judging what's possible and what's *too* simple. I think we're starting to touch here on what might be *called* moral questions around the use of models. It seems to me it's not simplification that's the problem so much as the intent of the person simplifying.

I think you're also right to link it back to the topic of risk. Because the upshot of the two kinds of complexity Yusuf has described is that, with human behaviour, you always have the risk of unintended consequences, unpredictable and emergent outcomes.

Which can be very uncomfortable if your job is to predict, plan and control.

Which makes me wonder.... Evie, you said a few minutes ago that the challenge for behaviour change is to map interventions to behavioural outcomes as closely as possible, via various internal states of the system. But given all this complexity, maybe that's an impossible dream.

I also wonder if this might be why some of the models in the field of behaviour change are less well specified.

Evie I'm not sure that follows. Yes, human behaviour is extremely complex, but that doesn't obviate the need to approach the world systematically.

Let's remember that complexity is also a feature of many physical systems. Take the weather, for example. Yes, there are always unexpected and unpredictable outcomes, but you can still create models with high predictive value if you collect the right data and model it in the right way.

The same is true with human behaviour. There are some areas where we have very clear evidence of overall patterns of behaviour in response to types of intervention. Like the formula for cigarette consumption price elasticity you mentioned earlier, Paola. Or the models linking sexual behaviour to the incidence of HIV which I was talking about.

So human behaviour is complex, but in some respects it is also very predictable. In fact, you could argue that it's the predictability of people that makes social life possible at all: we all have fairly good tacit models of the behaviour of others which guide decisions about our own social behaviour. Essentially what I'm proposing is a more formalised, explicit and rigorous version of that everyday understanding.

I agree we don't have formal models like the ones I just mentioned in as many areas of human behaviour as we'd like. There's plenty of work still to do. But that doesn't mean it's not possible in principle.

Yusuf I think there's one other issue you're missing here, however, which is time. You mention the example of the weather, but the predictive value of meteorological models declines pretty quickly over time.

The problem is that the gap between many behaviour change interventions and the intended outcomes is so long that it's arguably not even possible to talk about them as 'intervention' and 'outcome' any more. For example, suppose you're trying to establish the impact of Personal, Social and Health Education in schools on later sexual behaviour. It's a bit like trying to use a meteorological model to predict the weather in three years time.

I'm struck that the examples you give relate to quite immediate effects. For example, the relationship between price and consumption may not be a simple one, but I can believe that a change in price has a fairly immediate effect on consumption behaviour. Whereas something like education...

In fact, it's not just that the models are unlikely to be able to make predictions over these long time-spans. I'm not sure how you'd even gather data to build the model in the first place. Take the example of education again. Suppose you want to understand the long-term effects of educational choices on the economy. How do you gather the data? The dynamics of change are too slow for you to be able to sample the system. Instead, you have to start looking at proxies and predictors of outcomes: so, for example, you use exam results as a predictor of the longer-term economic outcomes you really care about. But as soon as you do that, you introduce noise into the system. You're not starting with the high quality data you need to build a model of the kind you're describing.

Evie That's a really interesting point. That's going to be a much bigger issue for certain kinds of intervention than others. So the impacts of something like price may be much easier to model than the impacts of something like education.

Yusuf And I think there's a real danger that people start believing the interventions that are easier to model are also ones that work better. Because I think people sometimes mistake greater confidence in the outcome for greater effectiveness. We're back to

Paola's point about risk: as human beings, the desire to feel like we're in control sometimes trumps the desire to actually get things right.

~ 9 ~

Paola I feel like the distinction we made between specific and *generic* models may be relevant to this topic of complexity. Evie, the successful models of human behaviour you've talked about relate to quite specific areas of human behaviour. When I then look at popular and well-evidence generic models, like the Theory of Planned Behaviour, it seems to me that they're rather different from what you're describing.

You see, I'm struggling to connect those generic models to the complexity of real human behaviour. Yusuf, you talked about a multiplicity of non-linear pathways. But it seems to me that our generic models of human behaviour typically show single, linear pathways.

Yusuf I'm not sure that's entirely fair. Many models explicitly include feedback loops. And they're simplifications as well: they're trying to get a handle on just one part of the complex picture. As Evie put it, they're platforms for further exploration.

However, I do think there could be value in taking a closer look at the different techniques that have been developed for modelling complex phenomena in other disciplines, and asking how we could make better use of some of those techniques in the field of behaviour change. I'm not sure we have a good enough grasp on what's in the modelling toolbox.

Because the reality is that lots of different disciplines are wrestling in different ways with problems that are too hard to model analytically. To take just one example, what could we learn from continuous flow dynamics and the way it uses iterative methods involving cellular automata?

And that's just one example. I'd love to see a project that set out to catalogue the different type of modelling technique available, and their differing applications.

Paola Perhaps we're back to the third type of model I suggested at the outset – the provocations to thought.

Evie What I preferred to call metaphors! I agree, though, there could be lots to learn from looking more closely at the way in which other disciplines model other kinds of complex phenomena.

So sticking with the example of continuous flow dynamics, consider the flow of air across an aircraft wing. At the trailing edge of the wing, you have lots of chaos and unpredictability, meaning it's impossible to model what's happening on a moment-by-moment basis. But if you then pull out to the aircraft as a whole, you can be completely confident about the overall lift on the wing. The regularities only become apparent when you pull out to the bigger picture.

I think there's an interesting metaphor there for human behaviour. Maybe if we look at individual behaviour it's a bit like the trailing edge of the wing: you just can't predict what's going to happen. But if we pull out to the population as a whole, we may start to see patterns.

~ 10 ~

Paola That's a really interesting parallel. And it flags up another important issue for me – this question of levels of analysis. The models you were talking about, Evie, are precisely models of behaviour patterns at the level of a population. They're not saying anything about what's going on at the level of individuals.

Whereas most of the generic models we have focus on the individual and what is going on between their ears. They're the products of a psychological perspective on behaviour, not a sociological one.

Yusuf I'm not sure I agree with that. I mean, it's a point that people often make: but I'm not sure it's actually a very fair one. Let's start with this complaint that the models focus on what's going on between people's ears. I think this is just a straightforward misunderstanding of many of the models we have.

For what it's worth, I suspect it arises from an ambiguity in the term 'context'. On the one hand, we use the word context to refer to all of the variables that we leave out when we build a model. Context is the thing we abstract from. On the other hand, when we're talking about human behaviour it is often useful to distinguish attributes of the individual – things like beliefs or intentions – from attributes of their social and physical setting. And the latter often gets called context as well.

Historically, psychology may sometimes have been guilty of confounding these two things, and treating anything that wasn't 'between people's ears' – i.e. context in the second sense – as something that could be left out of the model – context in the first sense. But I can also point to a long tradition of social psychology that has taken context in the second sense very seriously in trying to model behaviour. Many of the models we have clearly reflect this.

Of course psychological models involve abstracting from context – in the first sense of the term. That's what every model does. But that doesn't mean they're ignoring context in the second sense. In fact, I don't see how anyone who's serious about understanding human behaviour *could* ignore the importance of social and physical context.

Paola But models like that still work by turning social phenomena into attributes of the individual. Take social norms, for example. In a popular model like the Theory of Planned Behaviour, these become *subjective* norms, an individual's *perception* of a social reality.

Or take gender. People collect data on biological sex and call this gender. In fact, of course, even sex isn't binary as is usually assumed; but at least it is clearly a property of the individual. Whereas gender isn't: it's a product of the relationships between people. Gender only emerges as a meaningful construct if you look at the level of a community or society. If you try to reduce it to an individual characteristic, it stops being gender.

This is the other thought that was going through my head earlier, Yusuf, when you mentioned 'the interaction between the individual and their social context'. I suppose my starting point is a belief that the social represents a distinct level of reality, a distinct level of action and meaning, which needs to be modelled in its own right. It's more than just the sum of a series of contextualised individuals.

My concern is that if you only model at the level of individuals, you end up with a very partial picture. For example, I saw a study of a sex education intervention which targeted young people just before they became sexually active. At an individual level, the intervention had some clear impacts: levels of understanding increased, for example, and boys were less likely to pressurise girls into sex. But when it came to the hard medical outcomes – terminations of pregnancies, for example – there was no effect. And the reason for that, I would argue, lay not in the individuals but in social processes.

Yusuf I still don't really see what the problem is. I can account for that outcome at an individual level by noting that the theory of change which was behind the educational intervention clearly didn't pay enough attention to these contextual variables, and attributed too much importance to things like knowledge and attitudes. Which is a very common mistake, I agree. But it's not one that you're bound to make just because you model at the individual level. Making the individual your unit of analysis is not in any way the same as saying that only individual variables matter.

Paola It's interesting. To me the point I'm making seems quite obvious; but I can see that to you, your take also seems quite obvious. I suppose we're bumping up against some quite fundamental philosophical issues here.

Evie That's certainly how it sounds to me. I think you're getting into a question about reduction: can one level of analysis be reduced to another? And even that question comes in different flavours: ontological reductionism, epistemological reductionism.... Maybe we need to invite a philosopher of science along the next time we discuss these issues.

Paola I agree. And yes, the thing I'm resisting is what I perceive as a tendency to reduce the social to nothing more than a collection of individuals. Which maybe is being unfair to you, Yusuf?

Yusuf I'm not sure. Maybe I'm not really getting your point. It's another reminder of how important it is to keep talking about these things across disciplinary boundaries, and working hard to develop a common language.

Paola Absolutely. For what it's worth, I think I'd actually distinguish *three* levels of reality when we try to understand human behaviour. So there's a micro-level, the level of interacting individuals; a meso-level, the level of communities and institutions; and a macro-level, the level of an entire society. Modelling at each of these levels would bring something different to the overall picture. The dream, I suppose, would be to connect all three levels, and see how they interact with each other.

I think this matters when you look at what it takes to achieve behaviour change. Focusing too much on the micro-level, the level of individuals, leads in my view to an undue focus on interventions at this level as well. In reality, behaviour change typically involves interventions and changes across all three levels.

Take smoking, for example: at the macro-level, you had changes in the law; at the meso-level, changes in social norms and workplace practices; and at the micro-level, changes in the attitudes and behaviour of individual smokers. And all three levels interacted with each other.

Yusuf I think that's a good analysis. I also feel there's nothing in there that is problematic for the kind of approach I subscribe to. At the same time, it's clear to me that you feel my approach is too individualistic, that it fails to do justice in some way to these different levels of analysis, change and intervention. So I guess we'll just have to keep on talking about this one.

~ 11 ~

Evie There's another type of philosophical question which I think we may need to wrestle with. One point it seems we all implicitly agree on is that the study of human behaviour and behaviour change can and should be approached scientifically. A lot of our discussion of the role of models, and the interplay of theory and practice, has taken that point for granted.

But that raises a couple of questions. What do we think science is? And what bearing does that have on the way that we understand models?

Yusuf That sounds like a rather abstract point to me. Can you say a bit more?

Evie Well, let's think through a couple of examples. Suppose first that you're a Positivist. That means you believe that science is about observing the world, measuring it, and identifying regularities. If you take this view, then models are just ways of capturing the regularities you have observed.

If, however, you're a Popperian, then you turn this view on its head. From this perspective, models are expressions of patterns you *expect* to see. They're hypotheses, which you then go out and try to disprove by testing them.

A Critical Realist might take issue with both these views, and question whether there are any neutral, objective observations of the world. Models are something closer to interpretative stances – and you can never entirely step outside them and make 'objective' measurements. Your model shapes your observations, just as your observations shape your model.

Paola Maybe if you're a Kuhnian, and believe that science advances through the overthrow of paradigms in scientific revolutions, you'll see another role for models. It goes back to that third type of model I mentioned at the beginning – models which provoke thinking. The roles of models like these might be to throw up anomalies, unexpected results, the kinds of things that can lead us to question paradigms and initiate scientific revolutions. Maybe models play a role similar to that which the philosopher Ian Hacking ascribes to experiments: not testing theories, but creating new phenomena about which to theorise.

Evie It all depends what your view of science is. What is it you think we're actually doing here? How do we gain new knowledge, and what's the status of that knowledge once we've got it?

Yusuf And that in turn could shape how you go about building and using models... I think I understand the point you're making now.

Evie It's a question, really. I'm not sure whether it does make a difference. But if we're thinking about building that common framework for talking to each other about models, we need to explore the possibility.

Paola If we're doing that, then I think we should also re-examine the central role we've been giving to prediction. Evie, you suggested we focus our conversation on models that enable us to make predictions we can test, and you argued that that is central to the whole endeavour of science. Narrowing the scope in this way has been really helpful for today's conversation. But I've had this nagging doubt at the back of my mind: is prediction really the right goal for a science of behaviour change?

You see, I could argue that the fixation with prediction is a relatively recent phenomenon – that we're all still in the thrall of Newtonian astronomy, with its beautiful mathematics. But planetary bodies don't think. People do: they reflect on their own condition and environment, they have *their own models* of the world, which they also adjust in response to experience, and which influence their behaviour. Human behaviour exhibits a level of complexity that, I'd argue, is qualitatively different from anything else we encounter in the world.

And even if I'm wrong on that specific point, we all seemed to agree that the complexity of human behaviour is such that it's very difficult to predict anything beyond short timescales and automatic processes. So I'm still left wondering what's left of a science of behaviour change that puts prediction centre stage.

I'm not saying we should throw up our hands in despair, just that we might want to reconsider what we're trying to do. It seems to me that, even if we can't predict, we can still *explain*. We can understand, forensically dissect. We just need to recognise that those are different tasks, and stop fixating quite so much on prediction.

Evie I don't know if I really understand this distinction you're making between prediction and explanation. I mean, I know the words have different everyday meanings. But how do you make that work in a scientific context? How do you know your explanation is correct if you can't test it in some way?

Paola I suppose we might have to look at something like evolutionary science to get an answer to that question. After all, there is plenty of debate about different models of evolution, conducted on a clearly scientific basis. But so far as I'm aware they don't make any predictions.

Or better still, perhaps we should go and talk to historians. They are clearly in the business of explaining behaviour based on the evidence: but again, no predictions as such.

Yusuf As ever, Paola, they're interesting challenges you make. But I think I'm with Evie on this one. After all, what we're talking about here is not just explaining behaviour but *changing* it. If you can't establish some kind of predictive connection between intervention and outcome – be it ever so uncertain and probabilistic – then how are you going to decide what to do? What's the point of explaining what's happened in the past if it doesn't help you do things better in the future?

Paola Well, I supposed I'd turn that on its head and say, if in fact we *can't* predict the future, what do we achieve by *pretending* that we can?

We're just consoling ourselves with an illusion of control.

Besides, it seems to me there's a very real sense in which we can learn or fail to learn the lesson of history, without being able to make predictions about what will happen next. If nothing else, history tells you something about what *could* happen. We can't predict earthquakes, for example; but we know where to build buildings that can withstand them.

Maybe that's the kind of role models can play too. Not as predictive tools that give us control over the future, but as mechanisms that allow us creatively to explore different possible dynamics, and prepare for a future we can't control.

Evie And where does that leave the idea of behaviour change?

Paola I don't know! We'll have to pick that one up the next time we meet. But it's good to end on a note of controversy, don't you think?

Evie Absolutely. Plenty to take away and think about, and plenty to talk about next time.

Yusuf Agreed. I feel like we've made a lot of progress, but I'm still left with a great many questions.

Paola If nothing else, I think we've demonstrated the value of discussing those questions across disciplines.

Part 2
Responses to the dialogue

1. Use and usability: are theoretical models of behaviour change practical?

Marie Johnston

Emeritus Professor of Health Psychology, University of Aberdeen

Theoretical models have considerable potential for reducing muddle, enhancing models and guiding 'meddling' in the process of behaviour change. But is there a gap between current 'use' and potential 'usability'? There may be nothing quite so practical as a good theory, but only if the good theoretical model is used well in practice.

Models of behaviour change have several uses, a number of which are touched on in the Dialogue. For me, three functions in particular stand out (Johnston, 2014):

- *Reducing the muddle.* Theoretical models define constructs so that users know when they are investigating the same – or different – phenomena and can build a cumulative body of evidence which can be aggregated using evidence synthesis methods
- *Modelling the processes.* Theoretical models define the relationships between constructs so that the process of behaviour change can be modelled, allowing prediction and perhaps, more ambitiously, explanation of behaviour and behaviour change
- *Guiding 'meddling' to change behaviour.* By identifying causal determinants of behaviour, theoretical models may enable users to intervene to achieve better behavioural outcomes

In this paper, I raise some issues regarding the current use of theoretical models for each of these functions and raise questions about how usable our current theories are. I will illustrate my argument using mainly social cognitive theories – especially the Theory of Planned Behaviour (TPB), which is familiar to many people working in behaviour change (and easy to read about on the internet: people.umass.edu/aizen/tpb.html).

> *Useful models can be used to*
> *reduce muddle*
> *model processes*
> *guide 'meddling' to change behaviour*
> *...but only if 'used' well*

1. Reducing muddle: do our theoretical models operationalise and measure distinct constructs?

The minimum requirement of a useful model is that it should define clear constructs, which can be operationalised (i.e. turned into something that can be measured in practice), in a way that:

- reflects the content of each construct – i.e. has 'content validity'
- distinguishes it from other constructs

Constructs that cannot be operationalised in this way are not usable and may increase rather than decrease muddle.

> *Useful constructs can be measured but...*
> *Are there too many non-distinct constructs?*
> *Do we only measure the 'easy' bits?*

Do models of behaviour change as we currently use them meet this minimum requirement? Can the hundreds of constructs in them be operationalised in ways that reflect their content and distinguish them from each other? Examples of well-defined constructs do of course exist: but the evidence suggests that, in general, I think we're a long way from achieving these goals.

First, the proliferation of hypothetical constructs related to behaviour change presents a methodological challenge. There is growing evidence that, in the context of this proliferation, conventional psychometric methods of developing and evaluating measures of constructs may not identify distinct constructs. For example, various authors have proposed theoretical distinctions and overlaps between the TPB construct of perceived behavioural control (PBC) and the Social Cognitive Theory construct of self-efficacy (SE), and have proposed self-report items for measuring these constructs. However, when tested using Discriminant Content Validation (DCV) – a quantitative way of estimating content validity – it was evident that while SE items were satisfactory as measures of SE, PBC items were not satisfactory as measures of PBC, as they frequently did not measure PBC (Johnston et al., 2014). The fact that a key construct cannot readily be operationalised makes the TPB a difficult model to use (which might be a reason for preferring the more recently presented Reasoned Action Approach which incorporates SE rather than PBC into the Theory of Reasoned Action). Similar problems have been found with models of work stress: none of the measures of the key construct of 'effort' measured effort, but instead some measured 'demand', a key construct in the alternative model. (Bell et al., in submission).

A second problem lies in the restricted way in which many constructs, especially social cognitive constructs, are measured. Respondents are typically asked to rate the likelihood of, or strength of agreement with, a statement. Such ratings present gradings which are notoriously difficult to interpret (Gigerenzer and Edwards, 2003): for example, when I say that I 'strongly agree' with an intention statement, does this mean that I intend more strongly than someone else who only endorses 'agree'? On the other hand, if I say that I intend to perform the action 10 times, respondent A says 5 times and respondent B says 15 times, there is a quantitative metric that is clearly interpretable and fixes my position between A and B. Frequency of intention has been shown to have satisfactory content validity as an index of intention (Johnston et al., 2014) and is clearly encompassed within the definition, but is rarely assessed.

Thus some constructs may be well enough defined to be usable, but inadequately used in practice, while others have not been defined adequately to be usable as distinct measurable constructs. For theoretical models to contribute to the development of a cumulative science of behaviour change, they need to be both usable and appropriately used. We need to know the precise content of each construct and we need to measure or operationalise them to give a valid reflection of that content.

> *Confused measurement of constructs may increase muddle*

2. Modelling processes: do our theoretical models predict and explain differences between people and differences within people?

In addition to defining constructs, models also define the relationships between constructs: i.e. they examine how one construct may predict, explain or determine another construct. However issues arise concerning the ways in which models are used – or misused – to examine these relationships.

> *Useful models clarify relationships....*
>
> *within and/or between people?*
>
> *predictive or causal?*

The first issue is whether the theorised relationships account for differences between different people and/or differences within a person. If construct A predicts construct B, does this mean that:

- one can predict that individuals who are more strongly A will be more strongly B? (differences between people)
- for any given individual, one can predict that they will be more strongly B at times when they are more strongly A? (differences within a person)

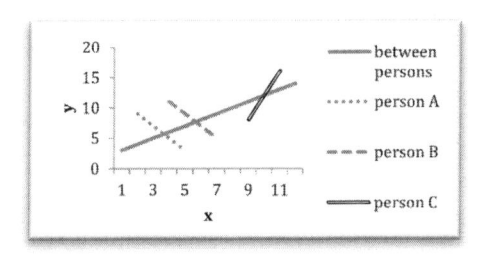

Figure 1 – a possible mismatch in evidence between and within persons

It is often assumed that relationships that hold between people will also apply within a person: but this assumption is fundamentally illogical and is an example of the 'ecological fallacy' or 'Simpson's paradox' (Loney and Nagelkerke, 2014). For example, Molenaar (2004) has found personality traits that are independent when investigated between people may not be independent within people: thus, knowing that person A is high on neuroticism compared with other people gives no information about whether they will be higher than others on conscientiousness (i.e. neuroticism and conscientiousness are independent), but it might still be the case that on days when A is more neurotic they are also more conscientious. In the same vein, it is reliably found that people with more perceived control engage in higher rates of the behaviour than those with lower perceived control, but this gives no information about how fluctuations in perceived control will predict behaviour within an individual; when investigated, variations in perceived control did not predict variations in behaviour within individuals (Quinn et al., 2013).

Figure 1 shows how very different relationships between constructs may be found between and within persons: the relationship between x and y is positive between people but negative for two illustrated persons (A and B) and positive for Person C.

The second issue is that, even if a variable does not predict behaviour, it may still be causal. An important causal variable may not significantly predict behaviour if there is a lack of variability e.g. if all respondents (or all occasions for an individual) show the same high or low levels. The classical example is that it would have been impossible to detect that smoking caused lung cancer in a population where everyone smoked. Similarly, in a population unaware of a health hazard, intention to change may not predict behaviour if intention is uniformly low; in a similar way, in a highly motivated population, variables that determine intention may not predict behaviour. Finding that a variable does not predict a behaviour may not rule it out as an explanatory and even causal variable. While these are extreme examples, models of health behaviour are often examined with measures where the average result is extremely high and the resulting lack of strong relationships may not be a good basis for rejecting the model as a basis for intervention. If intention does not predict behaviour but intention is uniformly low, it may still be valuable to work to increase intention. Reviews of the 'intention-behaviour' gap suggest that there is no 'gap' for those who lack intention – they are reliable in not enacting the behaviour.

Theoretical models are used extensively and successfully to predict and explain behaviour as a basis for developing interventions. However, one needs to be clear that the proposed relationships are not simply predictive but causal, and that the evidence for causal relationships applies within individuals. Finding a relationship between a predictor and a behaviour does not necessarily provide a basis for intervention; and equally, finding no relationship may not rule out the value of intervening to 'increase' the predictor.

The third issue concerns the ways in which the relationships between constructs are visually represented. Do we just use those parts of our models that are displayed in 'pictures'? Anecdotally, models which offer a pictorial representation of relationships appear to be more likely to be used, and used more comprehensively, than those lacking a visual image. For example, the TPB has an easily accessible image (people.umass.edu/aizen/tpb.html) which is frequently represented in publications using the model. By contrast, a model lacking this kind of picture is more likely to be used partially, with different studies incorporating different sets of its constructs and proposing different relationships between them.

Pictures can reduce ambiguity and make it more likely that different users will use the model in the same way and therefore contribute to a cumulative evidence base. In terms of usability, when it comes to understanding the relationships between constructs, 'one picture is worth a thousand words'.

On the other hand, pictures can sometimes create ambiguities. For example, even box-and-arrow pictures may not specify the nature of the relationships represented by the arrows – in some cases they imply causality and can therefore explain, but in others they are simply predictive. For example, in the TPB the arrow from PBC to behaviour is only predictive; the causal arrow is from 'Actual control' to behaviour, and PBC is predictive only to the extent that it reflects actual control.

Pictures may also fail to capture *synergies* that models propose between constructs. For example, according to social cognitive theory, self-efficacy alone does not increase behaviour; rather it is the combination of self-efficacy and another construct, valued outcome expectancies. Similarly, in fear-arousal theory, increasing fear without a plan of action may simply increase fear, and have no effect on behaviour (Peters et al., 2013). A picture which shows two boxes with arrows pointing to the third is ambiguous between cases like these and cases where each of the two boxes has an independent effect on the outcome.

> *'one picture may be worth 1000 words'*
>
> *... and so may mislead more readily*

3. Guiding 'meddling': how are our theoretical models useful in making decisions about intervention content and targeting?

Theoretical models are useful as a basis for intervention, helping us to identify whose behaviour to change, the constructs that need to be altered to achieve that change, and the active behaviour change content required of the intervention – that is: who, what and how.

> *Useful models guide intervention*
>
> *by identifying who, what and how to change*
>
> *But...*
>
> *What evidence is required?*
>
> *Is it enough to show that the model predicts differences between people?*

But do we collect the appropriate evidence for model-based intervention? For example, if we used the evidence of Figure

1 above with 'y' as a desirable behaviour, then the between-person evidence might suggest an intervention to increase 'x', while the within-person evidence suggests this would be harmful for persons A and B (while benefiting person C). Between-person evidence is a dubious basis for the development of an intervention, as interventions make changes *within* persons and therefore depend on understanding the factors that make an individual more likely to engage in particular behaviours (Johnston and Johnston, 2013).

This is clearly illustrated by variables such as gender or ethnicity, which vary between people but not within people. If it was found that gender predicted a given behaviour, this might suggest that one gender was more in need of intervention. With additional information, it might suggest a need to tailor interventions differentially to each gender. But it would give no information whatsoever about how an intervention should be developed: one would not attempt to convert women to men or vice versa. The same conclusion holds true for constructs which might vary within a person (e.g. constructs which represent how people think and feel such as intention or planning ability) but for which there is only between-person evidence. For example, if the only evidence available showed that people high on perceived control (between-person variation) were more likely to engage in a desired behaviour, one might design an intervention to increase perceived control; however, Quinn et al. (2013) found that some people did less when their perceived control was high (within-person variation) and that such an intervention might therefore actually harm them.

As noted above, between-person evidence may be useful in identifying individuals to target. This may be done atheoretically by simply collecting evidence for each individual. Alternatively, theoretical models may be helpful in classifying persons prior to intervention. For example, returning again to Figure 1, if persons like A and B are similar to each other but different from persons like C on a theoretical construct, say social deprivation, then two interventions might be designed – one for individuals with, in this example, low social deprivation, the other for individuals with high social deprivation.

Unfortunately, there is a dearth of within-person studies which could offer a valid basis for intervention design. For example, the TPB is widely used in behaviour change interventions: but evidence that people with more positive attitudes have stronger intentions and are more likely to engage in the behaviour is not enough. One needs evidence that, within individuals, fluctuations in attitudes lead to changes in intention, which in turn affect behaviour. (In statistical terms one would need evidence of *mediation* of the effect of attitudes on behaviour *within* persons before designing an intervention to change attitudes.) If, on top of this, there were evidence that another theoretical variable predicted the ways in which these within-person relationships varied between different groups of people, then it might also be possible to target interventions. For example, if the relationship between attitudes and behaviour only held for those with low intention to engage in the behaviour, one could target efforts to change attitudes at those with low intentions. (In statistical terms, one would need evidence of *moderated mediation* i.e. that the within-person effect of attitudes on behaviour was modified by intention.) This kind of evidence is not generally collected or used as the basis for behaviour change interventions.

> *Evidence needed to guide intervention*
>
> WHO: *To select recipients or tailor interventions – evidence of moderation*
>
> WHAT: *To target constructs for intervention – evidence of mediation from non-experimental within person studies*
>
> HOW: *To choose intervention techniques – evidence from experimental between-person studies*

While theoretical models are 'usable' in designing interventions, it's my view that they are often poorly used. As Michie and Prestwich (2010) note, they may simply be mentioned, or they may be used to identify targeted constructs for intervention, to select intervention techniques, to select recipients of the intervention, or to tailor the intervention for individuals. However, even when used to design or target interventions, the evidence from within-person studies is frequently lacking.

Am I suggesting that between-person studies are useless? Not at all: experimental between-person studies are essential in choosing effective intervention techniques (most obviously in randomised controlled trials, but also using the fractional factorial designs proposed by Collins et al. (2007) where the choice of techniques investigated may be guided by theoretical models). Nevertheless this may prove difficult as the links between theory and techniques are rarely specified; they are currently being investigated in a MRC-funded project, 'Theories and Techniques of Behaviour Change' (http://sbk.li/11811). As Azjen (2011) states, these links have not been made even for a model as widely used as the TPB: 'this is where the investigator's experience and creativity comes into play. The theory of planned behaviour .... does not tell us what kind of intervention will be most effective'. (A notable exception to this general rule is Operant Learning Theory, which has a vast array of associated techniques for changing behaviour.)

Conclusions

Theoretical models have considerable potential for reducing muddle, enhancing models and guiding 'meddling' in the process of behaviour. But do we have a gap between current 'use' and potential 'usability'? There may be 'nothing quite so practical as a good theory' (Cartwright, 1952) but only if the good theory is used well in practice.

Suggested further reading

For works cited, see References at the end of the book.

Johnston, M., Dixon, D., Hart, J., Glidewell, L., Schröder, C. and Pollard, B. (2014)'Discriminant content validity: A quantitative methodology for assessing content of theory-based measures, with illustrative applications', British Journal of Health Psychology, 19(2), pp. 240-57.

Discusses how conventional methods may fail to capture the valid content of the target construct.

Michie, S. and Prestwich, A. (2010) 'Are interventions theory-based? Development of a theory coding scheme', Health Psychology, 29(1), 1.

Discusses how theories are used in developing interventions.

Johnston, D.W. and Johnston, M. (2013) 'Useful theories should apply to individuals', British Journal of Health Psychology, 18(3), 469-73.

Discusses how theories that apply between individuals should also be applied within individuals.

2. In defence of the 'non-model': modelling the prevention of teenage tobacco use in Africa

Katherine Hardyment

Associate Director, Good Business

Precise models may be desirable in theory. In practice, even an imprecise model can provide a solid start point for action; and action can in turn generate more knowledge, which helps to improve our models.

The behaviour change work described in this piece is funded by The Bill & Melinda Gates Foundation.

Why does a teenager start smoking? Chances are you'll think peer pressure and role models are big issues. But doesn't it all depend on their context and experiences – different people responding in different ways to different influences?

The Dialogue on models of behaviour change throws up a lot of questions we've been grappling with in our behaviour change work with teens. As Yusuf says in §8, human behaviour is incredibly complex and contextual – but modelling that behaviour can be a powerful way to understand, predict and hopefully influence its course.

Three themes emerge in the Dialogue that we think are particularly interesting: the type of model and whether some 'models' are deserving of that name at all; why models at the 'less precise' end of the scale exist and have value; and – only hinted at, but important – how a model can evolve over time. We'd like to share some reflections on each, using insights from our behaviour change work in Africa as an example of how theory plays out on the ground.

The type of model – or perhaps it's not a model at all

Since 2013, we have launched a number of behaviour change interventions that use a social marketing approach to inspire teenagers in different African contexts to choose not to smoke. In each market, we create a behaviour change model through a three-step process. First, we develop hypotheses around key levers for behaviour change based on qualitative research into the knowledge, attitudes and perceptions of teenagers. Second, we design an approach that draws on relevant behaviour change principles to address these levers. Then we use ongoing evaluation of impact to test and refine our hypotheses and our approach.

The resulting logic model is not precise, analytical or quantitative. It's what, judging from her comments early in the Dialogue, Evie might describe as at the 'non-model' or 'bad' end of Yusuf's 'continuum of models', from 'precise' to 'less precise' (less precise being 'bad').

Yes, the logic model that we use may not be precise, but certainly it is useful. It allows us to plan activity according to the most influential variables, think through the causes of the behaviour we hope to influence, and map out and contextualise our proposed interventions for change. It provides the theoretical foundations on which we design activity. For example, we identify the peer pressure created by a widespread perception that most teenagers smoke (even though data indicates this is a myth – 90% do not smoke), so we design a viral social norms campaign for Facebook, sparking teens to tell their peers that they are part of the '#MostTeens' who don't smoke. An example of the teen selfies on Facebook inspired by this intervention is pictured.

It's interesting to note that this particular social norms intervention is an example of the interdependence of different levels of behaviour: the micro-level of individual choice, influenced by and influencing the meso-level of the community, both in the macro-context of society. As Paola says in §10 of the Dialogue, the dream is to accurately understand this interdependence – but it is a dream at present.

So call it what you will – logic model, framework, logic flow – setting out predictions of influence in a systematic way can be an invaluable way to design a strategic intervention. It's a solid start point.

Source: Facebook, 2015

A desire for data

It's not that a more precise model isn't desirable, it's that it's not possible.

There is very limited data on African teenagers' social context and risk behaviours. Business market research is lacking; teenagers simply don't have enough disposable income to make them a worthwhile focus for investigation. Research that has been done with this group tends to focus on issues very much on the government and international community's agenda – in particular, HIV/AIDS. Tobacco in Africa is the sleeping giant. It's big, it's dangerous, it's waking up and society is not prepared to respond – especially on the issue of uptake among teens, rather than cessation among adults (where more data is available).

Even if we did have more data, the number of different influences and scenarios at play when a teenager decides to try smoking would be near impossible to map accurately. In our qualitative research, teenagers struggled to recount all the different influences on their attitudes towards cigarettes – ranging from seeing popular girls in school holding cigarettes, to the (apparently huge) impact of watching pop idol Rhianna smoking in her latest music video. We know celebrities are influential – that's why we've spent so long getting them to vocally support our campaigns. But we struggle to know precisely how and how much they're important among all the other influences. This isn't only because of the interdependence and complexity of human choice, experience and perception in the context of social norms, peer pressure and a huge array of other social and cultural influences. It's also because of structural influences, such as the cost of a cigarette and a teenager's ability to get hold of one.

This is all far from the control system context that Evie describes in §2. It's an example of how, rather than simply thinking about picking a model according to what Yusuf describes as 'your purpose', we sometimes must pick a model according to what's possible.

But there is a silver lining here. One advantage of having a lack of information to create a model is that it limits assumptions about what the solution should look like. Our starting point was a brief to use the power of marketing to influence teenagers to choose not to smoke. This enabled us to navigate an issue that Paola rightly highlights (§6) of many practitioners approaching behaviour change work 'with an intervention already in mind'. Instead, the lack of data means we design our entire intervention around the results of the primary research, and evolve the model and approach as evidence of 'what works' is gathered.

Strengthening models with data – and experience

With time, our desire for data is gradually being met, as we create our own evidence base. We have just launched an intervention in a new African market – Uganda – for which a team at University College London (UCL), led by Professor Robert West, analysed the results of our baseline survey to inform the logic model for the intervention. Their work identified the statements of knowledge, attitudes and perception that correlate most strongly with smoking behaviour, but also are prevalent among non-smokers (for example, 'I believe that most people my age smoke'). This information informed the hypotheses for our logic model – it helped us to identify the beliefs and attitudes to address in the intervention, and to measure in monitoring surveys in order to track our impact.

It's worth saying, though, that quantitative insights can't give all the answers. Knowing what attitudes correlate with smoking behaviour doesn't tell you what influences brought about those attitudes, therefore directing you to the 'solution'. Nor can we guarantee that just because they correlate with smoking behaviour, they are also associated with a desire or inclination to try smoking for the first time.

Instead, the quantitative insights are another building block in the knowledge base we assemble as we design a new intervention.

This process of looking at all the information in the round – quantitative, qualitative and drawing on experience and expertise – is, I would argue, essential for building models and frameworks in complex systems. I first came across this idea of taking an inclusive approach to evidence back in my days studying Geography at Cambridge: I remember my lecturer in avalanches telling us how, after years of development drawing on more and more data, intelligent models designed to predict where and when avalanches would occur still couldn't out-predict models that factored in expert opinion. As with avalanches, so with human behaviour. Some of the most powerful insights that have helped us develop our interventions were gathered by simply talking to teenagers on the ground – not least because their expert knowledge of their own lives and situations enabled us to understand the data better, and refine our model.

Expertise is difficult to capture quantitatively – but it can and should have a place when developing models alongside hard data, whether for avalanches or behaviour change.

Trying to understand, predict and influence a teenager

As the dialogue rightly concludes, human behaviour is incredibly complex but this doesn't obviate the need to approach behaviour change work systematically. In fact, given our desire to use marketing – an intervention approach that Evie uses as an example of complexity in itself – our project is in even greater need of a systematic approach to ensure that planning is strategic, rather than on a whim. So models – let's call them logic models – do play an important role.

Trying to understand teenagers isn't simple, but every day we work on these projects we increase our knowledge of what we know, and what we need to know. It will take time to build even smarter models. We're working on it. In the meantime, amalgamating what we do know and predict into a logic model, and tracking the impact of interventions and contextual changes, is the best start point we've got for creating change today.

Suggested further reading

For works cited, see References at the end of the book.

Feet First (2014) film clip from Crowd Control. Available at: http://sbk.li/12921

Guaranteed to make you smile: two minutes of inspiration to use passion points like music and fun to change people's behaviour. We believe our campaigns win teenage interest because we follow this principle – it's about inspiration and motivation, not just education.

Jackson, R.R. (2014) 'Ebola may be in the headlines, but tobacco is another killer in Africa', The Guardian, 16 October 2014.

A short and unsettling summary of how women and young people in Africa are the new lucrative target for the tobacco industry.

Christakis, N. (2010) 'The Hidden Influence of Social Networks', TED talk. Available at: http://sbk.li/12931

A powerful TED talk by Nicholas Christakis that explores the role and significance of peer influence. We know peer pressure – positive and negative – is huge for teens, so a core part of our approach involves creating a positive network to which teens aspire to belong.

Bill and Melinda Gates Foundation: Tobacco Control Strategy Overview. Available at: http://sbk.li/12932

Social marketing can drive behaviour change, but it's even more powerful when combined with policy change. In this article, you can read how the Bill and Melinda Gates Foundation is taking a multi-intervention approach to the challenge of tobacco control around the world.

3. Model Conduct

Alan Cribb

Professor of Bioethics and Education, Centre for Public Policy Research, King's College London

Everyone would surely agree that both the development and use of models of behaviour can be done in ways that are better or worse – and that there would be value in clarifying good practice. But would it be possible to produce the same guidance for model developers and model users? Or might these two different kinds of activity call for different conceptions of good practice?

What follows is a fictional extract from the preface to a book that does not exist.

It is a response to those parts of the Dialogue where Evie, Paola and Yusuf are calling for more rigour in the way models are talked about and specified, and more guidance on the selection and use of models for behaviour change. I imagined a similar community of researchers – perhaps a few years later, and established in their careers – deciding to collaborate, as a panel of experts, on a text setting out standards of good practice. What would such a text look like and what would it cover?

Obviously I cannot answer that here. Instead I have focused on one issue that might arise in the production of such a text: is it possible to produce the same guidance for both model developers and model users?

This part of the preface is based on the idea that there was some fractiousness on the panel between those who wanted to provide one integrated set of guidance for both developers and users, and those who thought it necessary to differentiate between different kinds of good practice for different audiences. The extract assumes that the 'differentiators' prevailed, and consists of a self-justificatory piece written from that side of the argument.

This whole issue is prefigured in a remark of Paola's (§4):

> It strikes me there are two potentially competing agendas here. For the person who wants to bring about behaviour change, fiddling around with models to fit one's own purposes sounds like it might be a good idea. For the person who is trying to advance our understanding of human behaviour through systematic review, it's a huge problem. I wonder if this tension accounts for some of the difficulties?

An extract from the preface to *Good Practice for Behaviour Change*

One of the most insistent obstacles to the development of this work was disagreement amongst the panel as to the organisation of our guide. The whole panel agreed that the guide should cover both sides of the translation divide – i.e. it should indicate good practice in both model development and model application. But this aspiration led to strong disagreements. One group took the view that the guide should be as integrated as possible, with a single coherent set of guidance aimed at both pure research and at model usage in applied work. The other group insisted that different principles and forms of guidance were needed for different purposes. It is evident from a quick appraisal of the contents page that the latter group prevailed.

In broad terms, the integrationists took the line that there is no clear distinction between theory and practice, and that models can only be meaningfully developed, tested and refined in use. This being so, it would make little sense to try and separate out good practice for development and use. In addition to the dangers of incoherence, they were alive to the risk of double standards, or to the charge of hypocrisy if thought or conduct that was recommended in one domain was somehow laid aside or forgotten in other domains. By contrast, the differentiators took the line that model development and application are essentially different kinds of activity, which call for different conceptions and kinds of good practice. This being so, there is no inconsistency in stressing different principles, or in recommending different conduct, in the two domains. (One participant, who chose to leave the panel, developed the striking view that behaviour change models should never be applied outside of relatively limited and controlled research contexts.)

Our decision to organise the document in two parts, the first offering guidance for model development, the second guidance for model application, was influenced by three overlapping sets of reasons advanced by the differentiators.

1. Scientific comportment is not always fitting

Much of what counts as propriety in the part of the guide that relates to model development (Part 1) is related to scientific rigour – for example, the guidelines concerning research methodology, ethics, model specification and labelling. Without clear and consistent nomenclature, public syntheses of evidence bases and gaps, and so on, one cannot properly develop, compare and refine approaches to the modelling of behaviour change.

But these values cannot and should not be applied with the same steadfastness in applied settings. In large part this is a matter of practicality – there is only a certain amount of time and patience available for rigour in the real world. The clients of model developers will naturally care that the models they use are broadly useful, but they will equally naturally resist being incorporated into some never-ending research programme. Neither will they wish to fixate on nomenclature and labels. They may prefer to use terms that trip off their tongue or to 'personalise' model terms by re-casting them according to pre-existing missions or brands. Truth may be the core value in scientific research but something more like effectiveness is a candidate for the core value in applied work.

This does not mean that we wish to encourage dishonesty. It is, rather, that honesty involves an element of fittingness. If model developers are teaching students, they should be encouraging an unrelenting scepticism about the bases and reliability of their models. If they are talking to a client – who will typically be in need of some reassurance that the model will help them solve some practical problem – a different form and tone of honesty might be needed. Scientific rigour is part of good public relations, but it is not all of it. We do like to know that our doctor is fully fuelled by scientific scepticism before we allow her across the threshold, but we do not wish her to make a big display of it when she reaches the bedside.

2. The world is crazier than we think[1]

The world is more indeterminate than the models that represent it. The relative determinacy of models is, as has often been stated, their point: they can introduce much needed simplification into the way we understand and act in the world. But it also entails a need for caution when applying models – specifically caution in acting as if the world was model-like.

Sometimes real world cases and circumstances will be sufficiently circumscribed and/or stable for behaviour change models to be directly applicable. But it is not easy to know when these conditions apply. A hitherto reliable friend and adviser may apply the same sophisticated logic on Friday as on Monday, but Friday's advice may turn out to be poor advice because the world has changed during the week. When dealing with complex and open-ended systems, especially over long time frames, it is especially

---

[1] World is crazier and more of it than we think,
Incorrigibly plural. I peel and portion
A tangerine and spit the pips and feel
The drunkenness of things being various.
Louis MacNeice, from *Snow*. Available at: http://sbk.li/13991

important to be aware of the gap between models and reality. Indeed, the task of modelling some systems would arguably be so daunting, time-consuming and inherently unreliable as to be fruitless.

In many instances, while models might be useful aids to thinking, they will not do very much of the work. It is all very well saying that in these cases models make good servants but poor masters, but it has to be stressed that few people have the experience of managing servants, let alone the wisdom to do it well. Of course these difficulties also provide an incentive and an opportunity for model developers to improve both their models and their recommendations for how, where and when (not) to try and apply them. But by far the most important part of model usage relies upon the intelligent filtering and interpretation of any such recommendations rather than upon the following of them.

3. Knowing what might work tells you comparatively little

In the best cases having a good behaviour change model will provide a reliable basis for deciding what kinds of interventions might produce what kinds of effects. In short these models will tell us what does, or might, 'work'. However, as any thoughtful person appreciates, this kind of information, whilst potentially useful, only gives us a fraction of what we need to make a practical judgement. It is not that this kind of information lacks value, but rather that notions of usefulness can be assigned to it that are seriously misleading.

Models provide us with answers to only a small fraction of the questions we need answers to. In general terms, for example, we need not only to know 'does x 'work'?', but also: what range of things can and should count as 'working' (as being successful in some sense)? What other interventions, or alternatives to x, might 'work' in similar or different respects? What are the considerations in favour of or against different notions of success and/or different alternatives to x? How much of our time and resources should we be devoting to this particular area of success rather than something completely different? Where have these aims and priorities come from, and have we stood back from them, and thought otherwise about them, sufficiently?

These are all very familiar, routine and basic questions that need some kind of answers before we can sensibly act. The worry we have in mind here is that having a reasonably good answer to just one of these question can lead to distorted thinking: specifically, that knowing 'x works' may incline some people to do x even where, all things considered, x would be a foolish thing to do. It may reasonably be countered that only a rather stupid person would make this kind of mistake. But our worry is that many institutions and roles positively foster these forms of stupidity – encouraging people to think in very narrow terms and to pursue and demonstrate versions of success whether these are meaningful or wholly misleading.

Development and application

Enough of us have found these reasons to be persuasive for us to divide the guide into its two main parts – aimed at model development and model application respectively – and then into sub-sections based around more specific purposes and contexts. We are asking our readers to be flexible and to adapt their principles and manners as they travel across boundaries. In academic circles they will need to practise various kinds of narrow uprightness depending upon the species of rigour in play. Once they move into wider circles they will inevitably need to be more worldly, and ready to find common cause with, and make compromises with, multiple communities of interest. Some of the time these broader communities may share an interest in scientific progress and in honing the predictive strength of models. But they may often have a bigger interest in other things – things which may be laudable, or may be condemnable. Once outside the academic forum, the model developer needs access to multiple resources including a well-calibrated set of ethical scales and a hard hat.

In short we have chosen to stress the discontinuities, rather than the continuities, between model development and model use. People who are developing and testing models are simply doing something different from those who are applying models. The former are trying to get models right, the latter are trying to get something else right. Different standards apply when we are making things than when we are using them, and that is as it should be.

The integrationists are right to worry that this division risks sidelining some of the most important issues in model conduct. The vast majority of modellers are interested in both pure and applied work. They purposefully and explicitly work across academic and 'real world' settings. For them, getting models right will at the same time, and by necessity, involve getting something right in contexts of use (or at least being able to make some reliable claims). For that reason we have sought to cross-reference clearly and extensively. For example, the section (1.6) which focuses on the need for model developers to systematically specify their model type, assumptions, strengths and limitations (against the background of the appropriate model taxonomy and heritage grid) is very closely linked into the section (2.3) which recommends forms of published user guidance about the potential strengths, limitations and 'reach' of models. The intention, in part, is that it will be relatively easy for users, if they are so inclined, to dig beneath the guidance and to access the academic debates behind it.

Nonetheless we believe that there is merit in being conscious of the gaps between what is required in the spheres of research and practice. Not least these are gaps of governance and power. Just as model developers wish to accommodate parts of the world within their models, the resulting models (unless they are to live purely within research texts) need to be accommodated within the world. There are severe limits to how far model developers can legislate for this latter process and they will have to contend with many other, and typically much more powerful, legislators. This is why the concluding section of this report on vested interests and declarations of interests (3.2) directly addresses such power dynamics. It is important, from case to case and moment to moment, to think about who is governing and who is being governed.

On the one hand, model developers, if they are to be useful, will need to be flexible and negotiate; in so doing they need to be conscious of the degree to which they have become part of other people's projects. On the other hand model developers will want to create applications in their own image, steering policy-makers or practitioners to think in certain ways and metaphorically or literally 'buy' certain approaches; in so doing they must not only be mindful of the limits of their influence but also accountable for the power they are seeking to exercise.

Suggested further reading

For works cited, see References at the end of the book.

Midgley, M. (1991) Wisdom, Information and Wonder: What is knowledge for? London: Routledge.

A full length and in-depth reflection on the relationship between scientific specialisation and the broader purposes of knowledge.

4. Industrialising behaviour change

Richard L. Wright

Director of Sustainable Behaviour, Unilever

Industry can and will play an increasingly important role in behaviour change – but only if we can first 'industrialise' our models. That means making them accessible to non-expert employees, and also recognising the ways in which business can positively impact on behaviour – both via more traditional 'push' interventions, but also via interventions that are 'pulled' by consumers.

I've seen a lot of woodsheds in rural India that look a bit like toilets. They are the vestiges of toilet-building programmes that failed to address the need to change behaviour and convert the beneficiaries from open defecation to using the new facilities. The fact that people continue to defecate in fields makes it difficult and therefore unlikely that they wash their hands with soap; a simple act by which they can reduce the risk that they will become ill. In the UK it is easier to wash our hands with soap – but we frequently fail to do so – before meals that are likely to contain high levels of calories. Calories that will be converted to fat due to our sedentary lifestyle.

To address problems like these, I passionately believe that we need models to help practitioners become more effective at changing behaviour. Behaviour change is required to counter the epidemics of obesity and type 2 diabetes and to alleviate the stress we are putting on our environment. It has the power to help beat malnutrition and malaria and to reduce the prevalence of diarrhoea and pneumonia, which kill millions of children in low-income countries.

It is also my view that industry can, and will, play an increasingly important role in catalysing more sustainable behaviours. However, I question whether academic models of behaviour change are meeting all industry's needs. Further, I doubt that future scientific programmes that place greater emphasis on developing positivistic models – of the kind that, in the dialogue, Evie in particular seems keen to advocate – will do much to address these unmet needs.

Instead, I want to argue that industry needs help to empower non-expert employees to create cost-effective or even profitable behavioural change. Some of this behaviour change will occur as the result of designing deliberate interventions that are 'pushed' towards a target population.

Much will occur during the normal course of providing products and services that attract, or 'pull', customers towards them. 'Pull' interventions are less researched and less valued than 'push' campaigns; but work on their effectiveness is likely to be of greater industrial value.

Unilever Sustainable Living Plan and behaviour change

Let me start with an example that illustrates why I believe industry has an important role to play in catalysing more sustainable behaviours.

When developing Unilever's Sustainable Living Plan goals, we realised that we could dramatically reduce the overall greenhouse gas and water footprints of our products by catalysing changes in consumer behaviour. In addition, by promoting handwashing, safe sanitation and drinking water purification, we had an opportunity improve the health and wellbeing of some of the world's most vulnerable people.

In line with this, we made several ambitious commitments requiring mass behaviour change by 2020, including halving the water associated with consumers' use of our products and helping a billion people to improve their hygiene habits.

The level of these goals provides some indication of Unilever's scale: a vast global organisation employing 174,000 people in businesses ranging from deodorants and laundry powders to ice creams and soups. Two billion people every day use our products in over 190 countries. This reach means that, in principle, if we can enable consumers to make small changes in their behaviour then we can have a huge impact.

However, to achieve such ambitious goals we first needed to build the capacity of a large number of geographically disparate employees to help consumers change behaviour. The vast majority of these employees do not have a background in the behavioural sciences or access to experts.

To help enable the wider Unilever community develop behaviour change interventions we created the '5 Levers' process (Pradeep, 2011). This takes a team through a series of steps, starting with defining a specific behavioural challenge (e.g. 'Help 5- to 11-year-old children clean their teeth before bedtime'). The process goes on to cover developing an understanding of current behaviour and factors that may prevent or facilitate the behaviour change. Finally, the eponymous '5 Levers' are used to inspire intervention ideas.

We derived the '5 Levers' from a synthesis of many different theories and models. 'Make it Understood' includes communicating knowledge about the desired behaviour and establishing personal relevance. The other levers, 'Make it Easy', 'Make it desirable', 'Make it rewarding', and 'Make it a habit', include behaviourist principles on effective rewards, as well as the concepts of automatisation, social learning and social norms, and ideas from behavioural economics.

We have not rigorously tested the '5 Levers', nor do we claim that they are comprehensive or replace the marketer's art of creating compelling communications with the right look and feel to appeal to consumers. However, the process represents a good solution to one of the main problems in industrialising behaviour change theory. It enables us to drive best practice and appropriate many of the current behavioural theories on a global scale.

Profitable behaviour change

Unilever's Sustainable Living Plan is not an exercise in corporate social responsibility, but our business model. It describes how we intend to grow sales, while enhancing people's lives and not increasing the environmental burden that we, our suppliers, and our consumers place on the world.

This is an important point, because it specifies that *our actions will not be charitable but guided by enlightened self-interest*. For instance, we wish to help consumers in water-stressed countries through selling them 'easy rinse' laundry products. This enables consumers to manage this scarce resource and creates a return for our shareholders.

Expensive behaviour change programmes that need to be subsidised by the rest of Unilever's business are not in the plan. We don't have endless funds with which to implement behaviour change programmes that don't improve long-term profitability. Moreover, I believe that this is a strength rather than a weakness. If we can work out how to change highly-learned, habitual behaviours on a mass scale at the same time as improving profitability, then industry will commit to the long term. This sharply contrasts with situations where behaviour change is uneconomic and heavily subsidised by governments or donors. Unlike profitable programmes, subsidised programmes are susceptible to changing priorities and funding cuts.

This is the context in which I believe we really need real help from academia: help on how to achieve profitable behaviour change. Particularly for low- and middle-income countries, where profit margins are low, either we need low-cost ways of changing behaviour, or we need to offset the costs of interventions by creating revenue from the very act of behaviour change itself. I would categorise a self-sustaining business that changes behaviour as part of its existing business model as a 'pull intervention'.

'Push' and 'Pull' interventions

I would like to distinguish between two classes of behaviour change interventions by borrowing the terms 'push' and 'pull' from supply chain management and marketing.

'Push interventions' are where the intervener intentionally targets behaviour change with an identified population. Examples of 'push' methods are direct contact programmes delivered through schools, mothers' groups, or doctors' surgeries; and leaflets or letters sent to individuals or households. At Unilever we employ many 'push interventions' and the '5 Levers' framework can help teams create these kinds of interventions.

'Push interventions' are delivered in a prescribed way to a target population. They are 'bounded' in the sense that it is possible to identify what activities occur because of the intervention and what activities are coincidental. Finally, and importantly, because 'push interventions' select participants, they can be evaluated through randomised controlled trials (RCTs). Independent participants (or independent clusters of participants) can be selected and randomly allocated to 'Intervention' and 'Control' groups. Random allocation to groups is a critical property of RCTs as it ensures that differences in outcome can be ascribed to the effects of intervention rather than pre-existing differences between the groups. Haynes et al. (2013) argue that the use of RCTs to evaluate behavioural interventions represents good science, and I agree.

'Pull interventions' are less conventionally conceived as behaviour change interventions and, indeed, changing behaviour is unlikely to be the primary intention of the initiator. Important sources of 'pull interventions' are clubs, societies and interest groups, as well as the products and services offered by commercial enterprises.

For example, the RSPB attracts members who have an interest in birds or, even, just in being in the countryside. There is not necessarily an explicit intention to change behaviour. However, once people become members they may increase their participation in outdoor activities and voluntary conservation behaviours, as well as being subject to the RSPB's more intentional 'push' interventions where they encourage their members to feed garden birds, plant shrubs and trees, and create dead woodpiles for the benefit of nature.

Two examples of businesses that are making behaviour more sustainable as a 'by-product' of meeting consumers' needs are Clean Team in Kumasi, Ghana and Ocado in the UK. Clean Team is a small, service-based company that gives toilets to urban households and then collects the waste for a weekly fee. This provides a convenient alternative to public toilets particularly for older people. However, it also changes the behaviour of the whole family, making sanitation more hygienic and improving personal safety. Ocado, through its grocery delivery service, makes shopping more convenient while reducing the carbon footprint of the weekly shop. In the process, it also reduces the number of car journeys and encourages the re-use of plastic bags.

Businesses live or die by their ability to attract consumers and meet their needs. Behaviour change needs to be part of this, not an addition. When businesses do this well, they will engage people over the long term, creating greater opportunity for change.

Despite their potential power, I suspect, that none of the 'pull interventions' I have described were designed using behaviour change principles. However, it is my unproven intuition that all could have been improved through their application.

Application of behaviour change models to 'pull' interventions

Current models almost exclusively focus on 'push interventions'. It is more difficult for me to understand how the models apply to 'pull interventions'. This may be because the task of modelling such interventions seems to have some additional challenges associated with it.

First, models of 'pull interventions' would need to address what makes people initiate and maintain engagement with the intervention. Many current behaviour change models seem to assume an attentive and engaged target audience. By contrast, for some pro-environmental behaviours we have found that the challenge is in attracting the attention of a mass audience in the first place.

Second, 'pull interventions' may not be bounded in the same way as 'push interventions'. The activities of clubs and societies may be informal and partly determined by their membership. Business interventions will also be subject to change as they unfold – being tailored according to consumer demands and preferences. For both kinds of organisation, activities related and unrelated to the behaviour change will occur in parallel and continue on an ongoing basis. Both kinds of organisation may be highly effective behavioural change agents, but as 'interventions' they may be very difficult to characterise.

Finally, the targets of the behaviour change in a 'pull intervention' are a self-selected subset of the population, such as those interested in birds, or more convenient sanitation or shopping. This means that interventions are not amenable to RCTs. They violate a central tenet of randomised controlled trials: the random allocation to group. People in the 'Intervention' group are systematically different from those in the 'Control'. Satisfactory alternative paradigms for evaluating effectiveness, and cost-effectiveness, are not obvious and this lack of rigorous assessment means that 'pull interventions' are less valued as 'push interventions'.

I suspect it is these factors that explain why the field of behaviour change has placed disproportionate focus on 'push interventions'. They are easier to characterise and more amenable to RCTs that generate evidence concerning their efficacy and effectiveness. This in turn makes them more interesting to funders and journals.

Future models of behaviour change

'Push interventions' are, and will remain, important as means of changing many behaviours. However, 'pull interventions' are under-recognised and under-researched sources of behaviour change. They are of increasing relevance in a world that is increasingly digital. Behaviour change via internet sites, social networks, and mobile phones require 'pull', with people self-selecting themselves because the intervention interests them. We need to design these interventions to attract and hold participants' interest, and not just include good behavioural principles.

Better models of 'push interventions', with more tightly defined hypothetical constructs and well-characterised interventions will, in principle, allow the field to learn about what does and doesn't work. However, I believe that they will only provide incremental benefits to the practitioner who is already able to access theoretical principles through pragmatic frameworks, such as the '5 Levers' or MINDSPACE (Dolan et al., 2010).

It's my belief that dramatic shifts in our ability to make behaviour more sustainable will come through a greater understanding of how to realise successful 'pull interventions'. We need design principles, new interventions, and evaluation paradigms. We need to understand and improve their cost-effectiveness and we need to evaluate them with rigour, reporting outcomes in peer-reviewed journals. The opportunity for greater collaboration between industry and academia in this endeavour is both large and exciting.

5. Explanatory and predictive behavioural modelling

Nigel Shardlow

Director of Planning, Sandtable Ltd

An abundance of behavioural data and new techniques in machine learning makes it possible to build behavioural models that predict without explaining. Such 'purely predictive' models have their place in behaviour change. However, when the stakes are high – as they are for strategic decision-making – explanatory models that support causal storytelling (such as simulation models) are needed.

A few months ago I lost my sense of smell, completely. It turns out that, when you lose your sense of smell, people don't really show you that much sympathy. They don't think it's a big deal. It's actually a bit worse than it sounds, though. For a start, when you lose your sense of smell, you lose most of your ability to appreciate nice food and drink. All wine tastes about the same, plonk or grand cru. But there's also something else.

I found out about this other thing from a colleague at work who I'd told about my anosmia, as the medics call it. He sent me an article in the Guardian, which said something quite worrying. It reported the results of a study carried out by researchers from the University of Chicago that found that: 'Loss of the sense of smell predicted death [within five years] more accurately than a diagnosis of cancer, heart failure or lung disease'. (Costandi, 2014)

Think about this for a minute. In terms of outcomes, it means I should be more worried about dying if I lose my sense of smell than if I am sitting in front of a doctor who is telling me that I have cancer. This is extraordinary.

But the really extraordinary thing is that, when I read about the study, I wasn't worried about dying at all. Why is this?

Prediction and predictive models

Perhaps the main reason I wasn't worried is that the authors of the study don't provide a definitive explanation of the association between loss of smell and death. The study didn't look into the actual causes of death of the people who had died after losing their senses of smell. The authors say the loss is unlikely to be a cause itself, but rather an indicator that something else is wrong – but what that might be, and how it leads to death, their study didn't cover.

(To be fair to the authors, they do advance some hypotheses about what might be going on.)

The findings of the University of Chicago study are an example of prediction without explanation. Without an explanation of how I'm more likely to die, the prediction that I am more likely to die seems hollow. Because there is no explanation, it's hard to understand how it might happen. It's difficult to get worried about it.

The prediction is based on a statistical model (a logistic regression, in fact) of the relationship between two variables observed in the data: having a sense of smell and being alive after five years. This contrasts with a causal model in which the physical or physiological mechanism by which my death may be hastened is laid bare.

For all that the statistical model itself is just mathematical, our intuition must be that there is clearly something going on 'beneath' this mathematical relationship, something that connects, via some obscure pathway, anosmia to mortality. We just don't know for sure what it is at the moment, and that makes it easy to discount it, succumbing to what Daniel Kahneman has called a 'pervasive optimistic bias' in cognition (Kahneman, 2011).

Anyone working in the field of behavioural science will be familiar with the claim that more and more data is becoming available on human behaviour. Thanks to the internet, it is becoming easier to collect behavioural data, store it, and process it. So-called 'machine learning' techniques can then be applied to that rich and abundant data to create predictive models of behaviour that can be applied in a variety of contexts. As more data becomes available, we can expect to see even more predictive behavioural models of this kind.

A model that predicts behaviour but has nothing to say about how that behaviour came about – that has no explanation for that behaviour – is what we might call a purely predictive model.

In some disciplines that are working with behavioural models, such as data science, purely predictive models dominate. Indeed, the principal way in which practitioners judge the quality of the models they build is by looking at the accuracy of the predictions they make.

To take an example of a purely predictive model from a behavioural domain, consider movie choice in the context of Netflix, a movie rental business. Most people might think that a person's form and past ratings in choosing movies on Netflix would be a good place to start in trying to work out what movies they haven't seen that they might like to watch next. An intuitive and approachable way to start thinking about this problem would therefore be to build a model based on the notion of genre preference, by working out whether people watch more or less of a particular type of movie (romantic comedies, for example) than would be expected given the number available. Or, again, one could explore the idea that people's preference is driven by the actors in movies: so if I like *Taxi Driver*, which has De Niro in it, I'll probably like *Heat*.

The data scientists working on the Netflix problem don't go down this route. Instead, they use a proven mathematical algorithm, or a collection of algorithms, to build a mathematical and purely predictive model of the relationship between past and future film choice. In the end, what matters to Netflix is *whether* you enjoy the movies they recommend (and hence keep paying your subscription) – not *why* you enjoy them.

The best predictive models are based on data that includes only the following features: user IDs, movie titles, and ratings. That's it. One of the teams of data scientists working on the movie prediction problem suggested that, whilst they had access to additional attributes (such as cast, directors, etc.) those attributes 'could not help at all for improving the accuracy' of the predictive model they were building (quoted in Shmueli, 2010). Indeed, they suggested that including additional attributes might even degrade the model's predictive validity.

Model as representation and model as tool

One definition of a model you will find in the Dialogue (§1) is that a model is a representation. But the purely predictive models we have been discussing describe the mathematical relationship between an input and an output without saying anything about the mechanism of their connection. They are, at best, a partial representation of a state of affairs. Or, another way of thinking about this: the mathematical relationship between the input and output measurements says nothing about how input and output are actually connected to one another in the real world – if, indeed, they are connected. For this reason, purely predictive models are sometimes referred to as 'black box' models. You can see what goes in, and what comes out, but what goes on in the middle is opaque. Nevertheless, as the Netflix example shows, such models can still be useful.

In an explanatory model (a model that is not purely predictive) the description of the relationship between input and output attempts to represent the underlying causal mechanisms that connect them. An explanatory model is better or worse according to how well or badly it represents the mechanism.

Many of the psychological models that inform mainstream behavioural science aim to be both explanatory *and* predictive. For example, writing about the Theory of Planned Behaviour, one of its inventors says: 'True to its goal of *explaining* human behavior, not merely predicting it, the theory of planned behavior deals with the antecedents of attitudes, subjective norms, and perceived behavioral control, antecedents which in the final analysis determine intentions and actions' (Ajzen, 1991).

Explaining, for Ajzen, means elucidating the relationships between the immediate and more remote causes of behaviour: from behaviour itself, through the immediate intention, and back ultimately to attitudes towards the behaviour, subjective norms and control beliefs held about it. If all we were looking at were the relationship between the intention and the behaviour, we would be able to predict behaviour (when the intention was strong enough) but we wouldn't understand it – we wouldn't have an explanation of the behaviour. What makes the Theory of Planned Behaviour explanatory (not just predictive) is its attempt to capture the structured relationship between these various behavioural determinants in an interpretable way.

Purely predictive models in behaviour change

Whilst traditional behaviour change thinking has relied on models that are both predictive and explanatory, purely predictive modelling techniques do have a place in support of behaviour change.

In an example from our own practice, working with data from a study of behavioural interventions to promote handwashing with soap conducted in several small villages in India by members of the Hygiene Centre at the London School of Hygiene and Tropical Medicine (Biran et al., 2014), my colleagues at Sandtable used a machine learning algorithm to build a model to predict which households were more likely to adopt the behaviour based on certain observed socio-economic attributes (mean age of individuals in the household, family size, maximum level of education and land in acres). Knowing the values of these attributes for a household, we were able to use the model to predict to a reasonable level of accuracy how quickly inhabitants of the household would start washing their hands with soap after the initial intervention.

The model we used to predict initial adoption provided no causal explanation of how this or that attribute value combined with other attribute values to lead to adoption – or not. All it told us, in effect, was that the attributes were relevant, somehow, to adoption. How, we didn't know. But such a purely predictive model can still be useful in a behaviour change context in two ways.

First, and most practically, it can be used directly to target interventions in a population: it tells us which households are more likely to adopt first. Since there also appears to be some kind of normative effect in adoption, that means we might be able to save money compared with trying to target everybody. We can target the most receptive households first and allow the others to catch up.

Second, the purely predictive model helpfully points us in the right direction for the development of an explanatory behavioural model. It tells us that there may be *something* that causally links these socioeconomic attributes with adoption. It's then the role of theory development and further investigation to find out what that something might be.

Explanatory model or predictive model?

So, in a behaviour change context, which are we to prefer, explanatory or purely predictive behavioural models? The answer is, of course, that it depends on what you are going to be using the model for. In general, purely predictive models are perfectly acceptable for addressing short-term, tactical, repeatable problems; in strategic, commercial and policy contexts, explanatory models are typically required.

If I am a retailer, a black box model based on rich historical transaction data that tells me how many units of each product line people are going to buy across my stores each day of next month is essential to helping me manage inventory: as long as it keeps on working, nobody cares how it works. But a black box model that tells me that my customers will eventually drift away from my stores in the North East (implying I should close them now to cut losses) is going to be a hard sell to employees and shareholders. Strategic decisions need to be supported by a causal story – an intelligible explanation of how specific actions have led or will lead to their consequences. Similarly, if I am a policymaker I may be happy with a black box model that tells me how much money I need to spend on media to shift public attitudes towards contraceptive use in my advertising campaign; but I am unlikely to accept the results of a black box model that tells me that my policy of encouraging people to use condoms is having little effect on my objective of reducing teenage pregnancy. I need to know *why* my policy is failing, and what I can do about it.

In commercial strategy and policy it's important to understand the way things are, but it's also important to understand the way things could be. A prediction made by a black box model doesn't support reflection on ways in which the future might be different if certain things were different about the present. Only models that clarify the causal relationships between input and output support the kind of counterfactual enquiry involved in developing good strategy: getting to the heart of 'what might happen if' interventions were made, and hence which interventions to recommend.

Moreover, at a strategic level, leaders and policymakers have a deep need to engage their audiences – shareholders, stakeholders, citizens – in the decisions they are making. An important way in which they can do this is to tell stories about those decisions, and this means having explanations that make causal sense of the world.

Simulation models

I want to finish off with a discussion of another kind of behavioural model that combines predictive and explanatory elements and which also, to a much greater degree than many other forms of behavioural model, fosters the kind of causal storytelling I've been saying is important as a foundation for behaviour change strategy. (It's also the kind of model that Sandtable, the company I work for, happens to specialise in.)

A simulation model is a (normally digital) representation of a physical or social system that can be used to understand how the real system works and how it will behave in likely future scenarios. In a simulation model, the state of the model evolves according to a set of (normally time-based) computational rules that are systematically applied and re-applied.

When we built a simulation model of teenage pregnancy for the Department of Health and Department for Children

Schools and Families in 2009, we were aware of the need to furnish policymakers with explanations as well as predictions.

Based on public data on the sexual behaviour of teenagers drawn from the major Natsal survey on sexual attitudes and lifestyles (Johnson et al., 2001), as well as on a range of other sources, the model we built consisted of a simulated UK population made up of 4,000 individual computer-based 'agents' that behaved according to a set of empirically-derived behavioural rules (Department of Health et al., 2009). For example, individual agents could start and end relationships; decide whether to have sex or not with their partners; make choices about whether to use contraception; and decide which contraception to use.

By running the simulation, it became apparent that the received wisdom about the likely causes of teenage pregnancy – teenagers engaging in lots of short-lived hook-ups without condoms – was wrong. If the assumptions of the simulation were changed so that agents chose to use condoms every time they had sex, teenage girls continued to get pregnant. From this we concluded that condom use in one-night stands – in fact, condom use in general – made little difference to pregnancy rates. The principal contributor to teenage pregnancy rates, it emerged from the model, was a failure of the kinds of contraception in use, rather than a failure to use them.

If the various assumptions a simulation model makes are verified, it can also be used to predict. Most of the values of the attributes and variables used in the model are a matter of empirical investigation: how often condoms are chosen, how much sex occurs in one-night stands, and so forth. When these variables are driven by data, the model can be run forward in time and its results used as a prediction of what will happen to the outcome variables in the future: what happens to pregnancy rates if no action is taken at all?

What happens if we drive adoption of a different form of contraception?

Most importantly, perhaps, because simulation models are transparent in their operation, and have a clear representational relationship to the real world, clarifying its causal structure, they support deep engagement from business leaders and policymakers. They fulfil what Peter McBurney calls the 'mensatic' purpose of models: getting people round the table to discuss them and their implications (McBurney, 2012).

Ultimately, in the case of the sexual health simulation, the level of engagement secured amongst stakeholders who invested in the simulation led to a strategic recommendation to focus communication on fledgling relationships rather than one-night stands and to acknowledge the effectiveness of long-acting reversible contraceptives as an alternative to condoms (Department of Health et al., 2009).

An abundance of behavioural data and new techniques in machine learning makes it possible to build behavioural models that predict without explaining. Such 'purely predictive' models have their place in support of behaviour change initiatives. However, when the stakes are high, as they are for strategic decision-making, explanatory models that support causal storytelling, such as simulation-based models, are to be preferred.

Suggested further reading

For works cited, see References at the end of the book.

Jaccard, J and Jacoby, J. (2010) *Theory Construction and Model Building Skills.* **New York: Guilford Press.**

A thorough introduction to the enterprise of model building. Chapter 7 discusses the distinction between causal (explanatory) and predictive modelling.

Shmueli, G. (2010) 'To Explain or Predict?', *Statistical Science,* **25(3), pp. 289-310.**

A much more technical account of the distinction between prediction and explanation in the context of statistical science.

Epstein, J.M. (2008) 'Why Model?', Journal of Artificial Societies and Social Simulation, 11(4), p. 12.

Provides a list of reasons to build a model other than prediction.

6. The common language of story

Robert Holtom

Freelance Consultant and Writer

Models aren't the only tools we use to represent and understand behaviour. Story is a fundamental means of making sense of the world: and we regularly narrate our lives as we try to make sense of our own and others' behaviour. Model makers and storytellers have much to learn from one another, and could enhance their own work with a better understanding of the other discipline.

In the Dialogue on models of behaviour change, the trio of students discusses a wide range of models across disciplines. They broadly define models as representations of the world that always involve a degree of simplification or abstraction. Models, they agree, are tools used to map the world as it is and to predict and control events, especially human behaviour.

I suggest that there is another device that is often used to represent the world, discuss others' behaviours, examine the past and consider the future. This device forms a fundamental part of our everyday way of understanding behaviour. It is, of course, story. As anecdotes between friends, as exemplars in class, in fiction, film and theatre, in advertising and campaigning, stories are a powerful tool for representing and exploring the world. Like models, stories represent, they have a structure and they play an explanatory role in our lives.

The human condition and the common language of story:

Stories have been part of human society for millennia. Arguably the capacity for story begins in our body: the fact that our experience of the world is divided into past, present and future means the world is effectively narrated to us. Our senses acquaint us with the world – the three dimensional soundscape that our ears make possible and the visual field co-produced by our eyes. In unison with these senses our locomotive bodies take us from one place to another influencing how we get to know the world. Like colours and sounds, emotions also form part of our experience of our environments, alerting us to what is painful and pleasant, intensifying our experiences by painting them with feeling (Damasio, 2010). Even before words, ours is a rich experience of the world.

However, two further significant features turn this richly experienced world into one where genuine storytelling is possible. The first is our self-consciousness, the knowledge that we are body-bound individuals and distinct from others. We know of our selfhood. The second is language. We can use speech and other forms of language to share this intense and often overwhelming experience of the world. With communication others can come to know what we see, think and feel, others can know that we too experience the human condition. A condition marked by fragility, vulnerability, compassion, the need for community and independence, and, ultimately, mortality. The majority of us share this experience and it is immensely important to be able both to relate to it and to relate it to others.

Thus, a common language is necessary and I suggest that one can find such commonality in story. Many anthropological and ethnographic studies of stories from around the world have been undertaken. Vladamir Propp (1968) set himself the ambitious task of understanding Russian folktales, whilst Joseph Campbell (2008) examined tales of heroism from different cultures. These scholars discovered common elements in how stories are told, and these are now taught in many creative writing classes. You will be familiar with many of them, for example: the simple structure of beginning, middle, and end; the need for robust and well-developed characters that we can relate to as humans; and the use of plot with its inciting events and conflict. A further element explores the wants and needs of characters: the former linked to tangible gains they might want for themselves (e.g. a partner, a new house) and the latter referring to deeper psychological needs that, if met, would help a character become more fully human (e.g. self-belief, compassion).[2] Of course, sometimes a character might get what they *want* but not what they *need*, or vice versa.

Whether oral or written, stories explore the shared experience of the human condition – tales of love, hate, anger, revenge, passion, and altruism all speak to our knowledge of the world. However, we must take care when presenting sweeping generalisations about the role of stories across cultures. For example, Campbell's summary of the hero's quest as an archetypal story form he attributes to hundreds of stories, ancient and modern, has also been criticised for homogenising and simplifying a myriad of cultural variations. Indeed, the previous paragraph could be seen as such an exercise in generalisation. Nevertheless, I want to focus on points of commonality here, because humans do share many similarities across cultures and it's my contention that these manifest themselves in story. We must of course take care when crossing cultural borders, and be wary of appropriating and diluting diversity: but we can still hope to find patterns across cultures, rather than merely imposing simplifications.

Story as tool

If we agree that the common experience of the human condition has been represented in the common language of story, then we can also acknowledge that story plays a fundamental role in human life. We can observe this in the ubiquity of story across cultures and its many and varied uses: for example, Propp suggests that folk tales were tools to help people explore the growth and development of their psyche or personality, a literal example of folk psychology.

---

[2] I am grateful to the writer Kathryn Heyman for this distinction.

We see this also in the work of Jung (2003) as he famously explored the archetypes of mother, rebirth, spirit and trickster within myth, fairytale and scripture.

Stories are used to represent and simplify as well as expound and specify. Stories can home in on the minute details of someone's life and span centuries across a culture's history. Stories also play the important role of fostering empathy. Whether we are reading an autobiography or listening to our friend tell us about their day, story offers a vital tool that enables us to understand another's perspective (Zunshine, 2006). Stories can be orally and literarily transmitted and thus, through gestures and words, another's experience is shared with us and recreated as part of our experience. And just as emotion is part of our everyday familiarity with the world, so too will other's stories evoke felt responses. This, in part, is empathy.

Beyond autobiography and day-to-day accounts, stories can also present wholly fictional worlds and events that could never happen. Fiction, fantasy, sci-fi, fairytales, all invite us to relate to different worlds – but again, I suggest, this is not purely for recreational purposes. As we find the different characters of fiction in our own inner lives so we can use metaphor to better relate to ourselves, others and the world. We are being invited not to engage in a literal understanding of story but a metaphorical one. Jay Griffiths (2013) is a passionate advocate of the need to appreciate and understand metaphor, and she notes how children's makebelieve games reflect their easy relationship with metaphor. Bettelheim (2010) suggests that darker fairy tales can help children come to terms with their fears from a safe and symbolic distance, allowing them to solve the dilemmas of their inner and outer lives with story. It is not just children who benefit from metaphor. For example, scientists such as Einstein and Dawkins use metaphor to expound their theories, be they concerning quantum physics or selfish genes. 'Science is all metaphor', said psychologist Timothy Leary.

A sound grasp of metaphor and story thus equips an individual with the ability to better understand the world around them, as well as navigate their own life. Like models, stories represent human experience and behaviour – they map the human condition if you will. However, models are also regularly used to predict human behaviour, as a means of understanding what changes altering a certain variable might produce. Stories do play predictive roles, as many science fiction authors would contest, especially when their imaginings have become reality. However, whilst a model needs a rigorous relationship to the world to underpin its predictive power, a story can take a more circuitous and metaphorical route. And whilst models are judged on their explanatory and predictive powers, stories are often judged on their ability to inspire the imagination and emotions.

The criteria of judgment for models and stories are thus very different. Nevertheless, the importance of story as a tool should not go understated. Indeed it is likely that stories are already widely used within non-humanities disciplines.

Conclusion

Story is a fundamental means of making sense of our world. We regularly narrate our lives as we try to make sense of events. Story has general and specific power – recurrent structures and elements allow it to speak to our common experience of the world, whilst variations and inherent dynamism mean it can manifest a vast range of specificities as it twists and turns around different characters, locations and events. Given that story fosters understanding, empathy and creativity, it could perhaps be used alongside models as a tool for representing human experience and behaviour. A good story can also be used as an element in an initiative to elicit behaviour change, as stories have the power to compel and inspire.

Stories and models may often appear to be playing very different roles but, despite dissimilar structures, they are both used to represent and explain the world. Indeed, both modelmakers and storytellers have much to learn from one another and could enhance their own work with a better understanding of the other discipline. So, perhaps Evie, Yusuf and Paola would benefit from inviting Marcus, their literary friend, to the table as well!

Suggested further reading

For works cited, see References at the end of the book.

Mellon, N. (1998) *The Art of Storytelling*. Rockport, M.A.: Element Books.

An insightful introduction into the art of storytelling.

Mead, G. (2014) Telling the Story: The Heart and Soul of Successful Leadership. Hoboken, N.J: Wiley.

How to use story in a professional context.

Le Guin, U. (2012) *The Earthsea Quartet*. Harmondsworth: Penguin.

Four beautiful works of fiction, which use metaphor and fantasy to explore the human condition.

'Narrative and Proof' (2015) Podcast, The Oxford Research Centre in the Humanities. Available at: http://sbk.li/161341

A talk at Oxford University on the similarities/differences between narrative (in the humanities) and proof (in mathematics).

7. Probability and normativity: reconciling the two 'shoulds' of modelling

Chris Mills

Research Fellow, UCL Faculty of Laws

Modelling behaviour is often discussed as if it were solely a descriptive enterprise. In fact, modelling has a strong moral dimension, with action-guiding normative considerations playing important and distinct roles in the development and use of models of human behaviour.

Do models of behaviour just describe what people do and why they do it? Or do they also have something to say about what we *should* do? Do they also have a *normative* and *moral* dimension?

Much of the Dialogue focuses on the descriptive function of models of behaviour. For example, Evie's distinction in §1 between using models as 'maps' and models as 'blueprints' is primarily a distinction between two descriptive forms of modelling – explaining how things that either do or do not exist might function. If accurate, these models will tell us what is likely to occur given certain circumstances; a 'probabilistic should' if you will. These descriptive elements of modelling are well known, and as the discussion between protagonists illustrates, debate over them can easily get into deep philosophical water.

But modelling isn't solely a descriptive enterprise; it also has normative and moral dimensions. For example, we ask questions about how we *should* model a given behaviour, and use models to suggest how things *should* ideally function and which course of action we *should* undertake. These questions are not merely descriptive and their answers aren't simply explanatory. They differ in kind from the previous questions because they rely on norms, principles and reasons for their answers. Answering these questions is not simply a matter of statistical reasoning, but of evaluative and normative reasoning. Accordingly, let us call answers to these questions 'normative shoulds'.

As the descriptive aspects of modelling are widely discussed, I want to focus instead on the different roles that action-guiding normative considerations can play in modelling human behaviour, and how they relate to and are distinct from descriptive considerations. Specifically, I'd like to discuss three such roles:

- As evaluative guidelines for good practice in modelling
- As factors in real human behaviour which need to be represented in accurate models
- As conclusions drawn from models which explicitly seek to deliver moral recommendations

Exploring these three topics will give us a better grasp on the relationship between the descriptive and normative dimensions of modelling.

Evaluative Guidelines

When we design models, some of the most important questions we ask concern the process of modelling itself: how should we go about modelling? Which models should we use for any given project or purpose? What are the characteristics of a good model?

In the Dialogue, Paola's discussion of this point (§6) focuses mainly on ensuring that modellers understand the limits of their models, and more specifically, that they understand what their models necessarily omit. This is one way of considering whether a model meets the standards of a good model. If my model omits a feature commonly thought to be characteristic of a good model, this omission may reduce the likelihood that my model appropriately succeeds in its task. To become aware of what is missing from models and evaluate the reasons for the inclusion or omission of certain factors, modellers have to step 'outside' the confines of their model and consider alternative possible goals and methods. This is why I describe this kind of normative consideration as playing an external role in modelling.

There is a multitude of guidelines available to those who want to critically reflect on their modelling practice. Some of these guidelines differ between specialisms while others are universal; some are advisory while others are mandatory (e.g. Bailer-Jones, 2009). The aim of these guidelines is to improve the effectiveness of our models; but reflecting on which guidelines are relevant to the project at hand requires us to consider the aims of our project. Specifically, determining the content and force of these guidelines requires us to consider the suitability of our goals and method of enquiry. These considerations are evaluative.

In this broad sense, normative standards in modelling are inescapable. Clearly, a modeller should follow guidelines of good modelling. But determining which guidelines apply to which project requires us to consider our reasons for pursuing the project in the first place. Fundamental choices made by modellers concerning the shape and purpose of their projects play a dual role here: they determine the applicability of the relevant guidance, and they require us to reflect on what we think are good goals and suitable methods. For example, our rationale for employing one model instead of another may depend on what we are trying to achieve; but what we are trying to achieve itself requires justification. This task provides normative considerations with their first – external – role in modelling.

Modelling Moral Relations

In the previous section we saw that considerations of right and wrong play a role in determining guidance for modelling. This reflects the evaluative judgements we make of our goals and methods of enquiry. But normative and moral considerations also play an important internal role in the nuts and bolts of our models – for the simple reason that such considerations shape how real people behave.

When seeking to explain or predict human behaviour, one has to recognise the moral dimensions of human interaction. Without some representation of individual moral psychology and interpersonal moral practices, models of human behaviour will fail to track crucial causal factors in our decision-making (e.g. Doris et al., 2010). For example, a model which made such an omission would ignore how self-interest mingles with bounded rationality, how our notions of trust are subjected to social norms and collective beliefs, and how our sense of duty is filtered through emotions such as empathy, apathy, guilt, shame, anger and so on. Such a model would fail to explain how people engage with the moral landscape in their day-to-day lives. These factors matter when describing individual conduct and discerning patterns of behaviour. This ensures that modellers have reasons of descriptive accuracy to pay close attention to moral considerations as causal factors within their models. Thus, ensuring descriptive accuracy requires modellers to consider both evaluative standards of good modelling and moral standards determining the behaviour of the individuals they are modelling.

A classic example of this is altruism (e.g. Nagel, 1978). The possibility of truly altruistic motives has been debated by moral philosophers since the discipline's conception. The relationship between self-interest and altruism as motivators of human action informs debates across many different disciplines. The need to understand altruistic behaviour is clear: while some behaviour is selfish, some is undeniably selfless. We might expect individuals to behave in a self-interested manner much of the time, but cases of self-sacrifice (toward both friends and strangers) are common.

If it were the case, as some have argued, that all behaviour is ultimately selfish (and only sometimes instrumentally or indirectly selfless), then predicting behaviour would be much simpler. The causal chain for human interaction would have only one ultimate source: self-interest. Reflecting this, modellers would face the task of working out what the ideally or maximally self-interested individual would do, and then filtering that behaviour through relevant contextual factors to achieve an approximately realistic outcome. It's my view, however, that this picture is far too simple. The relationship between the two conflicting motivations – selfishness and altruism – is more complicated than this, and our models of human behaviour must reflect this fact if they are to be accurate.

Acknowledging the role played by moral considerations in human behaviour, and the need to reflect this fact in our models, provides an answer to Paolo's question in the Dialogue (§8) of whether modelling human behaviour is in some way special. In response, both Evie and Yusuf suggest that modelling human behaviour does not differ from models of other natural phenomena (such as gravity), because in either case we are seeking to discover and explain causal relations. The case of altruism, however, suggests that Paolo's question needs a more sophisticated answer. Even if the purposes of modelling human and non-human phenomena are the same, the factors involved are vastly different. Part of what makes human behaviour so fascinating is its moral content, and this, I suggest, makes the causal factors relevant to human behaviour qualitatively different from those relevant to other types of modelling.

Drawing Moral Conclusions

So far we have looked at two distinct roles that evaluative and moral considerations play in modelling human behaviour:

- First, they can offer us external guidance in the project of modelling. This kind of guidance is relevant to any form of modelling
- Secondly, they are internal causal factors which themselves need to be modelled. This point is relevant to the modelling of human behaviour in particular

Crucially, both of these roles are relevant to the descriptive enterprise of modelling behaviour. To better describe human behaviour, we need to engage with both types of consideration.

Things get more complex, however, when we turn to consider those who use modelling to draw moral conclusions: building models that are designed to tell us what we *should* do. This is a shift in aim from the models we have been discussing so far. This distinction between descriptive modelling and normative modelling mirrors a distinction between two common uses of the word 'should':

- The first type of 'should' is a *probabilistic* 'should'. This is the predictive form of a descriptive claim (i.e. X should occur as it is the most likely possibility). While non-predictive models seek to explain historical causal relationships between the relevant facts, predictive models seek to determine the likelihood of particular outcomes under certain conditions. From predicting the development of weather patterns, to the growth of epidemics, some of the most important insights we draw from models take this form.
- The second type of 'should' is a *moral* or *normative* 'should'. This type of 'should' communicates the view that, under certain conditions, we have reason to prefer particular outcomes or behaviour

over others (i.e. X should occur because we have most reason to bring it about). Given the disagreement over the descriptive function of modelling, it is easy to forget that this second type of 'should' can also feed into, shape, and be produced by many models.

We can illustrate this distinction between two types of modelling (reflecting the two types of 'should') by considering the field of economics (Caplin and Schotter, 2008). Economists commonly distinguish between positive and normative economics:

- Positive economics is *descriptive* economic enquiry that seeks to explain cause and effect in the allocation of scarce resources. Positive economic modelling might describe how various market factors influence individual decision-makers in their decisions concerning the distribution of resources. This process attempts to be as value-free as possible in its conclusion; relying on descriptive recommendations to explain what has occurred or suggest what is likely to occur.
- In contrast, normative economics is *prescriptive* economic enquiry, which seeks to determine what allocation of resources is the right allocation (usually according to some cost-benefit analysis). This process is designed to be explicitly value-laden; determining which decisions maximise some measure of wellbeing (such as revealed-preference satisfaction), or otherwise satisfy our preferred allocation and metric of distributive justice.

Normative economics is a driving force in public policy (e.g. Hausman and McPherson, 2006). It is a clear illustration of how morally desirable goals and principles can be included as components of a model. Arguably, the most obvious example of this is the inclusion of a 'utilitarian calculus'. Utilitarians famously state that we have a moral duty to act so that we promote the greatest good for the greatest number. This argument has been extremely influential in public policy, due to its flexibility, range and intuitiveness. Indeed, it is commonly argued that normative economics naturally mirrors utilitarianism by tending to rely on calculations of total increases in wellbeing in cost-benefit analyses, and modelling individual choice according to what brings about the greatest good for the greatest number.

However, the utilitarian calculus is not intended to represent the reasoning of individuals within the model. We rarely make choices with this calculation in mind, so suggesting that we represent individual choice in terms of this calculus will be descriptively inaccurate. But according to the utilitarian, normative economists can suggest that individuals *should* act this way. That is, they fail in their moral duties toward others if they fail to act in a manner that increases the overall sum of goodness. They have overriding reasons to act in this manner; a failure to do so is to act wrongly. Thus, the calculus is not describing the thought process of the individual, but rather the demands of morality itself.

This second element broadens the purpose for our models. Combining a sophisticated cost-benefit analysis with a thorough utilitarian calculus allows our model to offer us a number of normative insights that descriptive models cannot. Descriptive models explain and predict likely behaviour, while normative models can do this alongside conceptualising the demands of morality. The latter allows us to draw both descriptive and normative conclusions from our models: what people (probabilistically) should do and what people (morally) should do. By producing both sorts of conclusions, a model allows us to understand the differences between them; how individual behaviour under certain circumstances is likely to stray from the demands of morality and what changes in those circumstances will reduce this difference.

These insights are invaluable to real world decision-makers across policy areas, but they are commonly missing from descriptive models. Often, modellers aim to 'stick to the facts', constructing the most descriptively accurate model that they can and leaving the moral analysis to those who interpret the descriptive conclusions drawn from the model. But normative modelling appears to offer us a way of building this into the modelling process itself. Assuming we can model the demands of morality accurately, and doing so does not compromise the descriptive accuracy of the model itself, moral conclusions could potentially be drawn directly from the model itself.

Modelling the Demands of Morality

The utilitarian approach sketched here is useful for illustrating the possibility of normative modelling. In practice, however, it is both too simple and too controversial.

Even if we accept that utilitarianism provides us with the correct approach to the difficult moral questions facing policymakers, we might still disagree over the measure of goodness employed or the structure of the calculus. Utilitarianism is a broad church, and it is only one form of consequentialism – the approach to morality that weighs up the rightness and wrongness of actions in terms of their outcomes. Consequentialists are likely to call for a more complicated calculus.

More pressingly, we might deny that consequentialists offer the best account of the moral landscape (Scheffler, 1988). Many philosophers argue that outcomes are not the only way in which we should think about the relations between people, not least because the very thing that allows consequentialist theories to draw their conclusions – the fact that they impartially aggregate moral claims together – leads in many real situations to seemingly morally objectionable outcomes. Critics suggest that we might have reasons to reject such a theory due to some of its controversial assumptions.

Non-consequentialist approaches to morality propose a series of moral constraints that stand independently of the good that they bring about. *Contra* utilitarianism, they recognise action-guiding considerations that are independent of some calculus of wellbeing. How could we include such constraints within our models? Doing so requires a more nuanced approach, precisely because the relevant principles stand independently of the cost-benefit analysis favoured by normative economists. The utilitarian calculus neatly dovetails with a cost-benefit analysis, because both use the same units of analysis. Non-consequentialist constraints, by contrast, are more difficult to build into models because they work in a different way.

One recent approach to this challenge suggests that we can mimic non-consequentialist constraints by establishing a series of threshold functions:

> *An infringement of a constraint is not yet another 'cost' of the pertinent act or rule, to be considered along with other costs and benefits. Rather, constraints must not be infringed unless sufficiently large good (or bad) outcome are at stake. Following moderate deontology,*

> *threshold functions set the minimal net benefit of the action, policy, or rule that has to be produced to justify an infringement of a constraint (or to remove an option not to promote the good).*

Zamir and Madina, 2010, p. 104

This approach ensures that if a certain predicted outcome does not meet the threshold, then it is not a satisfactory option to be considered as a conclusion of the model. Further, this might be true even if it is the most beneficial outcome (and for this reason would be recommended from a purely consequentialist perspective). This approach offers us a different way of filtering out unacceptable conclusions within the model itself, rather than requiring decision-makers to apply the relevant moral principles after the fact.

This proposal arms us with another approach to normative modelling. Debate between these two approaches (and the possibility of others) is an important line of methodological study. But either approach shows how models can be used for normative purposes.

Suggested further reading

For works cited, see References at the end of the book.

Anderson, E. (1995) *Value in Ethics and Economics.* **Harvard: Harvard University Press,**

A detailed and compelling discussion of the potential for normative modelling.

Sen, A. (1991) *On Ethics and Economics.* **London: Wiley.**

A well-known critique of welfare economics that seeks to explain how moral thinking can improve the approach.

Smart, J.C.C. and Williams, B. (1973) *Utilitarianism: For and Against.* **Cambridge: Cambridge University Press.**

A well-written introduction to the debate over the nature and qualities of utilitarian thinking.

8. On epistemological and ontological incommensurability in modelling behaviour change

Michael P Kelly

Honorary Senior Visiting Fellow, Institute of Public Health, University of Cambridge

Psychology and sociology are often seen as offering incommensurate perspectives on human behaviour. But if you look hard enough, it is the similarities which strike you – along with the prospects for better modelling of human behaviour.

One of the more puzzling things about the modelling of behaviour change has been the failure of sociological and psychological explanations to be modelled together. On the face of it, it is rather odd that the two disciplines with behaviour or social action at their heart should have so little common ground and find it so difficult to engage with each other.

The conventional explanation for this state of affairs is that the differences between the two are such that it is impossible to bring them together. According to this conventional explanation, there are three significant differences:

- The first difference relates to the role of the individual. This is an *ontological* difference: that is, it relates to how each discipline sees the nature of being, and the kinds of entities it assumes exist. So one holds that the world can best be understood in terms of biological and psychological processes operating *within individuals*; the other sees *relationships between individuals* as the key to the nature of being
- The second difference is about cause and prediction. This is an *epistemological* difference: that is, it relates to the theory of what kind of knowledge best explains things and how that knowledge is acquired.
- The third is about the approach to variables, and is both *ontological*, i.e. about the nature of being, and *epistemological*, i.e. about the theory of knowledge and explanation being used

I'd like to look at these three supposed differences more closely, before going on to explain why, on closer inspection, it's the similarities between the two disciplines that strike me, not the differences.

Individual and social explanations

The focus on the individual in psychology means that the primary interest is often in what is happening in the mind or the brain or the body. The human is typically portrayed as an individual creature which responds automatically in various predictable ways to the external environment or is engaged in conscious reflective cognitive processing.

The importance of an *integrated* understanding of both the automatic and reflective systems has been central to recent scholarship (Strack and Deutsch, 2004). Human behaviour is conceptualised as an amalgam of conscious, reflective cognitive activity *and* automatic responses to cues in the environment.

At the same time, the drive to understand the underlying physical mechanisms and processes has been pursued with some considerable success as the neurobiological circuitry in the brain has been disassembled and the incredible ways in which sensory stimuli are processed has come to be better understood (Pinker, 1998). Psychology has also moved away from a mind-brain dualism to a more integrated understanding of the relationships between biology and the psyche (Damasio, 1994). In the process, however, the social has often become ever *more* peripheral in the explanatory picture. There are some important exceptions to this: for example, the exciting field of social neuroscience takes as its first premise that the defining characteristic of the human species is the *social* nature of human behaviour and that neuroscience only makes sense within that supra-individual framework (Cacioppo and Cacioppo, 2013). But this, I'd argue, is far from typical.

Sociology's starting point, by contrast, is not the individual but the primacy of the social. The argument is that the social is a distinctive and real phenomenon, which is separate from the material, biological and psychological realms and exerts real force on humans. For sociologists, human life is supra-individual and relational. To be human is to be in relationships with other humans, and behaviour emerges out of the interaction between people. Most sociology, in one way or another, focuses on various dimensions of relationships, be they class, gender, ethnic, industrial, institutional, international, community or family relationships.

So the two disciplines certainly appear to concentrate on different aspects of reality. According to the conventional explanation of the separation between them, this different focus reflects different *ontological* commitments. The two disciplines, it is argued, have different views on the nature of being. They believe in different kinds of entity. And as a result, there's no way of mapping the worldview of one onto the other – they are, in technical language, *incommensurable*.

Cause

Aside from the individual / social dichotomy, a second major fault line between the two disciplines is, according to the conventional explanation, their differing approaches to cause.

Much psychology tends to see human behaviour as having causes and, once those causes are known, as being reasonably predictable. Sociology, by contrast, tends to eschew the idea of fundamental determinist causes.

In fact sociology has built a considerable intellectual edifice demonstrating that determinist prediction of human behaviour is futile. This, it is argued, is because of the differences between, on the one hand, inanimate planets or physical and biological matter and, on the other, thinking human beings and the complexities of their affairs. For example, heavyweights like Giddens (1974) and Schutz (1953) are adamant that the idealised scientific predictive model cannot apply to the sociological study of human affairs.

So are psychology and sociology committed to irreconcilably different understandings of cause. Are they *epistemologically* incommensurable?

Actually, the model of simple determinism which some sociologists object to is an idea well past its sell by date – and one which psychologists too have questioned. It was based on very elementary understandings derived from Newtonian mechanics, long since understood as a special case in physics rather than an overarching predictive law. In biology and psychology simple determinism is rare and complexity rules the day. Complex causation in the social as well as the psychological realms seems an entirely reasonable idea.

My argument is that the notion that everything in the universe is subject to mechanisms of causation *except* human conduct is highly unlikely. However, that the mechanisms involved in human affairs will be different to physical laws or to simple cause and effect models seems highly likely. To assert that humans are so different to everything else in the universe is, in my view, a reworking of the doctrine of the soul and ancient theological debates about free will and determinism.

In recent decades social theory has developed an important framework to capture complexity called structuration (Giddens, 1979; 1982). In essence this describes the relationship between the society and the individual dynamically rather than deterministically. This type of sociological thinking therefore emphasises human agency: the human is conceptualised as a thinking, acting being whose thought and action takes place within the constraints imposed by social structures. Social structures are the product, or emerge out of social practices and human agency (Elder-Vass, 2010), but also operate directly as the social context within which human affairs take place. Furthermore, by virtue of the fact they are aware of the social constraints upon them, human actors give those constraints meaning and interpret the social world around them before they engage in social action.

The beauty of this approach is that it acknowledges human agency to be creative and ingenious, inventive and non-conformist. Behaviour, although patterned and linked to social structure, is nevertheless under some degree of individual control. Behaviour is not pre-programmed according to social position or some other social factor. I'll have more to say about structuration theory later, when I return to the similarities I see between psychology and sociology.

Variables

The third big difference between sociology and psychology cited by the conventional explanation of the split between them concerns their conception of variables. Sociology and psychology use different analytic concepts based on different understandings of what the fundamental building blocks of scientific explanation are.

This means that ideas do not translate easily from one discipline to another; or at least, in the translation, a good deal can be lost. Psychology, for instance, has developed methods which are particularly adept at dealing with variables which measure physiological or biochemical and behavioural changes. Much psychology uses controlled experimentation to distinguish effects of variation in the dependent variable from other effects. Sociology, by contrast, has tended to keep its distance from trials. One reason for this is that important social factors like social class, gender and educational background are about *relationships* between people and, although these can be easily turned into variables which are attached to individuals, in doing so they lose their relational and dynamic dimension.

As before, it's true that the two disciplines have different foci. Ideas do not translate easily between them – but does that mean translation is entirely impossible? Are they actually *incommensurable*?

Is an integrated approach possible?

So let's review the conventional explanation. The two disciplines, psychology and sociology, have developed quite different ontological and epistemological approaches; they have evolved distinct ways of describing the human condition; and there is a pretty compelling case for seeing them as incommensurable. Two disciplines each with a huge amount to say, but not to each other!

But pause and reflect for a moment. How can it be possible that what is essentially the same human behaviour can be accounted for so differently? Why is it not possible to get productive integration between them? Why so often do the two camps look at each other in apparent blank incomprehension? Why are the models so different?

It's my view that systematic knowledge about complex social/psychological phenomena is possible, that the disciplines can and should come together where there are substantive arenas of common interest, and that if you look it is the similarities which will strike you rather than the differences.

In short, my plea is that we see past the epistemological and ontological differences to the real world behind them. However, for this to happen, a number of common errors first need to be laid aside.

Setting aside some common errors

It's my view that the disciplinary rift between psychology and sociology are examples of a broader problem in the academic and scientific world that has emerged since the seventeenth century, when disciplinary specialism really got going.

As disciplinary specialisation kicked in, fields of study got narrower and narrower and lost sight of the fundamental point that the universe we inhabit is a totality, from the cosmological to the subatomic, and that that totality is a unity in which interactions occur across many different levels. Indeed, some commentators have declared that the search for understanding of totalities is pointless: reality is just too chaotic or disjointed for comprehension, they claim, and those systems of ideas which seek overall comprehension are but metanarratives devoid of scientific content and dangerous ideological illusions (Lyotard, 1984).

In such a world modelling would only ever be contingent, at best, and our chances of knowing anything with any certainty would always be out of reach. Indeed, if we persist in talking about complexity as if it is something which is unknowable or even chaotic then it will never be possible to find solutions to anything, or indeed to know anything very worthwhile at all.

It's my view, however, that this account of things is a consequence not of some fundamental truth about reality, but of the ways in which we happen to have structured our study of it over the last few centuries. The world as it is – including all the people in it – has an empirical and ontological unity. It and they constitute an obdurate material reality of which we are aware via our senses. Our senses provide us with incomplete information about that external world. But our incomplete awareness of it must not detract from its material, biological, psychological and social unity. It is real but our knowledge and understanding of it is partial. It is also complex and made up of many different elements or layers from the subatomic to the cosmological. These different layers are interrelated because they are in systemic interactions with each other continuously (Engel, 1960; 1981). This world, I believe, exists independently of human kind's ability to observe it.

Our ability to observe that world is imperfect, because our methods of observation are flawed. Human observers our fallible, our presuppositions, prejudices, biases and competencies act like lenses through which our observations occur, and we see the world as it appears to be rather than as it actually is (Kant, 1781/1787; Hume, 1748). Different disciplines use different methods to observe the world. Different methods of observation of the world produce different theories about the world. Different disciplines also make different theoretical *a priori* assumptions which precede observation. Not surprisingly therefore, very different disciplinary accounts and models of the world are developed. In turn these theories and methods vary in the nature of the assumptions they make about what constitutes an appropriate account of the world

– a theory of knowledge or epistemology. In short, different disciplines develop different ways of describing their bit of the world: but it must never be forgotten that that bit remains in a complex relationship with the whole.

So there is a conceptual distinction that has to be drawn between, on the one hand, a real material and social unity and, on the other, the sciences describing that real material and social unity, which proclaim disunity. Several errors follow from the proclamation of disunity:

- The first error is to assume that the empirical world is as disunited as the academic disciplines that describe it. If you assume a disunited world you are likely to be led to the argument that therefore explanations or models which integrate different layers are either impossible or so horribly complex as to be useless
- The second error is to assume that the method of observation of the world as it appears to be also reveals the way the world really is. In other words the discourse slips from description of what the observational method, whatever it is, shows to a belief that this description is a true account of the nature of reality. This is the classic error of naïve positivism. There is a distinction between the observer and the observed. What is there and what the observer sees is there are not the same thing. Once a discipline or a scientist forgets this distinction they are creeping towards ideology and away from science
- This in turn leads to the third error, which is to assume that the disciplinary version of the world that I hold to is not only different to the theories

others hold, but also superior to those other accounts
- The fourth error is to assert that the models of the world developed in a (usually my) particular discipline are ontologically and epistemologically incommensurate with other models to the degree that they could never exist in a unity

Automatic/reflective and agency/structure

If these errors are put to one side and the unity of the empirical world is brought into focus some intriguingly similar propositions emerge in certain aspects of psychology and sociology. I will focus here on just one area from each discipline to illustrate my point. In particular, the automatic/reflective dichotomy in psychology and the agency/structure dichotomy in sociology are not really very different in their overall implications. The psychological arguments do indeed major on the individual and the sociological ones on the social, and the language used is quite distinct, but the idea of a dynamic and emergent social and psychological system is inherent in both.

I am aware of little work which draws these strands of the two disciplines together. However, taking a non-discipline-bound look at the automatic and reflective system and agency and structure reveals some remarkable similarities.

Let's start with the psychological perspective. When using the automatic system the human responds to immediate cues in the environment, takes all sorts of short cuts in its thinking, doesn't work out costs, but seeks immediate gratification. In contrast the reflective system is that part of mind which is thoughtful, calculating, rational and orderly. The reflective system deals with costs and benefits, thinks about the long and the short-term consequences and outcomes of current actions, and foregoes pleasure now in the expectation of better rewards in the future.

There are physical stimuli in micro-environments to which the automatic system responds (see e.g. Hollands et al., 2013). For certain types of behaviour the automatic responses to the immediate situation or stimuli are easily delimited. So too are the mechanisms and processes involved (Damasio, 1994).

As well as physical environments, there are two other dimensions which evince automatic responses: subjective feeling states like pain, tiredness, fear and other emotions, hunger and thirst; and the *social* environment, made of up of people and groups in the immediate world of experience and also more diffuse social and cultural expectations. Here we begin to see the connections to the sociological perspective. What sociologists have noted over the years is that we are barely aware or conscious of many social stimuli in our immediate and broader environments yet they have a profound effect on our behaviour. The fact that we are barely aware is why the response to this aspect of the social environment is often automatic. The social environment includes such things as the language being spoken, the proximity of other social actors and, most importantly, rules, norms and folkways which are there as part of the cultural milieu and which constrain behaviour through automatic or semi-automatic types of responses with very little cognitive engagement on the part of the social actors involved. Many decades ago Schutz called this the taken for granted aspects of everyday life (Schutz, 1967).

The connections between the psychological and sociological perspectives really come into focus, however, when we turn our attention from the automatic system to the reflective system. In particular, there is a striking proximity between psychological ideas about the self, an idea which has been used with profit by writers such as Kahneman (2011), Damasio (1994) and Pinker (1998) in psychology, and Goffman (1969), Blumer (1969) and Strauss et al. (1984) in sociology. The reflective system is not just a processor. It has *consciousness*. It is aware of itself. As the calculations are made within the reflective system, it is conscious of its own intellectual processing and is also conscious of itself as a social being. Nested within the reflective system is the capacity for self-awareness and the sense of self (James, 1892; Mead 1934). Both James and Mead, whose works have been so influential in psychology (James) and sociology (Mead), sought to explain human conduct as more than simple reactions or responses or impulses. They realised there was more to human behaviour than the automatic responses to stimuli important as these were. The human, they argued, has consciousness. Mead and James described what they called the self as the seat of consciousness.

The self is the internal set of ideas that a person has about who and what they are. It involves them being able to distinguish self from other people, of being conscious of themselves existing across time and in different physical locations (of having an autobiography), and of being able to reason about their own internal states.

The psychological descriptions of the reflective and automatic systems and the sociological accounts of self both tap into the fact that humans are in part agents of their own destiny. The self is the basis of human agency. Without consciousness of self there would only be automatic responses to stimuli. Humans make choices and they do things; their actions are a force on the external world and on other people. Sociology has been particularly good in recent decades at exploring the power and importance of this human agency in shaping society or social structures (Giddens, 1979; 1982). Human agency produces social structure in the sense that the billions and billions of individual human actions (both automatic and self-conscious and reflective) produce social patterns that are regular, repetitive and reproduce themselves over time at the level of communities and society. These patterns are real things exerting real pressures on people (automatically and via interpretive conscious reflective processes). In other words although shaped by human agency, social structures in turn shape human agency. So although we are cognitive processors and agents of our own destiny, our agency is not exercised freely in a manner of our own choosing. Our agency is bounded by the consequences of our and others' agency and our awareness of that.

So structuration theory adds a further dimension to the notion of the reflective system by noting that, while social structures constrain behaviour and actions, human actors are conscious of those constraints, give them meaning and interpret the social world around them before they engage in social action. It is for this reason that simple predictions about the outcomes of actions designed to change behaviour are prone to such variance. The intervening factor is the thinking human actor. Humans, in other words, are pretty smart, as well as being very reactive to the world around them. This fundamental observation is basic to both psychology and sociology.

Conclusion

So in spite of the language, it is possible not only to see that the interests of these two disciplines are fundamentally similar, but also to construct an account in which ideas from each are integrated. Epistemological and ontological incommensurability melts away. And it is not just the two areas examined here. Interests in power and control, narrative, gender, class and ethnic differences, for example, are shared preoccupations.

Contrariwise, it is equally possible to argue that the preoccupations of the two disciplines are so different that it is not possible even to think about integration.

My view is that although the differences are both real and interesting, they actually tell us more about the nature of the disciplines and their history than they tell us about human behaviour. If we conceive of human behaviour as a unity – and indeed as part of a bigger unity from the cosmological to the subatomic – then a conversation between psychology and sociology seems not only possible but essential. From that conversation, some extremely promising lines of enquiry emerge, along with new prospects for better more fruitful modelling of human conduct.

9. Interdisciplinarity in the study of behaviour change: experiences, promises and challenges

Antonio Cabrales

Professor of Economics, Department of Economics, University College London

Angel Sánchez

Professor of Applied Mathematics, Grupo Interdisciplinar de Sistemas Complejos, Departamento de Matemáticas and Institute of UC3M-BS of Financial Big Data, Universidad Carlos III de Madrid

---

Interdisciplinary research holds enormous promise for the study of behaviour and behaviour change. In practice, it also creates challenges – both for teams that seek to cross disciplinary boundaries, and for existing disciplinary approaches to publishing, funding and career progression.

According to Wikipedia, *interdisciplinarity* 'involves the combining of two or more academic disciplines into one activity (e.g. a research project). It is about creating something new by crossing boundaries, and thinking across them'. By implication, interdisciplinarity is also an inherently transient activity: contributions from each discipline must eventually dissolve in a new field – although this process may take a long time. Talking *across* disciplines – as the participants in the Dialogue do – is an essential part in the process: but true interdisciplinarity means talking *past* disciplines.

So what does that look like in practice? What does it take for people who've invested their whole careers in one discipline to cross boundaries and create something new? How do we turn the rhetoric of interdisciplinarity into reality? And what are the pitfalls along the way?

These are big questions. In this paper, we'll offer a few tentative answers based on our own personal experiences of interdisciplinary research at the boundaries of complex systems, physics, economics and game theory, with a focus on understanding behaviour and change. Our tour will take us from unsuccessful or unsatisfactory collaborations to significant advances in the field of complex socio-economic systems achieved through a truly interdisciplinary approach.

We'll refer to ourselves throughout by our initials: AC, an economist working mostly in game theory, and AS, a physicist working on complex systems.

From multidisciplinarity to interdisciplinarity

Let's start with the most important requirement: for true interdisciplinarity, the interdisciplinary spirit must be embraced by *everyone* involved in the research.

Interdisciplinarity, let's remember, means more than just a willingness to talk to other disciplines. It should not be confused with *crossdisciplinarity* – defined by Wikipedia as 'explaining aspects of one discipline in terms of another' – and *multidisciplinarity* – 'drawing on knowledge from different disciplines but staying within their boundaries'. The mere fact that a team is able to solve or clarify problems by drawing on the expertise of researchers from different fields does not make that team an interdisciplinary one. For example, if the team is led by people who apply their own discipline's perspective to the material provided by the rest, then little is learned, and a new field is certainly not kick-started.

This is what happened, for instance (and these will be our only examples unrelated to behaviour), when AS used his knowledge of fractal geometry to understand the nature of new materials for optical memories, provided by an otherwise uninterested experimental team (Sánchez et al., 1992); or when he worked as a consultant on fractal tools to be applied to data from electrocardiograms, about which he had no knowledge – or, indeed, understanding of what the team was doing (Rojo-Alvarez et al., 2007). These are examples of multidisciplinary work – and if one is really interested in learning from other subjects and people, the experience turns out to be quite frustrating.

Our first joint project (Grujić et al., 2012) took us much closer to a genuinely interdisciplinary endeavour. The story starts with a team of theoretical physicists, led by AS, which was trying to understand how the structure of social connections between people may or may not foster co-operative behaviours in a dilemmatic context: for example, a context in which co-operating would lead to the best social outcome, but would be worse than not co-operating for self-interested individuals). The team realised that they needed a better understanding of how the behaviour of people in small groups varies depending on group size. To that end they contacted AC and another economist colleague. Subsequent joint work in designing a suitable experiment and analysing the obtained data showed clearly that co-operation in a social dilemma is very difficult as soon as there are more than two persons interacting. This result had immediate consequences for networked populations: in general, one should not expect much co-operation since most people have more than one connection.

So was this an interdisciplinary project? Almost, but not quite. For example, analysis of data played a prominent role in the project: but communication about some of the sophisticated modelling tools employed proved very difficult, making it hard for us really to cross the disciplinary boundaries. The physicists, for example, learnt quite a few things about the language and techniques employed by the economists, but they were unable to grasp those statistical tools. Every team member gained from the interaction in terms of knowledge about problems from another's perspective, but the contact between disciplines was not as fruitful as it could have been.

Interdisciplinarity and disciplinary conventions

Alongside projects like those discussed above, each of us has also had experiences where the full potential of interdisciplinary work has been realised.

One such project, for example, involved a study of how people behave in crowd computing structures – structures where individuals either offer their computing power in their home computers or carry out computations needed by a researcher or an organisation. The classic example is SETI, where many people contributed their computer time to search signals from extraterrestrial sources for indications of the existence of intelligent life elsewhere in the universe. Nowadays, however, the contribution of volunteers to crowd computing is being superseded to some extent by paid participants, who have an economic incentive to co-operate in the task – and may therefore, perhaps, be motivated to receive the incentive with the least possible effort. Designing a task distribution and incentive system that ensures reliable performance of the structure is a truly interdisciplinary task, requiring experts in economics, computer science and complex systems to join forces. Such was the team in which AS participated, as an expert in complex systems with some knowledge of economics and evolutionary dynamics (Christoforou et al., 2013a).

As it happened, the computer science team already had expertise in game theory, as they were using it to propose different incentive schemes to ensure that that participants were honest (that is, that they provided correct inputs even if computing involved some cost in personal effort or computer time). AS brought new disciplinary perspectives to bear by helping the team to replace this static picture with an evolutionary one, in which the person in charge of the process could implement additional supervisory policies over time to allow a more efficient design of incentives. Even though AS joined the team when the research question was already defined, his input enabled a new, interdisciplinary perspective to emerge in the team, allowing the introduction of constructs that only make sense from a dynamic perspective, such as the role of reputation in discriminating among participants that contribute to the task repeatedly (Christoforou et al., 2013b).

Nevertheless, the collaboration faced a number of challenges. A number of these related to the norms and institutions of different disciplines. For example, the pace at which the research proceeded was dictated by the conventions of computer science, for which the main venues for communicating results are conferences requiring submission of full (but limited length) papers to very strict deadlines. Driven by these requirements, the work advanced in bursts as the deadlines for relevant conferences, with intervening periods of no activity at all. Moreover, communicating the results solely through computer science conferences would have led to them being completely unnoticed by another key audience, complex systems researchers (particularly in physics and mathematics). Significant extra effort therefore had to be invested in preparing a publication in the appropriate journal in order to widen the impact of the work.

Similar challenges arising from different disciplinary conventions were apparent in another successful collaboration between economists, computer scientists and physicists – in this case, research on network topologies in which AC participated (Guimerà et al., 2002). The objective of the work was to understand how a given set of nodes (in this case people) and links (connections between those people) should be arranged to 'solve problems' in the shortest possible (average) time. For example, suppose one individual in an organisation conceives a project, but some other individual has a key input to make it successful, the nature of the skills each individual possesses is highly specialised and difficult to know without a direct connection. Any given person knows only whether she or the people to whom she's directly linked has the necessary skills. If none of them can, then the project has to be forwarded to other people in the organisation. Given the limited capacity of people to understand and process projects, a trade-off arises between centralisation and decentralisation. In a centralised organisation, projects find their destination fast, since the centre by definition knows what everyone can solve; but if lots of projects need processing, they will get held up in the centre's queue. In a decentralized organisation, projects spend a long time circulating in search of someone who can solve them; but congestion is less of an issue, as each node handles a more balanced load of projects.

Tackling this challenge required a genuinely interdisciplinary approach. The economists were instrumental in the formulation and formalisation of the problem, and in understanding the implications for actual organisations. The physicists, meanwhile, had a better understanding of the solution methods for this particular problem, and its connections with problems already solved in other disciplines. Both teams learnt new techniques and approaches from the enterprise. To date, it is still AC's most cited paper.

Despite the success of the collaboration, however, it is striking that almost eight years passed between the work's first publication and a version suitable for economists appearing in print (Arenas et al., 2010). The main reason for this delay was the resistance of a sub-discipline of economics profession (the microeconomists) to the use of numerical methods – though interestingly, another subdiscipline (the macroeconomists) uses mostly numerical methods. Another factor in the delay was the fact that the economics review process is much slower than in physics, due to the habit of economics editors and referees requiring detailed and complicated revisions, sometimes amounting to an almost completely new paper, with new designs, experiments and models. Even when teams achieve the goal of interdisciplinary working, the individual team members still have to publish their work in a world defined by disciplinary conventions.

A very different kind of collaboration saw AC working with sociobiologists to model the behaviour not of humans but of ants (Pollock et al., 2004). This work started at about the same time that the ELSE (Economic Learning and Social Evolution) Centre was created at University College London (UCL) by Ken Binmore, precisely to foster interdisciplinary work drawing on game theory and evolutionary approaches. Two visitors to the centre were AC and Gregory B. Pollock, a sociobiologist; and Pollock found himself explaining to AC how hard it was for his colleagues to understand a behaviour, observed in species of desert ants such as the Arizona desert ant (*acromyrmex versicolor*), which appeared to contradict self-interest. Specifically, when the ant queens co-found a nest, it is usually the one closest to the surface when building the nest who undertakes the dangerous task of foraging for the fungus garden (which feeds the queens) until there are workers to take over the task. Pollock and his colleagues had shown in previous experimental work that the way the dangerous foraging behaviour is enforced is through the refusal of other queens to forage: this refusal persists even if the surface excavator is experimentally removed. This 'punishment' to the refusing queen can even lead to death of the colony, which means the 'punisher' inflicts a very high cost to herself, and this is puzzling if one takes a narrow 'selfish gene' perspective.

The collaboration between disciplines here was critical to the success of this project for two reasons. The first is that the economist's position as an outsider, with no vested interest in the 'selfish gene' idea, made it easier for him to recognise that the standard disciplinary view was wrong. This is an aspect of interdisciplinary work we have not emphasised so far, but one we feel is very important. Bringing in outsiders with fresh ideas can be useful to broaden the perspectives of disciplinary insiders. Moreover – and this was the second reason why interdisciplinary collaboration was so important in this case – the outsider will bring with them a set of tools – in this case, tools from formal evolutionary game theory – which can help in understanding the particular problem under consideration.

In this case, the work consisted of modelling the interactions of the ants in more detail than had been done before, and finding a mechanism through which costly co-operation within groups (taking up foraging by the surface excavator) can be explained in evolutionary terms: namely, the intense competition between groups that interact locally. To be more precise, it is common for multiple colonies – the numbers can run into the hundreds – to start under the same vacant tree. Those colonies fight one another for exclusive possession of the tree – by raiding one another for brood once the workers emerge – until a single colony triumphs. Colonies that co-operate internally (the surface excavator, the more efficient forager takes the job) are more efficient (they grow faster and have more workers) in the external competition (because number of workers is very important in brood raiding) than those in which the surface excavator refuses (or there is squabble or delay) and is replaced by a less efficient ant. Thus, even if the co-operating groups are internally somewhat less stable, the external pressure can lead them to a higher long-term (stochastic) stability, something our research shows through simulations with ecologically plausible values. This fruitful interdisciplinary collaboration has gone on for many years, and a second paper involving another game theorist, Ken Binmore himself, appeared subsequently (Pollock et al., 2012), where the simulation analysis was complemented with other analytical results.

The emergence of a new field

As we noted at the beginning, interdisciplinarity is an inherently transient activity, which, if successful, should ultimately lead to the emergence of a new field. For this to happen, however, it is important for different disciplines to be involved from the outset, helping not only to find answers but also to define questions. An example of this is AS's involvement in a truly interdisciplinary research programme to define and set up the new field of behavioural human primatology.

Interestingly, this work arose from an earlier attempt by AS to propose, to a different group, behavioural experiments with primates. This collaboration failed because the results did not agree with the theoretical perspective and related experiments of the primatologists. Owing to an agreement that all the data would remain the property of the primatologists, the results could not be published and the collaboration stopped abruptly. The team had failed to break down the disciplinary boundaries.

Subsequently, AS contacted another researcher, who has a BSc in zoology and a PhD in psychology, and who works with primates. They started their discussion in a small workshop on the evolution of co-operation, and followed it up in private – eventually leading to a position paper setting out a full project (Cronin and Sánchez, 2012). As this project has developed, further collaborators have been recruited as required (in particular, an economist). The team has carried out its first set of experiments on human behaviour inspired by primates and is preparing the results for publication. In the future, the team expects to bring in expertise from computational social sciences and paleoanthropologists, to use their findings to shed light on the origin of the first human societies in what will be a fully-fledged interdisciplinary approach.

The challenge and promise of interdisciplinarity

The examples above illustrate our own experiences in addressing issues of behaviour and behaviour change in interdisciplinary settings, experiences that have taught us about both the promise and the challenges of working in this way.

Beginning with the challenges, one lesson we have learned is that collaboration is not always easy. There are many problems that can derail an interdisciplinary team: communication difficulties; different disciplines working at different paces and disseminating their results in different ways; disagreement on the interpretation of the research; obstacles to dissemination arising either from conditions established at the beginning, or from the dominant position of the partner who is presenting, and so on.

However, while one must approach every new endeavour with caution, our many positive experiences suggest that problems such as these need not be major concerns. Much more worrisome, in our view, are lack of support from the funding bodies and obstacles created by academic career structures:

- With regard to funding, the evaluation of interdisciplinary proposals is generally dealt with badly. Often an interdisciplinary category under which one can file a proposal does not even exist. Even if it does exist, the evaluators are still disciplinary researchers. Invariably, therefore, this kind of application ends up being presented mostly in the language of just one of the disciplines involved, with a marginal contribution from the others. More satisfying and potentially fruitful approaches to interdisciplinary working, such as starting a project with a new field already in mind, are typically doomed in terms of fund-raising. Suffice it to say, as an example, that in a typical EU call for grants, with a success rate between 5 and 10%, receiving just one report from an evaluator who claims that the proposal is out of scope is more than enough to have it rejected.
- Turning to career structures, the unfortunate truth is that working on interdisciplinary research is more often than not an obstacle to progression in a career in academia. Promotions are generally associated with a specific field and, again, evaluation difficulties plague the problem of choosing the best candidate.

These are two key areas in which science policymakers need to take action if they are serious in their oft-proclaimed desire to promote truly interdisciplinary research.

When it comes to the study of behaviour and behaviour change, we believe that interdisciplinary research has to be promoted. As the examples we have considered show, behaviour, which happens in a context, needs to be considered in that context if the conclusions of the research are to be of any use. For instance, complexity science shows that contagion (of infectious diseases, behaviours, etc) through social interactions depends crucially on the structure of the network of social contacts. This means that even if the contagion *mechanism* is the same in all cases (propagation of a virus, imitation, etc.) the *context* of the population changes the global outcome, in a manner that knowledge of the interaction alone cannot predict. On the other hand, details also matter, so peculiarities of the disciplines involved – ranging from computer science to biology through ecology and managerial science – must be taken on board from the outset, by involving the appropriate expertise of individuals motivated to overcome the challenges of collaboration. When that is done, the rewards, both in personal terms and in terms of project results, are significant.

Furthermore, the more researchers become used to interdisciplinary work, the more we will learn about *how* to work together, and the closer we will be to solving the issues mentioned above. That is why it is our fervent hope that science policymakers undergo a true change in behaviour in their support for interdisciplinary research.

Suggested further reading

For works cited, see References at the end of the book.

Dzeng, E. (2013) 'How to inspire interdisciplinarity: lessons from the collegiate system', The Guardian Higher Education Network Blog. Available at: http://sbk.li/191781

A perspective from a general internal medicine fellow working on her PhD and trying to take an interdisciplinary view that nicely complements the view we present here.

Pfirman, S. and Begg, M. (2012) 'Troubled by Interdisciplinarity?' Science Careers, Science. Available at: http://sbk.li/191782

The authors largely expand our discussion that interdisciplinary research doesn't fit into traditional academic structures, and show how to become aware of the pitfalls and prepare yourself to succeed in such an arena. Their recommendations include building skills for interdisciplinary collaboration, extending your mentorship team, bolstering your interdisciplinary CV for disciplinary review, and preparing for the complications of writing and submitting interdisciplinary grant proposals.

Shapiro, E. (2014) 'Point of view: correcting the bias against interdisciplinary research', eLife 3 e02576. Available at: http://sbk.li/191783

Discusses the problems related to the evaluation of interdisciplinary research and the bias in favour of disciplinary proposes, and proposes actions to counteract this bias.

10. Changing professional behaviour with cognitive engineering

John Fox

Professor, Department of Engineering Science, Oxford University

The design of cognitive prostheses – tools, such as the many kinds of software that are designed to improve human performance in cognitive tasks – can be seen as a 'straightforward engineering problem'. In fact, like so many other kinds of behaviour change tools, the design of a cognitive prosthesis requires an interdisciplinary approach, and is a key theme in the emerging discipline of cognitive engineering.

In §1 of the Dialogue, Evie draws a distinction between two types of model: those which are used to understand things that already exist or happen in the world, which she compares to maps; and models of things that we want to make exist or happen, which she compares to blueprints. As an example of the latter, she might have in mind the models often constructed by engineers and other technical professionals seeking to develop optimal solutions to real-world problems.

Evie's distinction seems plausible: but does it hold when we look specifically at problems of behaviour change? In this paper, I'll explore a specific behaviour change challenge: the design of cognitive prostheses, such as software that is designed to improve on human performance in a range of cognitive tasks. In particular, I'll focus on software that is designed to optimise the behaviour of healthcare professionals in clinical tasks like reasoning, decision-making and planning. I'll argue that tackling this class of design problems requires an interdisciplinary approach – exemplified by the emerging discipline of cognitive engineering – which blends the 'blueprinting' perspective of the engineer with the 'map-making' perspective of cognitive psychology and neuroscience.

Cognitive prostheses in healthcare

Psychologists and behavioural scientists have for many years been aware of the inevitability of human error, and even irrationality, in our personal decision-making and in professional practice. Forty years ago, cognitive scientists Donald Norman and Tim Shallice (Norman and Shallice, 1976) outlined five types of situations in which routine human patterns of behaviour are often insufficient to produce optimal performance:

1. Situations that involve planning or decision-making
2. Situations that involve error correction or troubleshooting
3. Situations where responses contain novel sequences of actions
4. Dangerous or technically difficult situations
5. Situations where we should avoid a habitual or routine response

Most if not all of these are typical in clinical practice – and probably in all professional behaviour. It's only recently, however, that healthcare practitioners and policymakers have started to recognise the sub-optimality of normal human reasoning, and the potential for making improvements on it (e.g. Kohn et al., 1999; Vincent, 2001; Gawande, 2014).

The realities of modern clinical practice have exacerbated the predicament of healthcare professionals and their all-too-human reasoning capabilities. On the one hand, they struggle to keep up with the rapidly expanding knowledge base of medicine, new clinical research and the constant need to update professional practice and skills. On the other, they face the remorseless pressure of public expectations regarding quality of service, better care outcomes and safety. Such pressures inevitably lead to error, and in recent years the evidence of growing levels of avoidable patient harm and even deaths due to medical mistakes, as well as inefficient and inappropriate use of resources, has become incontrovertible.

'Cognitive prostheses' represent one potential response to these challenges. The basic idea is simple enough, and can be illustrated with an analogy. Imagine that you are shortsighted (many of you won't have to imagine): your sub-optimal vision can be improved by the use of 'visual prostheses' like glasses or contact lenses. Wearing these, you can see much better than you would have done otherwise. In the same way, cognitive prostheses are designed to support common cognitive tasks, such as acquiring and communicating relevant information, interpreting it correctly, making decisions well and transparently, planning tasks appropriately and managing professional and organisational processes effectively and safely.

A straightforward engineering problem?

How does one go about developing a cognitive prosthesis? On the face of it, this may seem like a straightforward engineering problem, drawing on the many established techniques for:

- supporting 'rational' reasoning and decision-making (e.g. logical and statistical techniques)
- managing complex processes (e.g. business process modelling and workflow management systems)
- carrying out tasks optimally (e.g. with respect to criteria of costs, benefits and harms).

It certainly seems that way to many engineers and technical professionals. Software engineers, for example, typically approach behaviour change by defining a set of 'use cases' that identify the problems to be solved, selecting the appropriate techniques, specifying the required functions, and then implementing, testing and deploying the required prosthesis using one of various established software development methodologies. For example, this was exactly the expectation of Anthony Finkelstein, Professor of

Software Engineering at University College London (UCL), in a discussion of the use of engineering models in designing systems to promote behaviour change (Finkelstein, 2014).

Unfortunately, the real processes of human reasoning, decision-making and planning are very different from 'normative' theories of these tasks – theories that describe the way we *should* reason and make decisions, if only we weren't human beings, and which typically come from mathematics, computer science or other technical roots. It's true that mature normative theories of this kind have been used successfully in business domains and other settings: but in healthcare, and in other situations where human expertise is important and needs to be kept 'in the loop', the adoption and impact of technologies based on these approaches have been much more mixed. There are in fact few if any 'off the shelf' normative theories that have been shown to reliably guide design of the kinds of cognitive prostheses we seek. Prostheses developed in this way are often unsuccessful in mitigating the kinds of problems we encounter in a human-centred, complex and knowledge-intensive field like healthcare.

For example, some colleagues and I were recently asked by a major hospital group in the USA to help them to develop and deploy computer-based services to support doctors and nurses in their work. Their clinicians were signed up to the need for better care, and accepted the need for well designed 'care pathways' to guide and where necessary change their routine practice. The highly capable informatics division of the hospital group was therefore asked to develop the necessary systems. They based their design approach on 'clinical algorithms' (a form of flow diagram) and well-established software engineering methods of the kind outlined above. In due course the team delivered a functional and impressive prototype, running on a modern touch-based tablet, for their clinical colleagues to assess. To their surprise the feedback was negative: the users liked the presentation but found the clinical algorithms medically unintuitive and too rigid to use in practice. They also found that the effort required to use the pathways was not compensated for by benefits that would assist the clinicians in their work or reduce pressures on them.

In this case, as in many others, the 'optimal solution' to the behaviour change problem, developed using a 'straightforward engineering' approach to correcting shortcomings in human clinical practice, turned out not to be optimal at all. In terms of our earlier simple analogy, it was as if the team had designed perfect glasses or contact lenses that no one then wore.

Puzzled by this outcome, the development team became interested in our interdisciplinary approach to developing cognitive prostheses. At the heart of that approach, which is called *cognitive engineering*, is a simple principle: to design a successful cognitive prosthesis, we need to start from an understanding of human cognition, and in particular the 'executive functions' described by Norman and Shallice (1976) and studied in cognitive psychology, neuroscience and AI. (Reasoning, problem-solving, planning and execution, working memory and task flexibility are all examples of executive functions.) To put it in Evie's terms: we need a map before we can draw up a blueprint.

The cognitive engineering approach

Cognitive prostheses are designed to correct errors and shortcomings in human reasoning, decision-making and planning. The causes of these human errors and shortcomings have been widely discussed – most famously by Kahneman and Tversky's heuristics and biases programme and its successors (see e.g. Kahneman et al., 1982) – and it's not surprising that developers of cognitive prostheses have focused on ways of eliminating perceived causes of mistakes.

But I believe this is too restrictive. For the cognitive engineer, it's important to understand, not only human *error*, but also the many ways in which humans *succeed*. Notwithstanding the identification of human biases and even criticisms of human 'irrationality', human cognition also has many strengths – strengths which can be inspiring for an engineer seeking to match human flexibility and versatility, the depth of our understanding of the world we inhabit, and the many kinds of knowledge that we can bring to bear in a moment. In contrast, technologies developed as solutions to 'straightforward engineering problems' are often seen by the professionals they are intended for as inflexible, naïve or irrelevant to perceived needs. Consequently, however technically sophisticated and 'rational' they appear to be, they are dismissed and fail to change behaviour.

What does this mean in practice? Through our own work, we have developed three cognitive engineering principles as a design framework to support the development of cognitive prostheses, which I'll discuss briefly in the rest of this paper (more detail can be found in Fox, 2014):

- Start from the best theory of high-level cognition available
- Employ the theory to analyse the professional tasks that are being undertaken
- Understand the role of knowledge in these tasks, and how it is being represented and used

Underpinning all of these principles is the basic insight that, to improve on human cognition, we need to understand its strengths as well as its weaknesses.

Principle 1: modelling high-level cognition

Our recommended starting point for the cognitive engineer is a model of the thing we wish to optimise: high-level human cognition. In our approach we start from the proposition that human thinking in general (and medical expertise in particular) is the expression of a complex interplay of many cognition functions, often referred to collectively as 'executive functions' or the 'executive system', which is responsible for capabilities like reasoning, decision-making and planning. Our attempts to understand these capabilities in engineering terms led to a generalised model of human and artificial 'cognitive agents' (Fox et al., 2003; Fox et al., 2013). Key elements of the model are as follows:

- Cognitive agents engage with their environment (perceiving, acting and communicating with other agents with which they may need to collaborate, as in a clinical team)
- From these engagements, cognitive agents form and modify beliefs about a current situation, leading to goals that guide their behaviour over short or long periods of time
- Other cognitive functions include abilities to *reason*, make decisions under uncertainty, formulate plans and schedule actions
- Expert cognitive agents draw upon substantial (sometimes prodigious) bodies of knowledge about this, both general knowledge and specialist knowledge of particular domains like medicine
- All these processes are subject to different kinds of cognitive control, including 'reactive' control

(situation-driven) and 'deliberative' control (goal-driven)
- A feature that distinguishes the behaviour of human cognitive agents is our ability to reflect upon our beliefs, decisions and plans and the rationales for them – a characteristic which is not typical of conventional software systems but which is important for an agent if it is to be adaptive (able to review and modify its decisions and plans as circumstances change)

Our analysis offers an enumeration of some of the main cognitive process that underpin executive processes which are characteristic of professional expertise. From a design point of view the analysis shows that cognitive performance depends upon a range of capabilities that are at once a source of versatility and flexibility, yet also shed light on the origins of errors that undermine human effectiveness and are potential targets for the design of prostheses.

Beyond this generalised model of high-level cognition, however, our observations over many years of clinicians working in diverse settings, and systematic investigations of clinical expertise in the lab have led us to conclude that no one model or theory of expertise gives us a uniquely correct framework for design. Instead, we have found we need a number of different kinds of models of expert behaviour to understand and emulate the sophistication and power of human cognition.

Principle 2: task analysis

The second challenge for a cognitive engineer is to analyse the tasks that are being undertaken by the professionals who will use the cognitive prosthesis. While an analysis of high-level cognitive functions reveals many distinct sources of error, and suggests mitigations for those errors, it does not offer a good way of thinking about the professional tasks that the cognitive functions are orchestrated to perform and which the prosthesis should support. To address this we developed a task analysis language called PRO*forma* (Sutton and Fox, 2003). This allows us to break down a complex professional task into its component parts using a small set of formal task models, notably decisions, plans and actions.

Other task analysis techniques have been developed for such purposes as workflow modelling and the design of human-computer interfaces, but these languages are typically designed only to *describe* a task of interest, while PRO*forma* task models can also be *enacted* by a computer. Furthermore, a PRO*forma* model of expertise is easy to understand, and can be deployed as a tool to support less expert individuals – for example, by taking them through a task in the same sequence of steps that an expert would follow. Last but not least, because PRO*forma* is grounded in a model of high-level human cognition it allows us to develop not just an effective engineering solution, but a naturalistic solution that emulates real human expertise that is easy for people to understand, while still eliminating many causes of human error. A cognitive prosthesis designed in this way, I would argue, is much more likely to change professional behaviour.

Principle 3: understanding how knowledge is represented

The third challenge for the cognitive engineer is to understand how knowledge, including expert knowledge, is represented and used by the human professionals for whom the cognitive prosthesis is intended.

Computer science and artificial intelligence have developed a number of computational techniques for representing general and specialist knowledge. Furthermore there are an increasing number of formal theories of domain-specific knowledge that allow us to understand the conceptual and logical structure of the knowledge of experts in a specialist domain, and to develop powerful techniques for emulating their expertise.

The figure below shows an example of the kinds of structure I am talking about here: the 'knowledge ladder'. Though it is a simple picture we have found it to be a useful pedagogical device and a practical framework for guiding the design and implementation of knowledge bases (Fox, 2005). The knowledge ladder has emerged progressively over many attempts to formalise medical knowledge and expertise, though the framework does not appear to have any features that limit its use in other domains.

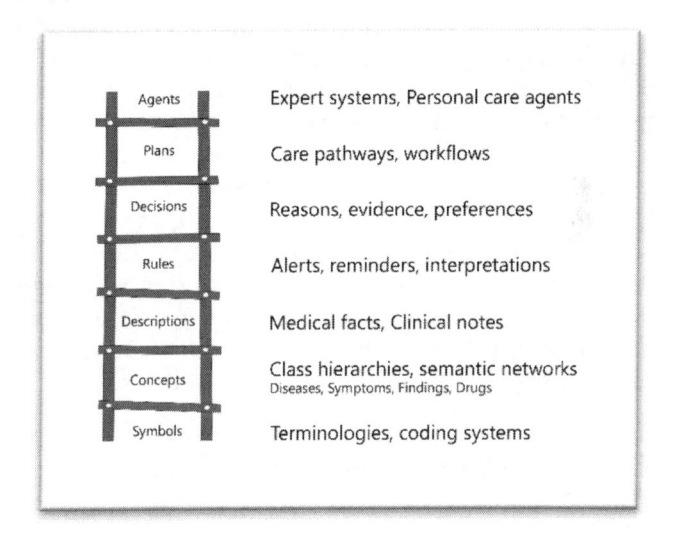

Rung	Examples
Agents	Expert systems, Personal care agents
Plans	Care pathways, workflows
Decisions	Reasons, evidence, preferences
Rules	Alerts, reminders, interpretations
Descriptions	Medical facts, Clinical notes
Concepts	Class hierarchies, semantic networks; Diseases, Symptoms, Findings, Drugs
Symbols	Terminologies, coding systems

In common with other AI knowledge representations, the knowledge ladder has a layered structure in which each type of knowledge has a well-defined relationship with the layers immediately below and above it. This arrangement has substantial engineering benefits: it offers a logically precise way of understanding an otherwise vague notion like 'knowledge', and has proved to be a valuable tool in designing general task models like those written in PRO*forma* which have been routinely adopted in specific clinical domains.

Conclusion

The three principles are the central components of a design methodology that we call CREDO, which facilitates rapid design, implementation and deployment of cognitive prostheses to assist in clinical and other kinds of thinking, and help to mitigate sources of error and modify inappropriate or out-of-date behaviour. The CREDO framework has proved effective in supporting many different kinds of tasks, ranging from capturing and interpreting data (e.g. about a patient), evaluating a situation (e.g. normal or abnormal) or assessing an action (e.g. risky or safe), to making recommendations for diagnosis (e.g. about the presence or absence of a condition) or treatment (e.g. this drug or that). A PRO*forma* agent can also guide a clinical workflow or support a multidisciplinary clinical team. The cognitive engineering framework facilitates the design of simple and intuitive user interfaces, and empowers users by providing evidence-based explanations for all recommendations and tasks.

Crucially, CREDO – and the cognitive engineering approach that it exemplifies – is also proving to be a successful platform for building and deploying diverse applications which can *change* professional behaviour in healthcare, and potentially in other fields as well. The secret to its success, I would argue, lies in its interdisciplinary approach to design: it draws on concepts and techniques from modern cognitive science, yet is sufficiently formal and precise that it can satisfy the needs for clarity and precision expected by professional engineers and designers.

CREDO is only a first step in developing principled foundations for cognitive engineering of systems that can enhance and change professional behaviour. Nevertheless, its successes to date have convinced me of the larger point: that behaviour change is not a 'straightforward engineering problem', but one that requires an interdisciplinary response to provide 'maps' as well as 'blueprints'.

Suggested further reading

For works cited, see References at the end of the book.

Norman, D.A. (1986) 'Cognitive Engineering', *User centered system design*. Available at: http://sbk.li/1101911

An old but still important essay by a pioneer of cognitive science and engineering that motivates and explains his perspective on human-centred design.

'Cognitive Science', Wikipedia. Available at: http://sbk.li/1101912

A fast tour through the main themes and concepts of cognitive science, which provides the multidisciplinary foundations for the field of cognitive engineering.

11. Economic models in interdisciplinary studies of behaviour change: helpful abstractions or spurious distractions?

Michelle Baddeley

Professor in Economics and Finance, UCL Bartlett Faculty of the Built Environment, University College London

What contribution can economics make to our understanding of behaviour change? To answer that question, we first need to understand some of the key dilemmas that characterise the discipline of economics, and the origins of these dilemmas. By taking a more interdisciplinary perspective, behavioural economics shows potential in overcoming these dilemmas, and enhancing the contribution of economics to interdisciplinary dialogue about behaviour change.

In 2010 a group of economists wrote a letter setting out the case against austerity, signed by many highly respected figures, to *The Sunday Times*. In response, another group wrote a contradictory letter to I, again with many highly respected signatories. Almost as if this were a Prisoner's Dilemma game of self-interested groups delivering the worst possible outcome for everyone, the net result was that economics as a discipline lost credibility. If the most feted economists in the world could not come to a simple agreement about something as important as whether or not governments should be spending money during a recession, what could economics – and macroeconomics specifically – really contribute to human wellbeing and welfare?

The incident is just one example of a wider trend since the financial crisis, which has seen the discipline driven into strictly divided camps, at least in the context of popular debates – broadly pro-market versus broadly pro-government, even though each economist's views are probably more nuanced than this simple distinction suggests. Widely reported arguments about the empirical basis of each camp's position have not helped bolster the public's support for economists' analyses. For example, Reinhart and Rogoff's claims about the impact of fiscal deficits on economic growth, were shown to be based on significant errors in the data analysis (see Cassidy, 2013); and Piketty's analysis of the relationships between inequality and economic growth was criticised by *The Financial Times* on the grounds that some data were flawed (see Irwin, 2014). No camp can be excluded from the criticisms: both sides claimed that their conclusions were confirmed by empirical evidence – even though the reality was that, in both cases, the empirical evidence was mixed and the data and/or its analysis significantly flawed.

What are the non-economists to make of this? That economists do not know what they're talking about? That they are offering us, not helpful abstractions, which can help us to make sense of behaviour and behaviour change, but spurious distractions with data presented and analysed selectively to support particular ideological positions and political stances?

As an economist, I believe that my discipline can contribute significant insights to interdisciplinary analyses of behaviour and behaviour change. But economists also face a number of complex dilemmas when modelling human behaviour, and these dilemmas have shaped the discipline, and have driven some profound disagreements.

In this paper, I'd like to highlight three key dilemmas, which have shaped the discipline of economics and its approaches to modelling behaviour:

- how to create models – typically mathematical models – of phenomena which are inherently complex – in large part due to the influences of human psychology
- how to develop reliable methods for the empirical testing of theory and hypotheses
- how to deal with situations of unquantifiable uncertainty, as opposed to quantifiable risk

Modelling inherently complex phenomena

A key hurdle for any economist is that economies, and the people and organisations that make up the building blocks of economic models, are inherently complex, reflecting a complex reality. Economic systems are driven by human reactions, political forces, psychological responses and social influences; different groups of people interacting in different ways, in different contexts, with differing goals, and driven by differing incentives – social and behavioural as well as monetary.

In his biographical essay about pioneering economist Alfred Marshall, John Maynard Keynes captures the breadth and complexity of the challenges an economist faces in capturing economic realities:

> *The master-economist must possess a rare combination of gifts [...] He must be mathematician, historian, statesman, philosopher [...] He must understand symbols and speak in words. He must contemplate the particular, in terms of the general, and touch abstract and concrete in the same flight of thought. He must study the present in the light of the past for the purposes of the future. No part of man's nature or his institutions must be entirely outside his regard. He must be purposeful and disinterested in a simultaneous mood, as aloof and incorruptible as an artist, yet sometimes as near to earth as a politician [...] a dealer in the particular and the general, the temporal and the eternal, at the same time.*
> Keynes, 1924, p. 322

In response to these challenges, most economic modellers have constructed models as simplified abstractions, derived logically from underlying assumptions. The current convention in mainstream economics is to formulate these models as *mathematical* representations, simplifying from a complex reality by focusing on a relatively small number of key variables.

Necessarily these models abstract from the complexity of reality: indeed, this is part of their intention – which is to simplify and, by doing so, to enable understanding. An immediate problem emerges, however, when there are many paths to simplification, and the choice of path chosen becomes a subjective decision, perhaps moulded by the researcher's pre-conceptions and political opinions that underpin their 'correct' way of thinking about the world. Given the very large number of possibilities for explanatory variables, the economic modeller is forced to concentrate on a small number of key variables, selected from a wide range. But how far should this process of mathematical abstraction and simplification go? Too far, and the model will become so divorced from reality that it is no longer useful. Not far enough, and the model will itself be too complex to help us understand what is going on.

This is the first fundamental dilemma facing the economic modeller. Mankiw summarises its essence:

> *A good theory has two characteristics: internal consistency and external consistency. An internally consistent theory is one that is parsimonious; it invokes no ad hoc or peculiar axioms. An externally consistent theory is one that fits the facts; it makes empirically refutable predictions that are not refuted. All scientists, including economists, strive for theories that are both internally and externally consistent... Yet like all optimising agents, scientists face tradeoffs. One theory may be more 'beautiful', while another may be easier to reconcile with observation.*
> Mankiw, 1989, pp. 88-9

As a discipline, economics has been criticised for failures on both sides of this trade-off. On the one hand, the economic models used today can appear strange and mysterious to non-economists. It is difficult to understand them and their foundations without a strong background in economics. Economics, at its best, is practical science, but if it becomes too esoteric, if it fails to simplify enough, then its usefulness in terms of understanding and shaping behaviour will be limited.

On the other hand, economic models are often criticised as lacking external consistency (i.e. empirically, the real-world does not mirror the theory) and intuitive plausibility. Other criticisms focus on underlying assumptions that are unrealistic in terms of our own experience of how real people and businesses behave.

There are elements of both kinds of criticism in John Maynard Keynes's commentary on the mathematical models of his day:

> *Too large a proportion of recent 'mathematical' economics are mere concoctions, as imprecise as the initial assumptions they rest on, which allow the author to lose sight of the complexities and interdependencies of the real world in a maze of pretentious and unhelpful symbols.*
> Keynes, 1936, p. 298

Disagreements about how to simplify and abstract, and about how far that process should go, account for much of the disagreement within economics.

For example, consider the theoretical models associated with one school of economics – what is broadly known as neo-classical economics. These models simplify reality by leaving out many of the factors that prevent perfect competition in reality, and assuming smoothly operating markets and flexible prices. These are the economic models that most people know about, even if they do not understand them.

In reality, most economists would agree that unfettered markets do not work well in the real world because market failure is endemic – which does not mean that government failure can be ruled out. In a modern mixed economy, careful judgements are needed about how to balance the risks of market failure versus government failure. Nevertheless, there are reasons why many economists still choose to start with the assumptions of perfect competition – for example that prices respond quickly and flexibly to relative shifts in supply and demand without any buyer or seller having any power over market prices and output – even when they don't think it's particularly realistic. Some would argue that mathematical models are simplifications that help us to understand how economies work. Others argue that a model of perfect competition provides a benchmark ideal – it is not likely to be seen in the real world, but if we know what the essential ingredients are for a world of perfect competition, then we can move the real world towards it, e.g. by constraining monopolistic behaviours and by enabling the better circulation of information. Overall, there is a lively debate within the economics discipline about whether or not, or how far, the perfect competition model can help us.

On the other hand, there are large numbers of economists who reject the assumption of perfect competition completely, and develop different approaches to simplification and modelling – and in some cases question whether any simplification at all is justifiable. Some retain essential assumptions that enable mathematicisation: for example the new Keynesian school use the rationality assumption associated with neo-classical economics because it enables them to characterise and mathematicise economic behaviour in a relatively simple way. Alongside that, they incorporate more realistic assumptions about, for example, 'sticky' (inflexible) prices and imperfect information.

Testing economic models

An empirical defence of mathematical economic models and their underlying unrealistic assumptions (e.g. that people are rational, that prices are flexible) is that these models generate testable predictions, and that the world operates 'as if' these assumptions were true (Friedman, 1953). If we want to understand and test economic models, the argument goes, then we need to construct relatively simple representations.

One reason why pro-market approaches remain popular is their simplicity. For example, Gary Becker controversially used abstract rational choice economic models to characterise a wide range of behaviours from marriage and divorce to crime and addiction[3] – an approach since popularised in books such as *Freakonomics* and *Super-Freakonomics*. The power of this approach lies in the fact that assuming all people are rational and self-interested makes modelling their behaviour a lot easier. Moreover, the approach has concrete implications for policy and interventions to drive behaviour change – provided complex human behaviour in the real world really is 'as if' the simple model were true.

This invites an empirical question: to what extent do mathematical representations such as rational choice

---

[3] See Becker (1976) for an outline of some of these models.

economic models actually enable us to predict real-world economic behaviour?

If we want to answer that question, and establish whether the real world works as if these otherwise unrealistic models were true, then we need powerful tools for empirical testing - and the now enormous field of econometrics provides a wide range of tools and techniques. A key problem for economists is how to test their models to ensure that they properly capture reality, but there is little common ground even when models are tested using purportedly objective data and econometric methods.

Risk and uncertainty

In economics, there is a useful distinction between conceptions of quantifiable risk - or Knightian risk - and unquantifiable uncertainty - or Knightian uncertainty. (The distinction is attributed to Knight, 1921; see also Keynes, 1921.) Knightian risk arises in situations which are governed by quantifiable laws and/or easily replicable scenarios that can be captured using frequency distributions. For example, rolling dice and betting on a double six is a situation of quantifiable risk: it's not possible to know what will happen, but it is possible to get an objective, quantifiable measure of probability. Risk may also be quantifiable if events can be captured by a frequency distribution; for example, via the law of large numbers, exam scores from large numbers of students sitting the same exam with an objectively determined number of correct and incorrect answers will tend to follow a normal distribution. Most economists would acknowledge that situations characterised by quantifiable risk are often unlikely - especially when information is incomplete - and modern economic theory and econometrics are increasingly embedding Bayesian methods in which probabilities are updated as new information accumulates.

Knightian uncertainty, by contrast, is about what's unknown and, possibly, unknowable. Many economic and financial phenomena emerge in unique situations in which we can neither apply probabilistic laws, nor assume that outcomes can be captured by frequency distributions. Unquantifiable Knightian uncertainty reflects the fact that there are many possibilities and drivers, and innumerable sources of interactions between people and contexts. This sort of world does not fit well with the assumptions about statistical stability implicit in conventional econometric analyses – conventional econometrics allows for randomness but the randomness takes a controlled and specific form: the statistical characteristics of the probability distributions which underlie random variables, e.g. the means and variances, are stable and thus inferences can be made and tested using statistical techniques. In a 'non-ergodic' world, complex unrealities are not quantifiable (Davidson, 1996).

For example, consider a business investing in an innovative new product that has never been marketed before. It is virtually impossible in such a situation to quantify the likelihood of success, because there is no prior experience on which an entrepreneur can draw, and no prior information on which to base an estimate of success. A businessperson may well come up with a numerical estimate of likely profits, but such numbers will be spurious, often without objective basis.

Unquantifiable uncertainties are endemic when it comes to economic and financial questions, both in the discipline of economics and in its subject matter. This means that the economic modeller's job is hard, harder than modelling many physical systems. For example, in engineering systems the parameters are fixed: an engineer can make a well-judged prediction about how many cars might be produced from a given car manufacturing plant in a day. By contrast, a macroeconomic policy-maker will find it difficult accurately to judge what inflation, unemployment or GDP growth might be in a year's time, because these variables are determined in a highly complex system which is affected not only by relatively fixed physical parameters but also by the unpredictability of human psychology. More research is needed in understanding the difference between uncertainty and risk in these scenarios, because they are often the most transformative, with the widest implications for individual businesses and industries, including workers within those industries. One way in which this might be achieved is by moving beyond standard econometric modelling towards computational modelling of complex systems, embedding insights from mathematics, computer science and planning – e.g. agent-based modelling.

New directions for Economics: What role can behavioural economics play?

What can we conclude about whether economic models are helpful abstractions or spurious distractions? The simple answer is that, at their best, economic models are helpful abstractions, but a wider, more outward-looking, orientation can help to reduce the danger that they become spurious distractions.

The increasingly popular sub-discipline of behavioural economics has a key role to play in this, because behavioural economics is by its nature outward-looking; it combines economic insights, for example about incentives and motivations, with insights about the other forces that drive decision-making and behaviour from other social sciences, as well as the natural sciences, including psychology, sociology, philosophy, evolutionary biology, behavioural ecology and neuroscience.

To what extent can behavioural economics smooth the way in discovering some common ground and/or more objective evidence – to give a more solid basis for models of behaviour change? Behavioural economics can combine the rigour seen in rational choice models with a richer understanding of how real people behave. Real-world applications include problems associated with poor planning, procrastination and disproportionate short-termism, and behavioural economics has contributed to policy debates around issues from pension provision and organ donation to online security and privacy protection. There are also applications in the context of addiction and other health choices connected to a poor diet and lack of exercise.

So far, however, there has been little emphasis in the behavioural economics literature about overarching questions of methodology. The focus has been on collecting evidence, using – for economists – relatively innovative methods borrowed from the medical and biological sciences (e.g. experimental evidence, including randomised controlled trials (RCTs)). One of the main advantages of behavioural economics is that it moves beyond a monodisciplinary approach. But it suffers from economics' general disadvantage in that it is already dividing into camps, depending on the extent to which assumptions of rational behaviour are modified or abandoned. In engineering behaviour change, the nature of rationality must be a key question, and whilst behavioural economics is on its way to finding some answers, the question is not yet resolved. Is rationality bounded by limits on information and cognitive processing ability, as emphasised by Herbert Simon; or is behaviour irrational, as emphasised in popular accounts e.g. by Dan Ariely? The debates on the nature and extent of rationality are enormous and much more work is needed in exploring the boundaries of rationality. For me, Herbert Simon's work is one of the most promising starting points in unravelling this complex question.[4]

Another area of potential lies in how behavioural economics embraces multidisciplinary approaches – and its collaborations with scientists. Economists' dependence on mathematical abstractions in formulating their models was a loophole meaning that economists have not engaged strongly with standard scientific methodologies – in terms of forming testable, falsifiable hypotheses, testing them using robust empirical methods, and revisiting the theory if not confirmed by the evidence. Again the implications for models of behaviour change are potentially profound because experimental methods, including RCTs, are strongly grounded in established scientific methodologies. Nonetheless potential problems remain – reflecting tensions within scientific discovery more generally.

The problem is that the process of empirical testing is not so simple. Scientists are no less prone to social influences and peer pressure than economists – the focus is on finding novel results – and there is little incentive to replicate others' findings – there is no glory in it.[5] But with a better understanding of models and methodologies, behavioural economics has the potential to combine analytical rigour with intuitive plausibility – enabling us better to understand and mould behaviour change, and to generate significant real-world impacts in terms of welfare and wellbeing.

---

[4] See Simon (1957) for a collection of his key papers.
[5] See Baddeley (2013) for an analysis of some of these problems in economics, and science more generally.

12. A social practice perspective

Dale Southerton

Director, Sustainable Consumption Institute and Professor of Sociology, University of Manchester (former Director, Sustainable Practices Research Group)

Daniel Welch

Research Associate, Sustainable Consumption Institute

Much current policy implicitly assumes a 'portfolio' model of behaviour, which conceptualises human activity as individualistic, voluntary, and deliberative. The social practice perspective challenges these assumptions, with significant implications for behaviour change models and interventions.

The Sustainable Practices Research Group (2010-2013) was funded by the Economic and Social Research Council, the Scottish Government and Defra

The Dialogue draws our attention to the importance of bringing implicit models of behaviour into the open, and the role that explicit models can play as guides for analysis (see for example §3). A social practice perspective draws into relief an implicit model of the human subject and of behaviour that is so common it often goes unacknowledged. The alternative, explicit model of social practice has important consequences for how the problem of behaviour change is framed, how we conceptualise social change, and how we think about evidence and evaluation.

An implicit model of behaviour

Let's imagine a typical morning for a character that embodies that common, implicit model. Let's call her Portfolio. Portfolio wakes around 7am, which is when she chooses to set her alarm on weekdays, and decides to have a shower – she likes to feel refreshed in the morning. She decides to leave the house and drive to work at 8.15am to beat the worst of the traffic. She usually decides to leave for home by 5.15pm for the same reason. Most days she likes to have lunch at her desk, so she decides to pop into the deli on the way to pick something up.

Now meet Practicia. She embodies the social practice perspective. Practicia wakes around 7am too. Her daily routine bears a strong resemblance in its general patterning to that of other daytime employees in the UK, and is part of a collective schedule determined by institutions and infrastructures: in this case normal office hours and the rush hour commute. She takes a shower as she does every morning – just like over half of UK adults. She leaves the house to drive to work at 8.15am, before the rush hour traffic gets too bad. She usually leaves for home by 5.15pm for the same reason. That's no surprise – 20% of all car journeys in the UK are taken between 8am and 9am or between 5pm and 6pm. Like more than half of UK office workers, Practicia usually has a sandwich at her desk for lunch, and her usual habit is to pop into the deli on the way to pick something up.

Portfolia embodies a voluntaristic and individualistic model of behaviour, implicit in behavioural economics and much social psychology, and thus in conventional behaviour change strategies. Hindess (1990) has called this the 'portfolio model'. In this model of behaviour the human subject possesses a more or less stable portfolio of values, attitudes, norms, interests, desires and so forth, and selects from them to decide on their course of action. Behaviour is assumed to be driven by this 'portfolio', variously understood as: norms (in classical sociology), attitudes (in social psychology), or preferences or interests (in economics) (Welch and Warde, 2015). The portfolio model emphasises the deliberative character of behaviour and frames behaviour change as a problem of individuals' capacity to exercise change, and of the barriers – attitudinal and contextual – to those behavioural choices.

This implicit model is found in particularly acute form in understandings of 'the consumer', the imaginary figure at whom much sustainable consumption policy is directed. Shove (2010) has lampooned this dominant policy approach to sustainability as an overly simplistic 'ABC' model, in which Stern's influential Attitude-Behaviour-Context model is reduced to a linear relationship of Attitude-Behaviour-Choice. Such a model restricts behaviour change policy to information provision, changing incentives and social marketing for the purpose of attitudinal change.

From the perspective of Practicia's morning routine, this implicit model fundamentally *overestimates* the role of choice in routine behaviour and *underestimates* the extent to which individuals' autonomy is constrained by infrastructures, institutions, and conventions. And we can add, by access to social, cultural and economic resources (Southerton et al., 2004).

Social practice: an explicit model of human activity

Let's now take a look at the explicit model of human activity found in a social practice perspective. In this model, human activity is understood primarily as the performance of *social* practices. A simple definition is that practices are 'blocks of activities' that people share: sets of 'doings and sayings' (Warde, 2005). Practicia is performing a number of dynamically linked social practices in her morning routine – including showering, driving, and eating – and her day will pan out through a range of work practices (e.g. writing reports) and leisure practices (e.g. playing tennis). Her routines do not simply represent her behaviour as an individual but represent social practices that are widely shared.

We can think of practices as shared in two ways:

1. People perform practices together. Many practices require the participation of others to be performed satisfactorily: this means most practices are inherently social, and that many are subject to the context-specific rules and conventions of social interaction.
2. Practices are recognisable entities distinct from the many individuals that perform them. Because sufficiently large numbers of people perform them either at the same time (but not necessarily together – such as rush hour commuting) or in

broadly similar ways, we can recognise there is a *thing* called driving, even if we do not drive ourselves.

Performing socially shared practices entails the reproduction of cultural conventions and norms, the deployment of socially learnt skills, and the use of common tools, technologies and infrastructures. For example, driving as a practice requires: the material components of the car and the road transport infrastructure; the embodied know-how of the skill of driving; understanding of a host of meanings and ideas, including formalised rules such as speed limits, the symbols used on road signs, and conventions such as flashing one's headlights; and, often, emotional engagements and cultural values, such as in the equation of driving with autonomy and freedom.

Two influential frameworks which sort this bewildering array of components into generic categories are offered by:

- Warde (2005, p. 134), who defines the categories of practice components as: understandings (know-how and practical interpretation); procedures (rules, principles, instructions); and engagements (an array of ends and projects, as well as emotional and value orientations).
- Shove et al. (2012, p. 23), who distinguish three types of practice element: materials, competence and meanings. The inclusion of material elements emphasises how practices are always deeply interwoven with objects, tools, technologies and infrastructures. Competence draws our attention to the skills and know-how necessary for the successful performance of a practice, while

meanings include norms, cultural conventions and expectations.

Thinking in terms of generic elements is important because it suggests ways in which practices are interconnected. They are interconnected because they share elements – infrastructures being the most obvious example – and because the existence of one practice often has implications for many others. For example, encouraging the practice of commuter cycling requires not only the provision of cycling infrastructure but also the provision of showers in the workplace to accommodate conventions of cleanliness and 'freshness'.

The fundamental move of a social practice perspective for understanding behaviour change is that practices become the central unit of analysis, and in terms of policy, the central unit of intervention – rather than individuals (and their attitudes and preferences), or other analytical categories such as interests, values, or attitudes. The social practice perspective re-frames the question from 'How do we change individuals' behaviours?' to 'How do we change practices?'

A key implication of this is that much of what passes as the 'value-action' or 'attitude-behaviour' gap – the centrepiece of so much policy analysis and intervention – is in fact an artefact of the implicit portfolio model of behaviour. This is not to deny that people have values or attitudes, nor that they act on them. But it is to challenge that model as the principal (or indeed only) paradigm through which we should understand human activity.

With respect to consumption, a further fundamental re-framing is suggested: that people consume in the pursuit of social practices (for example, sharing a meal, playing sport or gardening) and not in pursuit of consumption *per se* (Warde, 2005). Furthermore, much environmentally significant consumption of energy and resources in the use of goods and services occurs in the accomplishment of everyday routine tasks (for example, doing the laundry, showering or commuting) – what we might call *inconspicuous* consumption, as opposed to the *conspicuous* consumption usually associated with 'consumerism'.

Researching practices

In the Sustainable Practices Research Group (SPRG), we set out to explore processes of change, stability and normalisation empirically, through the lens of social practice theories. Our 'Keeping Cool' project, for example, investigated the processes through which air conditioning has increasingly become a normal expectation in a variety of indoor environments in the UK, including hospitals, offices and hotels. The 'need' for air conditioning in many cases was not to keep people cool, but rather to keep office and hospital technologies cool. Thus a standardised indoor temperature is being engineered into our built environment and, in doing so, is coming to shape a wide range of normalised social practices, such as nursing and office work, as increasingly energy-intensive.

Another environmentally negative process of normalisation was found in a project exploring the creation of new environmental standards for UK homes. The project showed how the 'Zero Carbon' standard defined a certification of energy efficiency measures at one moment in time. This moment takes today's 'normal' ways of living as its benchmark, but fails to consider that social practices are dynamic. This static understanding of everyday life is likely to reproduce current practices and actually constrain changes towards more sustainable forms of everyday practice.

Research such as this reveals processes through which cultural expectations and standards emerge and shape social practices (see www.sprg.ac.uk for more examples). Recognising that social practices are dynamic and that interventions are therefore aimed at a moving target is an important insight from our research. Importantly, we also found that different practices exhibit different dynamics of change and variation. For example:

- The 'Changing Eating Habits' project compared shifts in eating habits as Anglo-French couples moved to France or England. While these were moments of transition in individuals' lives, changes in eating habits were most strongly shaped by broad cultural conventions, including patterns of sociability and the social norms associated with the host culinary culture
- The 'Drinking Water' project, compared bottled water drinking in the UK, Germany, Italy, India, Mexico, and Taiwan. This revealed the diverse interactions between natural, socio-economic and political systems, and how these interactions shape institutions, which in turn account for the diversity of bottled water drinking in the national contexts
- The 'Patterns of Water' project analysed how people perform a range of domestic practices that consume water: gardening, bathing and showering, and doing the laundry. We found that diversity in practices bears little relation to socio-demographics, household composition or attitudes and values. Nevertheless distinct groupings of 'practitioners' were identified (such as the over 50% who showered seven or more times a week, and the less than 10% who bathed every day), suggesting novel targets for intervention

Interventions in practice

Existing examples of policy or interventions explicitly informed by the social practice perspective remain limited in number (for an exception, see Darnton and Evans, 2013). However, one way we might assess its utility is through its capacity to explain the success or failure of existing initiatives, all of which are, of course, themselves interventions into social practice. In an international review of thirty policy interventions for sustainable consumption, Southerton et al. (2011) found that the vast majority were framed by the portfolio model of behaviour and sought to 'change the behaviour of autonomous consumers – whether by providing economic incentives, correcting information efficiencies, seeking to re-frame attitudes, or removing the barriers' to individuals' behaviour change (p.118). By contrast, the most successful initiatives, while not explicitly based on a social practice perspective, targeted a fuller range of components of practice – rather than simply the assumed *drivers* of individual behaviour.

What, then, would behaviour change policy informed by a social practice perspective look like?

The key insight is perhaps that interventions would address as full a range of the components of practices as possible. Most existing interventions, by contrast, address only a limited range of components. For example, social marketing generally addresses meanings only, training generally addresses competences and regulation generally addresses only procedures or the material underpinnings of practice. It is worth noting that the successful initiatives Southerton et al. (2011) examine tend also to be those on a more ambitious scale.

However, we should not simply conclude that more ambitious policies produce better results. Hargreaves (2011), for example, conducted an ethnographic study of a workplace environmental behaviour change programme. The programme was a conventional one, seeking to change attitudes in order to change behaviour, and was relatively successful in terms of behavioural outcomes. However, Hargreaves found that the 'environmental attitudes' of participants were largely unchanged. Rather, the changes in practices became invested with meanings of loyalty to company culture. Hargreaves's analysis of the programme provided a more robust account of how and why it achieved results than the implicit portfolio model of behaviour under which the programme had been conceived. Similarly, through empirical research into changing eating habits, Halkier (2010) found that interaction within social networks and practical procedures were often more important than individual normative commitments. Examples such as these underscore the value of the social practice perspective for behaviour change policy even when interventions address only a limited range of the components of practices.

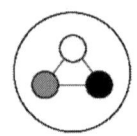

Figure 1: Shove et al.'s (2012) three elements of practice: meaning, competence and material

At the level of 'nuts and bolts', the social practice perspective implies a number of distinct kinds of intervention which policymakers could make use of. Building on Shove et al.'s (2012) three elements of practice (meaning, competence and material), Spurling et al. (2013) suggest three complementary types of intervention: recrafting practices; substituting practices; and changing how practices interlock.

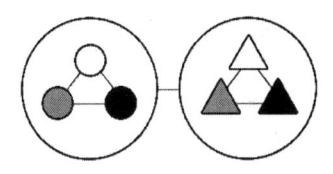

Figure 2: Re-crafting practices: changing the elements of practice (Spurling et al, 2013)

'Re-crafting practices' suggests changing elements of practices and as such is not dissimilar to some existing forms of intervention. However, its starting point is a systematic analysis of the dynamic relationships between practice elements to inform where those changes are best made. As Southerton et al.'s (2011) review of initiatives suggests, successful interventions often intervene in as full a range of the elements of practices as possible. An example of such an integrated approach (although not framed in terms of practice theory) is the New Nordic Diet, a Scandinavian programme aimed at promoting a novel, healthy and sustainable cuisine (see Spurling et al., 2013). This addressed the multiple elements of practice simultaneously:

- Material: the programme promoted the use of sustainable, healthy foods originating from the Nordic region
- Competence: the programme offered cookery courses in the new dishes
- Meanings: the programme was conceived as an identity movement, and enrolled fashionable restaurants, celebrity chefs, media and other organisations to actively recruit practitioners

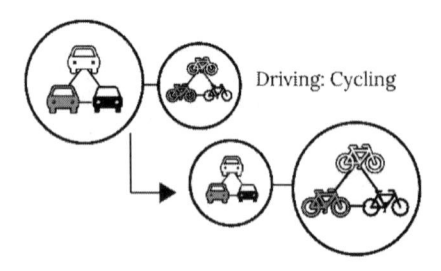

Figure 3: Substituting practices: different practices compete for time, space and resources (Spurling et al., 2013)

The second intervention type, of particular pertinence to sustainability, is 'substituting practices'. This approach asks policymakers to think how alternative practices might fulfil the same role as (and therefore replace) existing practices, draws attention to how different practices compete for time, space and resources, and highlights how infrastructures and conventions lock the evolution of social practices into particular paths.

Commuter cycling and commuter driving, for example, compete for many of the same resources, including people's time, space on roads, and spending on infrastructure. A practice based analysis might recognise that *commuter cycling* is a particular variant of cycling practice comprising of different elements to leisure cycling. If cycling is to compete for commuters then it is this variant of cycling that should be the focus of policy.

An example of an intervention aimed at substituting cycling for other forms of commuting is Transport for Greater Manchester's Cycling Hub scheme. The city centre hub, located conveniently for transfer to rail, tram and bus services, offers commuters cycle parking spaces, lockers and showers (recognising that commuter cycling intersects with the cultural expectation of cleanliness at work). The Hub also contains a bike shop offering on-site servicing, recognising that reliability is an important aspect of commuter cycling, and skills training for this specific variant of the practice, for example providing confidence in urban traffic (Spurling et al., 2013). Elements of meanings, materials and competence are thus all addressed.

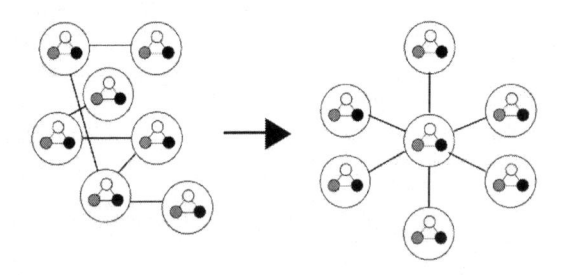

Figure 4: Changing how practices interlock

The third intervention type, 'changing how practices interlock', builds on the ways in which practices interlock with one another. There is both a spatial and a temporal aspect to this. Crucially, practices interlock through sequence and synchronisation (recall the morning routine outlined above, with both its necessary sequence of activities, and synchronized practices, such as rush hour driving). Temporal interlocking, through sequence and synchronization, presents novel opportunities for achieving substantial shifts in practices by positively harnessing the complex interactions between them. Furthermore, as many social practices *are* so interlocked, *any* form of intervention may produce change that ripples through interconnected practices.

New kinds of urban space, for example, potentially enable interlocking practices of working, commuting, eating and socialising to be radically reconfigured. The recently refurbished Liverpool Central Library, for example, is a new kind of city centre space which might bring about such changes. Plentiful desk space, electric points, computers, internet and print facilities, and different forms of workspace (meeting rooms, games areas, reading rooms, lounge areas) create a place for new practices of working to develop. Such 'community hubs', in which people can work 'from home' but in the same venue, address some of the social and practical challenges of working from home, such as isolation, or the absence of suitable resources and spaces (e.g. office space, meeting rooms). In terms of sustainability, such spaces potentially reduce both commuter travel and the increased energy consumption associated with home working (Spurling et al., 2013).

The wider implications

Different models of behaviour lead to different framings of problems, suggesting plausible and possible targets for intervention, whilst excluding others (Spurling et al., 2013). The portfolio model – implicit in much current policy – suggests conventional initiatives of information provision, changing incentives and social marketing for attitudinal change. It also reinforces a particular ideology in which responsibility for changing complex social problems is laid at the door of individuals' behaviour (Shove, 2010). The social practice perspective offers an alternative, explicit model that recognises the complexities of everyday life, can account for routine and inconspicuous forms of consumption and provides a process-based account of social change.

Applying this model, we propose four critical insights into the policy framing of 'behaviour change':

- First, coordinated policies are needed which seek to effect (or at least recognise) suites of practices. The greatest gains will be found where changes

fostered in particular practices, or elements shared across practices, are likely to spill over and positively affect other practices
- Secondly, habits and routines are cultural, not personal – and certainly not irrational deficiencies of human action. They are formed and sustained through the organisation of practices: change how practices are organised and you change habits and routines
- Thirdly, because practices continually change, they represent moving targets for policy. To shape them, we need not one-off interventions, but a programmatic, reflexive and responsive approach to policy. The interconnectedness of practices also suggests it is not easy to predict the effects of interventions, or to model processes of change, however much policy makers may wish it otherwise (Evans et al., 2012)
- Finally, a new evidence base is required, one focused on accounting for varieties of practices. Data sources analysing 'doings' exist in the form of nationally comparative time diaries and a range of qualitative and survey instruments. Yet in the context of sustainable consumption, where 'evidence' fixates on the measurement of the environmental impacts of specific goods or services, supplemented with some data on aggregate purchasing patterns and pro-environmental attitudes, we have a long way to go.

Suggested further reading

For works cited, see References at the end of the book.

Spurling, N., McMeekin, A., Shove, E., Southerton, D. and Welch, D. (2013) Interventions in practice: re-framing policy approaches to consumer behaviour. Sustainable Practices Research Group Report. Available at: http://sbk.li/1122221

This report draws together insights from the Sustainable Practices Research Group for policymakers and behaviour change practitioners. It critiques three problem framings commonplace within current policy and provides a fuller account of the three types of social practice-based intervention outlined above.

Evans, D. et al., (2012) 'Sustainable Consumption, Behaviour Change Policies and Theories of Practice', in Warde, A. and Southerton, D. (eds.) *The Habits of Consumption*. Collegium, 12. Available at: http://sbk.li/1122222

This short paper considers the practical potential of social practice approaches to sustainable consumption policy.

Strengers, Y. and Maller, C. (eds.) (2015) Social Practices, Intervention and Sustainability: Beyond behaviour change. London: Routledge.

This edited collection is an important contribution to the social practices and sustainability literature, and includes a detailed application of the types of intervention introduced above to sustainable transport policy.

13. Clearing the pathway to change: a new psychodynamic perspective

Peter Fonagy

Freud Memorial Professor of Psychoanalysis, Research Department of Clinical, Educational and Health Psychology, University College London

Liz Allison

Director, UCL Psychoanalysis Unit

Chloe Campbell

Research Fellow, UCL Psychoanalysis Unit

What can psychoanalysis bring to an interdisciplinary dialogue on behaviour change? A new direction in psychodynamic thinking shifts the focus from the dynamic unconscious to interpersonal processes and the critical role played by epistemic trust in our ability both to learn about our social world and to change our behaviour. To promote behaviour change, on this account, we may first need to reopen an individual's ability to receive and accept social instruction.

What can psychoanalysis bring to – and learn from – an interdisciplinary dialogue on behaviour change? If Evie, Yusuf and Paola, the characters in the Dialogue, had invited a psychoanalyst to join them, where might their conversation have headed?

Many of you will probably be expecting us to talk about instincts and drives, particularly sex and aggression, and the ways that these might shape personality, mental disorder, unconscious motivations, neurotic fixations and resistance to change. These are the explanatory forces that have hitherto dominated psychoanalytic thinking. But how do we use this psychodynamic 'map' – as the participants in the Dialogue might call it – to navigate behaviour change? Classical psychoanalytic models have tended to lay emphasis on helping the client to acquire insight into their unconscious motivations, but without explaining how this promotes change. This has left those trying to manage system-wide change puzzled about how insights into human motivation based on individual psychotherapy could possibly be of relevance to bringing about behaviour change other than through unconscious influence (e.g. Vance Packard's *Hidden Persuaders* (Packard, 1957)).

The model we suggest in this chapter reflects a new and different direction in psychodynamic thinking, which is concerned with human communication and the interpersonal process by means of which we *learn to learn* about the world and the meaning of behaviour. The vicissitudes of this learning process, we suggest, can profoundly determine the degree to which we are likely to be willing to modify our behaviour on the basis of what is communicated to us (Fonagy, Luyten and Allison, 2014).

Critically, our conceptualisation of behaviour change is essentially a relational one: before a person's priorities for action can change, we suggest, a *conversation* has to take place, a dialogue between a listener and a communicator (the agent of behaviour change). The success of this conversation depends on the qualities of the relationship between the two – particularly the capacity of the listener to be open to or listen to the communication that is designed to elicit behaviour change.

We are using the term 'conversation' here to refer to any interchange of information, ideas, etc. between people. In this sense conversation may be external (between people) or internal (inside someone's head); actual or just in fantasy; in spoken or written form; within a school, a business, a family, a country, including but in no way restricted to management or healthcare contexts.

Across all these possible settings, however, some common principles apply. In particular, we will argue in this paper that behaviour change is brought about by a particular form of *social instruction* – even when that instruction is from the self to the self as part of an internal conversation. Behaviour only changes if the individual involved is able to accept that social instruction as relevant (to them) and valid. Under certain conditions, however, the channels for receiving and learning from social instruction become blocked, and the individual becomes closed to conversations that might direct a change in behaviour. To successfully promote behaviour change, we will argue, we need first to identify the common factors that enable the reopening of an individual's ability to receive and accept social instruction (Fonagy and Allison, 2014; Fonagy and Luyten, in press).

To refer back to the questions covered in the Dialogue, we would suggest that what the psychoanalytic approach described here brings to the interdisciplinary approach is an understanding of the mechanism at work in linking change at the micro-level with wider meso- and macro-level change. This mechanism, we suggest, is the evolutionarily driven human capacity for epistemic trust, which is what opens the channel for communication and learning about the social world – cultural norms and expectations that govern behaviour on everything from how to use tools and technology to prevailing values and beliefs. We shall explain epistemic trust in more detail below; but in terms of the interdisciplinary approach that characterises this book, we suggest that the unique contribution of the psychoanalytic perspective we are offering lies in its conceptualisation of the significance of the individual's openness to social communication, and the insights it provides into how to stimulate and rekindle this openness to communication – necessary, in our view, if there is to be any possibility of sustained change.

Social instruction and epistemic trust

According to social anthropologists (sociobiologists) it's a mere 300,000 years since *homo sapiens*, having got up on its hind legs, had to face the challenge of passing on knowledge about how to create the tools that these freshly-freed hands were capable of creating (Wilson, 1976). Tools, especially tools that can create tools, are opaque in their purpose and require explication (hence language) to enable the learner to conserve this information for ensuing generations.

How can our children rapidly acquire the huge amount of cultural knowledge relevant to them, which has accrued over countless generations, while filtering out misleading, inaccurate or deceitful information (Gergely, 2013)? How is this kind of social instruction possible?

Based on the work of Sperber and Wilson (Sperber et al., 2010; Wilson and Sperber, 2012), we assume that openness to the reception of such social knowledge depends on *epistemic trust* – by which we mean trust that interpersonally transmitted knowledge has personal relevance and can be generalised beyond the immediate social context. If circumspection is the default position that protects the child from being misled, the young human needs to be able to identify the specific conditions under which their generalised 'epistemic vigilance' when listening to others should be suspended or inhibited.

Epistemic trust is a special kind of attentiveness, a knowledge transfer highway that enables social learning in an ever-changing social and cultural context and allows individuals to open their minds to benefit from the accumulated knowledge of their social environment (Fonagy and Allison, 2014; Fonagy and Luyten, in press; Fonagy, Luyten and Allison, 2014). Epistemic trust designates a communication as coming from a reliable trusted source, which gives the instruction the quality called *internality*: that is, it is experienced as personally relevant, is taken on board with a sense of ownership, and is understood as being in keeping with one's own intentions.

The key to an individual's acceptance of a piece of social knowledge as relevant to them is the authority that the communicator has with that individual. We can understand this as a sort of compromise position between two extremes. On the one hand, we could in principle use our inductive and deductive reasoning capabilities to differentiate accurate from inaccurate information: but in practice this is not always possible and, perhaps more importantly, involves considerable effort. On the other hand, it would not be wise to be uncritically receptive to everything we are told, by anyone; being selective about which individuals we invest epistemic trust in enables us to relax the natural epistemic vigilance that protects us against misinformation (whether accidentally or intentionally) from an unreliable or untrustworthy source (Sperber et al., 2010).

Natural pedagogy and the role of ostensive cues

This account of social learning and epistemic trust leans heavily on Gergely and Csibra's theory of *natural pedagogy* (Csibra and Gergely, 2009). Gergely and Csibra argue that human communication evolved to enable us to deal with the fact that we are born into a world which is bristling with objects, customs, opinions and techniques for survival that are cognitively opaque, in other words, whose function, use or rationale is not immediately obvious. This is known as the *learnability problem*, and the theory of *natural pedagogy* maintains that, in order to solve it, we evolved instincts for teaching and learning.

Natural pedagogy is a uniquely human adaptation to enable culturally relevant knowledge to be transmitted from one person to another. Csibra and Gergely propose that the teacher/communicator uses special signals, known as *ostensive cues*, to alert to the recipient that what is being conveyed is relevant to them, and should be understood as a generalisable piece of cultural knowledge. For example, they have shown that infants have a species-specific sensitivity to certain nonverbal ostensive cues (Csibra and Gergely, 2006, 2009, 2011), including eye contact, turn-taking contingent reactivity, and the use of a special vocal tone ('motherese'). By using ostensive cues, both in infancy and beyond, the communicator explicitly recognises the listener as an agent. Receiving this special attention prompts the listener to pay special attention in turn: *ostensive cues trigger epistemic trust*. They signal that it is safe and appropriate to relax epistemic vigilance.

In particular, the knowledge conveyed in this pedagogic state acquires what we earlier called *internality*. For example, when we learn to use an implement of our culture, such as a 'fork', we forget who taught us: the knowledge is internalised, and becomes our possession, our inheritance, our tradition, our identity. Of course, other information conveyed to us may also be listened to and understood: but unless it is communicated against a background of epistemic trust, we will not internalise it, and the presence of the communicator (symbolic or real) is necessary to ensure that instructions are followed.

We believe this distinction is key to thinking about behaviour change. An individual who experiences epistemic trust in relation to the communicator is far more likely to take the knowledge being conveyed on board, own it and allow it to guide their future behaviour. In fact, we postulate that regardless of the content of a particular intervention, change is unlikely to occur in the absence of epistemic trust.

The distinction also invites an obvious question for anyone interested in behaviour change. If epistemic trust in relation to a communicator plays such an important role, then how can we (re)establish it? In order to answer this question, we first need to understand how epistemic trust is established in early development, and the circumstances under which the 'epistemic superhighway' of social knowledge transmission may sometimes become blocked. In particular, we need to take a closer look at the process via which a caregiver responds to the infant's signals.

Epistemic trust and attachment

In normal human development, secure attachment to a caregiver and epistemic trust are established via some of the same interpersonal processes. Studies of attachment have shown that secure attachment is driven by the caregiver's generally sensitive responsiveness to the infant's expressive displays, which leads the infant to feel 'agentive'

– that is, feeling that they are being treated as an individual whose reactions matter. The behaviours that communicate this general responsiveness to the infant also act as ostensive cues: they designate the attachment figure as a reliable informant and generate the epistemic trust that forms the necessary foundation for the child to acquire further knowledge from their caregiver. Epistemic trust and attachment have common roots.

The capacity of an individual to form attachment relationships, based on their attachment history, is also an important indicator of their ability to change their own behaviour on the basis of instruction.

- On the one hand, there is considerable evidence to suggest that the quality of an individual's attachment history predicts the extent to which they trust the communication they receive from another person, and this explains the greater flexibility of individuals with secure attachment histories. Secure attachment is associated with greater trust, insecure attachment with chronic anxious expectations of rejection or the dismissal of the importance of attachment relationships.
- On the other hand, even in adulthood, insecure attachment remains associated with disadvantages in learning from experience (Ayoub et al., 2009; Fernald et al., 2011; Goodman, Quas and Ogle, 2010; Rieder and Cicchetti, 1989). Particularly, adult attachment insecurity is likely to be associated with a greater likelihood of cognitive closure, a lower tolerance for ambiguity, and a more pronounced tendency to dogmatic thinking (Mikulincer, 1997). Individuals who are insecure in their attachment are also more likely to save intellectual effort and adopt stereotypes

(Mikulincer, 1997). The same predisposition to knowledge inflexibility is revealed by insecure individuals' tendency to make judgments on the basis of early information and to pay insufficient heed to subsequent data even if it is incompatible with the configuration first created (Green-Hennessy and Reis, 1998; Mikulincer, 1997). Insecure individuals, who fear the loss of attachment figures, also anxiously hold on to their initial constructions. They are less likely to revise their knowledge in the face of information that challenges their assumptions (Green-Hennessy and Reis, 1998; Green and Campbell, 2000; Mikulincer, 1997; Mikulincer and Arad, 1999), as if they not only had less confidence in the robustness of their bond to their attachment figure, but also feared the loss of epistemic trust.

In sum, we propose that the epistemic connection provided to us by evolution in order for us to learn from experience appears to be partially closed to those whose attachment to their caregiver is insecure.

Implications for the behaviour change process

In the absence of epistemic trust, the capacity for change is limited. Conversely, significant behavioural change can be facilitated by establishing epistemic trust with the listener in order to open the individual to social communication. How can we help this to happen? In brief, we need to ensure that the listener receives the key ostensive cues that facilitate epistemic trust and open the listener's mind to internalising (coming to own) the instruction as relevant to them and governing their behaviour.

This, of course, invites a question: how are the ostensive cues that mothers use in communicating with their infants relevant to adult behaviour change? Remember, the essence of an ostensive cue is to make the listener feel their own agency is respected. To open the mind of a listener, to help them internalise the communication, they have to feel that the communicator has attended to their understanding of the situation. Exactly the same principle applies in the case of adults.

For example, John Hattie is Professor of Education at the University of Auckland, New Zealand. Over 15 years of research he synthesised over 800 meta-analyses relating to the influences on achievement in school-aged students (Hattie, 2013). No small dataset this: 60,155 studies, about 245 million students, 159,570 effect sizes, influence of some programme, policy, or innovation on academic achievement in school (early childhood, elementary, high, and tertiary). Was there a set of predictors of good teaching outcomes? What makes a teacher effective? The findings were clear: it is the teacher's ability to see learning through the eyes of their students (and consequently students seeing teaching as the key to their ongoing learning) that made for effective behaviour change. The key ingredients were: the child's awareness of the learning intentions (the objective of the lesson); knowing when a student is successful; and having sufficient understanding of the student's understanding.

To generalise to adults and other behaviour change contexts, our relational model of behaviour change, informed by psychodynamic attachment theory, suggests that:

- the communicator needs to be able to see the request for change through the eyes of the listener

- listeners need to see the information as key to their ongoing learning about their culture

This is what establishes epistemic trust and ensures robust behaviour change.

The greatest effects on social learning occur when communicators become learners in the context of their own teaching: they are constantly aware of how they might be experienced, and on the lookout for possible changes that might improve their effectiveness, and for when a relationship is established that enables listeners to learn to teach themselves. The attributes that seem most likely to support behaviour change – self-monitoring, self-evaluation, self-assessment, self-teaching – are also the developmental outcomes associated with greater resilience. When learners become their own 'teachers', behaviour change becomes sustainable.

So what can we do to trigger the epistemic openness that enables an individual to take in (internalise) social communication? We believe that the listener's experience of agentiveness through contingent responding (ostensive cueing) is the key. *The listener has to feel listened to before they can listen.* We take the view that the experience of feeling that I as listener am accurately seen – along with all the expectations, beliefs and emotional experiences that I bring to the conversation concerning change – is the critical element that enhances our ability to learn. The experience of our subjectivity being understood – of another human being having our mind in mind – is important because it establishes epistemic trust and opens us up to learning. Only then does what we learn have the potential to change our perception of our social world and our consequent behaviour.

One of the major themes of the Dialogue is how we might use models in a way that makes them both more productive and more theoretically rigorous. The psychoanalytic approach described here, based as it is on clinical experience, research findings and theoretical considerations encompassing attachment, mentalising and natural pedagogy, seeks to introduce to the interdisciplinary table a new approach to what makes the communication of social knowledge (i.e. a modification in behaviour) meaningful at the level of individual subjectivity.

Suggested further reading

For works cited, see References at the end of the book.

Bateman, A.W. and Fonagy, P. (eds.) (2012) *Handbook of mentalizing in mental health practice.* **Washington: American Psychiatric Publishing.**

A comprehensive introduction to mentalizing theory and its clinical applications.

Fonagy, P. and Allison, E. (2014) 'The role of mentalizing and epistemic trust in the therapeutic relationship', *Psychotherapy,* **51(3), pp. 372-380.**

This sets out more fully the theory of epistemic trust in the context of therapeutic change.

Gergely, G. (2013) 'Ostensive communication and cultural learning: The natural pedagogy hypothesis', in Metcalfe, J. and Terrace, H.S. (eds.) *Agency and Joint Attention.* **Oxford: Oxford University Press, pp. 139-51.**

This is a valuable outline of the Theory of Natural Pedagogy, which underpins our thinking on epistemic trust.

Wilson, D. and Sperber, D. (2012) *Meaning and relevance.* **Cambridge: Cambridge University Press.**

This provides a full account of the latest thinking on communication and the transmission of knowledge and beliefs.

14. How can we use literature as a tool for understanding and changing behaviour in complex contexts?

Maurice Biriotti

CEO of SHM and Professor of Medical Humanities, UCL

Models involve a necessary simplification of reality, and while simplifying often helps us work out what to do, it can also get in the way. In many situations, changing behaviour means embracing complexity, not abstracting from it. When that is the case, literary texts can provide an alternative way of thinking about behaviour and behaviour change.

This paper is based on personal experience. My job is to figure out how to change behaviours in a number of public and corporate settings. The recent explosion in different approaches to behaviour change has been a treasure trove for someone in my profession. There is no question that the various models of behaviour change that have emerged over the last few decades have proved effective and socially useful under certain circumstances.

However, I think it is also clear that there is no single, sure-fire method for effecting behaviour change – different models seem to work in different situations. And sometimes behaviour is so fragmented or contradictory that no model works. One example of this issue that comes up regularly in my work is when I'm faced with trying to resolve situations of deep conflict. In these contexts, effecting behaviour change remains beyond the reach of most current approaches.

As all the characters in the Dialogue agree, models involve a necessary simplification of reality: and while simplifying often helps us work out what to do, it can also get in the way. Should we just accept that we sometimes can't model behaviours? If so, does that mean we are powerless to think about behaviour change in these more complex situations? Or are there other ways we can approach the problem?

I'd like to argue that, when we are faced with more complex situations underpinning challenging behaviour, there is no substitute for thinking about complexity. But that does not mean we're powerless. One possible answer may lie in an activity that is increasingly marginalised and under threat in our academies and daily lives: reading and analysing literature as a serious endeavour. Literary texts, as opposed to scientific and analytic models, embrace ambiguity, complexity and contradiction. It's my experience that the insights they provide can be invaluable in giving us a framework for making sense of the most complicated behaviours.

Models and their uses

Before looking at how literature can help us understand and change behaviours, it is worth saying a little more about models of behaviour change.

In many situations, they can, of course, be invaluable. For instance, in supporting a current study at a hospital in Ireland, a team of researchers and designers in my company have used the lessons from different models of behaviour change to develop a mobile application to help mothers make choices that improve nutrition in early life. The models we have at our disposal can tell us a great deal about many aspects of human behaviour and possible ways of changing it. In particular, they can help us to design interventions of the following four types:

1. Rational: behaviour change happens through intensifying the rational (making logical, informative arguments for why a particular behaviour is undesirable or wrong).
2. Emotional: behaviour change happens through playing on people's emotional responses, intensifying the aversive nature of negative stimuli or the appealing nature of positive stimuli to elicit or reinforce behaviour.
3. Cognitive: behaviour change is achieved through exploiting the mind's architecture and setting up choices so that people are naturally inclined to behave in a certain way – people are 'nudged' into a particular behaviour.

4. Social: behaviour change is effected by creating an environment in which behaviours are either favourable, and encouraged, or unacceptable, and discouraged.

One of the main reasons why models of behaviour are so helpful is because they abstract from and simplify complexity, and allow us to focus on just a few key variables in an otherwise bewildering situation. This is their great strength – but also, I'd argue, their signal weakness in contexts where we can't afford to turn our backs on complexity.

Complexity in practice

To explain why I think the study of literature can help us to make sense of the kind of complexity that models of behaviour change cannot account for, it will help to focus on a specific case from my own experience.

It's an example of model-defying complexity that I frequently see, and which arises in the context of big outsourcing deals between companies. It starts with company A, a company which is good at selling a certain product, but acknowledges that it is not so good at running its IT function. Company A therefore decides to outsource all of its IT processes to company B, a specialist IT company. At the beginning of the deal, the business relationship generates excitement, energy and the promise of real innovation and mutual learning. Yet within around six months the relationship has gone sour and broken down: there are financial, commercial and technical problems, and these problems are generating a great deal of friction. The situation can soon begin to feel 'intractable'.

I've seen this happen many times. But why? Why on earth should these relationships break down when each party is committed to doing what they do best? Due to the popularity of outsourcing arrangements, not to mention the amount of money at stake, there has been no shortage of attempts to answer this question.

Some of the complexity, of course, arises from the fact that the relationship we need to examine here is not just between two companies, but also between the different people involved. So let us now imagine that there are two principals in each company, who each have thousands of people working for them and distinct feelings about the arrangement.

- In A, the sales company, we have Amerjeet, the finance lead, and Anita, the HR lead.
- In B, the IT company, we have Ben, the commercial lead, and Belinda, the technical lead.

Ben (the commercial lead) is motivated by profit. He is often frustrated by contractual obligations that get in the way of commercial benefit for both parties. By contrast, Belinda (the technical expert) is driven by safety. She cares most about avoiding risk, and often this means sticking to the letter of the contract. As Ben and Belinda approach negotiations, it transpires that there is quite a difference between their two positions. In company A, meanwhile, Amerjeet (the finance person) is fundamentally driven by justice. If he suspects his company is being taken for a ride, he will happily get the courts involved. Anita (the HR colleague), on the other hand, is driven by an interest in people. She never liked this outsourcing deal in the first place – some people lost their jobs, and she was the person who had to break the news to them. She would be perfectly willing to use any excuse to make the whole thing fall apart.

Now imagine the whole deal comes under pressure. Performance is not going well, and both companies feel they are losing money. Ben tries to save the day by arguing for an injection of cash that goes beyond the letter of the contract. When Amerjeet accuses Ben of sharp practice, the distrust towards Company B spreads across Company A. Belinda is outraged that her good work is being besmirched. She begins to hide behind bureaucratic behaviours. Anita starts to get complaints from her people and her indignation turns to high-handedness. Far from playing fast and loose with the contract, Company B become even more contractual; Company A begin to display a loathing that is ever more thinly veiled; and so on...

When we face complex situations such as these, the behaviour change models we have often simply don't offer a solution, or even a way of thinking about the problem. For one thing, in people's minds at least, behaviour has become linked to a matter of principle, a moral dimension that feeds the intractability. For another, far from the benign social effects that some contemporary behaviour change models rely on, the dynamic nature of the cycle of distrust in such a case feeds negative behaviours that can spread across thousands of employees in two companies like wildfire.

Using literature as a technology for thinking

In cases where models don't offer a solution, it is tempting to accept that this is simply not a case in which we have tools to help us think about behaviour change. But my experience is that there is another way.

It's my view that the study of literature can help. Whether you are thinking about your favourite novel or a great work of Shakespeare, the narrative is often driven precisely by what happens when motivations clash. Of course, we read literature for pleasure and for stimulation, but literary texts are a powerful and remarkably flexible 'technology for thinking': they allow us to deal with enormous complexity, and articulate contradictions effectively, in a way models cannot. And there is a wealth of literature to tap into – people have been writing about the complex challenges they face for several thousand years.

To illustrate how literature can help us think about behaviour change, let's remember the example of companies A and B and in parallel consider a literary text, Sophocles' play *Antigone*. If you don't know the play, you'll find a summary of the plot in the box.

Each of these perspectives takes into account the importance of principle: Antigone and Creon don't just behave the way they do because of habit – they believe in their respective positions. Models that depend on rational or cognitive approaches (types 1 and 3 in my earlier categorisation) have little currency in the face of deep-seated principle, and an emotional approach (type 2) is as likely to fan the flames as to quell the disquiet. Many corporations, and for that matter governments, have tried to impose behaviour change on a population without understanding this dimension, and the results are often poor and sometimes shocking.

The plot of Antigone

Antigone is the daughter of infamous parents, Oedipus and Jocasta – the ill-fated mother-son relationship. The relationship between them produced two girls, Antigone and Ismene, and two boys, who also feature in the story. In the wake of a plague, Oedipus loses control of his kingdom and seeks to find out who was responsible for this crime. Upon discovering he himself was responsible, he goes into exile and leaves his kingdom to Jocasta's brother, Creon (his brother-in-law and uncle). There is then a question about what will happen to Oedipus' children. The two sons find themselves on different sides of a bloody war and kill one another in battle. In the aftermath, Creon, the new king, decides that only the brother who was on the winning side – the side of the state – deserves to be buried.

At the beginning of the play, Antigone has just heard this news. She feels that not burying one brother would defy the sacred laws that outweigh the rules of the state. She resolves to defy the law and bury him anyway, against the advice of her sister who knows the consequence of such disobedience will be death. So Antigone buries the body. In case family relationships were not already complicated enough, it transpires that Antigone is engaged to be married to Creon's son, Haemon. When Antigone's actions are discovered, Haemon begs his father not to punish Antigone for what she has done. After all, she was only trying to do the right thing by burying her brother. Creon does not agree: he is the King and he demands obedience. It becomes clear that he is going to go through with his plan to punish Antigone, and he orders her to be buried alive. When he begins to change his mind, he goes to find Antigone to set her free but discovers to his horror that she has already killed herself. Haemon, in a fit of rage, tries to kill his father, and then kills himself. Finally, Creon's wife kills herself too. It's a classic setting of the theme of 'universal' laws versus the laws of the state.

In addition, the literary text does not just lay out different positions in the form of a philosophical argument. It also describes the *interplay* between the different worldviews, and demonstrates the dynamic effects of a vicious cycle out of control (a counterproductive version of a social dynamic – type 4 in my earlier categorisation). One of the striking features of *Antigone* is that – in contrast to the logic presented by approaches such as game theory, which suggest that 'players' are all playing the same 'game' – the characters are not only in disagreement but also playing *different* 'games', each with a wholly different idea of what success would look like. The text provides what we might describe (with Paola in the Dialogue) as a 'map' of this kind of conflict – albeit a map of a kind no model of behaviour change can supply.

Reading such a text and making that process a paradigm for understanding the situation of our two warring companies allows us to focus on a different set of questions for behaviour change – questions that are not well covered under the existing models:

- How can we understand the situation in such a way that we do justice to all parties' sense of what is right?
- How do we map the dynamic between the players and figure out where best to try to stop the vicious cycle?
- How do we address both behaviours and the underlying principles and motivations that drive behaviours?
- How do we get all parties back to a common set of goals and principles that can underpin the right behaviours in the future?

By using the analysis of literature as a paradigm, we have a way of articulating and crystallising complexity without erasing the ambiguities, inconsistencies and unpredictability of human behaviour and human interaction. Models in social science tend to take individual experiences and abstract them into generalisations and statistics that can make models workable. A literary approach goes the other way. It takes abstract ideas and major social concerns, and turns them into particular situations and stories, bringing them to life through individual narratives and interpersonal dynamics. Such an approach may not have the sure-fire certainty of a model applied to a well-known situation. But it does provide a third way between the precision and predictability of the model on the one hand, and staring uncomprehending at human complexity on the other.

I'm happy to report that an elaborated version of the solution based on reading *Antigone* helped companies A and B avoid financial ruin, the law courts or the eruption of mass violence (all of which were much closer outcomes than either party would dare admit in public at the time).

The approach is painstaking and requires a great deal of interpretative skill. And of course there are thousands of literary texts and literary critical approaches that can be chosen. But we do at least have the beginnings of a different approach here.

Conclusion

Any kind of behaviour change is hard enough. Even when people know they need to change, when they want to change, when there are social pressures on them to change, still change can be elusive. In many such situations, models of behaviour of the kind discussed in the Dialogue offer a way forwards. In others, by contrast – the kind of situation I've been focusing on – models can't help us. We need to face up to the complexity, not abstract from it. It's in situations such as these, I believe, that literary texts offer us a paradigm through which we can see issues somewhat more clearly. For instance:

- We can see that deeply embedded matters of principle make an appeal to reason difficult to pull off. One person's reason can be another person's madness. We see this in the character of Antigone, who defies the notion that self-interest is a foundation stone for reason and ignores her sister's 'reasonable' entreaties.
- We can see that warring factions often can't be dealt with in the same way. When people really see the world differently, simply trying to adjudicate and decide between right and wrong fails, because it doesn't take into account the fact that points of view can be right or wrong depending on the lens you look through. In addition, *Antigone* shows us that so-called mollifying influences – in Antigone's case, Haemon and Ismene – are unlikely to soften, but can actually serve to intensify and heighten disagreement
- We can see that sometimes two parties we imagine are far apart, and therefore in need of being brought together, actually can't leave each other alone. Antigone and Creon's seemingly divergent attitudes put them on a collision course with each other that creates a kind of unhealthy magnetic pull. Conflict can create a sort of claustrophobic proximity. We tend to think we can only change conflictual behaviours by bringing people together, but at times of intractable clashes of principle, we may in fact need to create space or find a way to separate them.

By applying principles such as these in the case of the real companies A and B, we came up with a methodology that worked not only for the principals but also for the hundreds of thousands of people involved in the instances of bad behaviour.

This is just one example of how we can use a literary text as a technology for thinking about complexity in behaviour and behaviour change. The text doesn't provide a panacea or a simple answer, but it does create a world of its own in which you can crystallise complex thoughts and feelings and figure out what to do with them. It's not a new approach – in fact, it's very ancient – but its applicability suggests that a strong case can be made for not ignoring a wealth of extraordinary resources we have in our literary heritage.

Of course, I could have said a lot about the limitations of literature as well. The outcome really does depend on the text you use, and in reality there's never a one-to-one equivalence between text and reality. Literature is also open, as we know, to endless interpretation and reinterpretation.

But drawbacks such as these are part of the point – in really complex situations, there's no substitute for the messy process of getting engaged with intricacy and contradiction. My point is simply this: that help is at hand. It just comes from a source that in my experience has never been more valuable just at a time when it's never felt more under threat in our culture and our institutions.

15. The role of forecasting models in transport planning – an historical perspective

Peter Jones

Professor of Transport and Sustainable Development,
Centre for Transport Studies, UCL

Models are neither developed nor used in a vacuum: they have a history, which shapes and constrains what we do with them. Sometimes we need to re-examine that history to understand where we have ended up.

In §7 of the Dialogue on models of behaviour change, Paola draws attention to the way in which uncritical use of models can potentially mislead us. Earlier (§5), Yusuf draws attention – in passing – to the need for clarity about the 'heritage' of a model. I think there's a deeper point to be made here: that models have a history of development and use, and that sometimes we need to re-examine that history to understand why we may have ended up with something that is not 'fit for purpose'.

I'm going to explore this point by looking at a specific example: transport modelling and policy in the UK. Mathematical forecasting models have played a central role in transport planning and policymaking in the UK and most developed countries over the past 50 years, resulting in a fascinating interplay between modellers' constructs and policymakers perceptions – with models sometimes leading but at other times largely lagging behind and hindering policy formulation.

At its heart, a transport forecasting model consists of a set of mathematical formulae describing the relationships between: various measures of traffic and travel behaviour (e.g. car mileage or average work trips per person); the supply of transport services in the context of local land use patterns (affecting availability, prices, travel times, etc.); and the demand for travel, represented by the socio-demographic characteristics of the population (occupation, gender, car licence ownership, etc.). Such models were originally derived from engineering principles (such as vehicle capacity and flow), but quickly took on board core concepts from economics (such as utility maximisation).

Over time, the measures of behaviour that have been used have changed and broadened; and with increasing computing power the models have become more sophisticated in a number of ways, including:

- increasing spatial disaggregation (from large areas down to point locations)
- increasing temporal disaggregation (from daily aggregate values to real-time movements)
- greater granularity in the assumed decision-making unit (from group averages down to single households or individuals)

Despite this increasing sophistication in the models themselves, however, the ways in which those models influence policy formulation (often implicitly) remains poorly recognised and poorly understood. That, I suggest, is where history can help us.

US imports for a UK policy context

The reliance on mathematical models to inform national and urban-level transport policy-making and investment decisions in the UK can be traced back to the early 1960s – a time when car ownership was starting to grow rapidly, and when it was anticipated that within a few decades most people would own a car. Reports such as *Traffic in Towns* (HMSO, 1963) highlighted the pressure that the growth in car numbers would put on traditional road networks and urban structures, and the difficult choices that would have to be taken in order to accommodate cars in cities. Policymakers needed a way of forecasting future demand for car use and road capacity, and a means of testing the likely effectiveness – and economic justification – of potential major road investment strategies.

Early computer-based travel forecasting models were imported from the United States, which had experienced rapid growth in car ownership and use several decades in advance of the UK. These imported models were welcomed by most transport professionals, who believed that the anticipated growth in car ownership and use would swamp traditional inter-urban and urban street networks unless there was a major programme of road investment, and that to plan this programme they needed to understand complex patterns of movement at both city and regional scale – an undertaking much too complex for conventional, junction-based manual methods of analysis.

The use of computer-based models also resonated with political priorities of the time. The Labour government of 1964 to 1970 was seeking to modernise the country – the Prime Minister, Harold Wilson, spoke memorably of the 'white heat of the technological revolution' – and welcomed objective, scientific solutions to problems and the use of emerging computer technologies. This was also a time of major city reconstruction and urban house building, with a strong focus on the 'new'.

What was *not* generally recognised by professionals at the time, however, was that these imported models were neither culturally neutral nor 'value free' – nor, in many respects, appropriate for UK conditions (Thomson, 1969).

In fact, there were important conceptual biases built into the models. The modelling methods had been developed for the United States, where there was a much stronger and more fully embedded car culture than in the UK. In particular, the models assumed that, once a person had access to a car, they would use it for virtually all of their travel. Effectively the models were *designed* to forecast increases in car ownership and use, and to encourage solutions which would enable unconstrained levels of car use, requiring major urban freeway construction – as was to be found in most American cities at that time. They were also very strategic in nature, ignoring local trips and focusing on the longer distance ones which would be attracted to high capacity, limited access roads. The models only forecast non-local car 'trips' (i.e. the number of one-way car driver journeys in a city) – ignoring local car trips and those on foot, bicycle or public transport.

This did not translate well to large UK cities – and particularly London, where the models soon predicted that, even with four high-capacity ring motorways at different distances from central London, demand would greatly outstrip supply. At the same time, the negative consequences of early urban motorway construction in London quickly became apparent. In particular, Westway, connecting White City and Edgware Road, was constructed between 1964 and 1970 as a 3-lane elevated motorway; it required extensive housing demolition and resulted in stark neighbourhood severance and high levels of vehicle air and noise pollution. This led to a strong negative public reaction, and a successful 'homes before roads' campaign, which ousted a Conservative administration at the Greater London Council and replaced it with an anti-car and pro-public transport Labour administration led by Ken Livingstone.

Taken together, these developments quickly led to the recognition that unlimited car use would not be possible, at least in larger cities like London, and that potential car traffic would need to be constrained in some way (by default or by design) – both due to the physical impossibility of accommodating full car use, and as a consequence of the negative public reaction to early urban motorway building.

Adapting the models

This recognition posed two major conceptual and practical problems for the existing US-derived forecasting models. First, there was no built-in mechanism to constrain the growth in car traffic that was predicted as a result of the forecast increases in car ownership – so 'manual adjustments' were necessary. Second, and related to this, there was no mechanism to estimate the extent to which people with cars would, for certain trips, choose to use public transport, or cycle or walk instead of driving.

To address these problems, the American vehicle-based models had to be modified to accommodate the fact that car owners would not make all their journeys by car. This was achieved by modifying the basic unit of analysis – from *vehicle* trips to *person* trips – and introducing a 'mode choice' sub-model which estimated people's willingness to use alternative modes of transport (especially public transport), given the relative times and costs involved.

Unfortunately, this approach of 'bolting on' a mode choice sub-model to what at its core remained a strategic vehicle-based model is far from ideal, and has led to biases which are still to be found in many operational transport forecasting models nearly half a century later. Although there have been successive 'expansions' of the original vehicle-based models over time, their car derived origin is still the 'ghost in the machine', and has distorted thinking in many ways.

The legacy of history

The way in which travel forecasting models developed in the UK from their car-based origins has left, as its legacy, three enduring conceptual problems:

1. The standard mode choice model is inherently flawed, as it forecasts travel mode decisions on a trip-by-trip basis. This clearly makes no sense for most journeys from home – people don't usually decide to drive to work and then take the bus

home! – and so weakens the reliability of the forecasts and the strength of the policy advice.
2. Walking and cycling are poorly handled in most travel forecasting models, which still focus more on 'strategic' trips and deal less well with more 'local', non-motorised journeys.
3. Overall household or person trip rates are assumed to depend on car ownership, income and household size, and not to be influenced by transport network conditions.

On top of this, it is worth noting a number of operational limitations which have shaped the relationship between models and policy. For example, early transport forecasting models were run on large, mainframe computers: it could take many days, and cost a great deal, to complete just one city-wide forecast (based on one assumption about future population size, location and characteristics, and one land use/transport plan). This had two major consequences.

- First, very few alternative growth forecasts or investment options for dealing with anticipated transport demand were tested, due to time and cost constraints. Indeed it was quite common just to use one growth assumption and test two alternative investment plans (one 'pro-car' and the other 'pro-public transport'). This greatly limited the development and testing of more sophisticated policy packages.
- Second, to reduce computational complexity, early models used some basic simplifying assumptions, which were all too evident to the early model developers, but forgotten by later generations who simply 'pressed the button' and ran the models,

assuming them to reasonably reflect travel behaviour.

These days, of course, constraints on computer processing power have, for many practical purposes, disappeared. But the legacy of those early simplifying assumptions, remains, and the practical limitations of the early days of transport modelling have had a major constraining effect on shaping transport policy over several decades.

One striking example of this constraining effect on policy concerns the influence of road capacity on behaviour. For simplicity, early models assumed that, once the number of car trips between an origin zone and a destination zone had been estimated, these estimates would not be affected by any subsequent changes in road network conditions. For example, if road capacity was later reduced to introduce bus priority or increase pedestrian crossing times, it was assumed that the pattern of car trips would be unaffected and that congestion would therefore grow rapidly. This assumption of a completely inelastic 'fixed origin-destination matrix' became hard-wired into transport models, and came to be seen as a reliable forecast of traffic behaviour – instead of what it really was, a legacy of the need to make simplifying assumptions when computers were much less powerful. This in turn delayed by a decade or more policy attempts to reduce capacity for general road traffic in large urban areas. For example, when the policy decision was taken to redesign the Vauxhall Cross junction in London and reallocate capacity to buses, cyclists and pedestrians, the model used, true to form, forecast a huge increase in vehicle delay. It was only by experimenting on the ground – taking out lane capacity incrementally, gradually moving traffic cones across a traffic lane – that it was confirmed that traffic behaviour was in fact elastic and responsive to network conditions. This opened the way for later, more dramatic road capacity reduction schemes, such as the redesign of Trafalgar Square.

Another example of the enduring effects on policy of early computational limitations concerns the complex, reciprocal relationship between transport and land use. As a way of simplifying, most early transport forecasting models looked only at the influence of land use patterns (e.g. where people live and work) on travel demand, and *not* at the influence of major transport investments (e.g. the M25 or the Jubilee Line Extension) on land use patterns. This meant that there was no understanding of where and when transport could stimulate development and regeneration, and as a result medium and long-term travel volumes have been greatly underestimated in areas of large potential demand – parts of the M25, for example, are the busiest sections of the British motorway network, while the Jubilee Line Extension is carrying much higher flows than were anticipated.

Recent developments

Many of the limitations discussed here have been recognised by academics for some time, and there have been efforts to refine forecasting concepts and methods, although their translation into practice is much slower and fragmented. Such developments include:

- Switching from trip-based models to tour-based models, using sequences of trips starting and ending at home (or at the workplace), thereby enabling travel mode choices between, say, car and train to be much better modelled (e.g. Omer et al., 2010)
- Introducing feedback loops, so that road network conditions start to affect the number, and origins

and destinations, of car driver trips (Department for Transport, 2014a)
- Developing fully integrated land use/transport models, which take account of the impact of improved accessibility on land use patterns and densities (Department for Transport, 2014b)

As well as seeking to address the limitations of the models bequeathed to us by history, academics have also sought to make sense of new phenomena. One recent development which has been seen as a particular challenge to conventional transport forecasting models is the advent of 'peak car': evidence that the decades-long growth in car use has levelled off (pre-recession) and is actually in decline in cities such as London, Paris and Vienna. What is particularly noticeable is a sharp decline in car ownership and use among young men – even in the United States – which has not been picked up in conventional forecasting models. Evidence such as this is leading to a strong academic challenge to the economic paradigm which has dominated transport modelling for several decades – particularly by sociologists, who have developed a 'mobilities' paradigm (Urry, 2007) covering all forms of movement of people, goods and ideas. This alternative paradigm recognises that transport behaviours take place within complex socio-technical clusters and associated social and business practices, which can change the nature and meanings of travel, including the role of the car.

Great progress has also been made in *communicating* the outputs of transport models. One of the practical limitations of the conventional transport models that are still widely used is that their outputs are largely unintelligible to the average layman or politician. Results in the form of large tables of numbers or performance ratios mean little to most people, and can be off-putting – meaning that transport professionals end up acting as 'gatekeepers', the only people able to interpret the numbers and their implications. In recent years, however, this has changed radically, thanks to the twin developments of microsimulation models (able to forecast the behaviour of millions of individual vehicles or people), and the capacity to present realistic visualisations. These developments – both the result of dramatic increases in computing power – have greatly increased transparency. At the same time, concerns have been expressed that these visualisations are so powerful that they distort decision-making, with local politicians and others paying insufficient attention to the background, quantitative outputs.

A final development – which has yet to have much impact on practical transport planning and policymaking, but has the potential to transform our thinking – is the re-conceptualisation of travel as an output of daily activity choices (e.g. Bhat and Koppelman, 1999). In theory, this approach has much to commend it: it explicitly models travel as a derived demand, and in principle can forecast such things as how travel patterns change as costs increase (e.g. by combining several trips into one tour from home), or how the internet substitutes electronic communication for travel. To date, however, there have been very few operational activity-based models, despite increased computing power and the availability of data.

One might speculate that this is partly because such models cannot be developed as a 'bolt-on' to traditional models: we would first have to remove the ghostly car from the machine, and start from a different perspective altogether. This is a big 'ask' as it involves overcoming the inertia of history and writing off much past sunk investment.

As I have sought to illustrate in this brief review of the history of transport models in the UK, models of behaviour are neither developed nor used in a vacuum, but are shaped and constrained by history.

Suggested further reading

For works cited, see References at the end of the book.

Jones, P. (2014) 'The evolution of urban mobility: The interplay of academic and policy perspectives' IATSS Research, 38(1), pp. 7-13.

The paper discusses how advances in forecasting models have been associated with major changes in urban transport policies in several countries.

PTV Vissim micro-simulation modelling capabilities. Available at: http://sbk.li/1152601

An example of the level of detail and realism with which the travel behaviour of people using different methods of transport in an urban area can be simulated. Other products are available (e.g. Paramics).

Boyce, D. and Williams, H. (2015) *Forecasting Urban Travel: past, present and future.* **Cheltenham: Edward Elgar.**

The definitive history of urban travel forecasting, written in a very comprehensive and readable fashion.

16. Explanatory models and conviction narratives

David Tuckett

Director, Centre for the Study of Decision-Making Uncertainty, UCL

Behaviour change is often approached as an exercise in applying models of behaviour to people we think need to change. But those people have their own models: ways of making sense of reality which in turn shape their behaviour and relationships. A model shapes the behaviour of the person who believes it as much as it does the behaviour of the person it's supposed to be about: and changing behaviour is often about promoting dialogue between different people's models.

In §8 of the Dialogue, Yusuf comments on the complexity of the system we are trying to model when we seek to understand human behaviour. One point he might have made is that human beings *themselves* have models – ways of making sense of their own reality – which in turn shape their behaviour and relationships. The point is not a new one. Freud showed us that the reality created by the subjective unconscious makes sense of what is otherwise nonsense. Max Weber used the concept of *verstehen* – understanding the meaning of action from the actor's point of view – to emphasise that it is *experienced* reality that is the determinant of action. The challenge from both these giants is to *make sense of how the other is making sense*.

For a long time my interest (as economist, medical sociologist, psychoanalyst and finally decision-scientist) has been in the boundaries between imagined reality, experienced reality, social reality and demonstrated realty. When I think about how to bring about behaviour change I start by conceiving of the patient (or other agent) as an authority on her own illness (or situation). Effective action in fields such as finance, health decision-making or high level decision-making in government and business requires that decision-makers and decision-enablers (i.e. educators, therapists and behaviour change specialists) adopt a very subtle and balanced attitude to what they think of as each other's reality – one which takes seriously the challenge of Freud and Weber.

In this paper, I want to explore the idea that behaviour change might be an exercise not only in *applying* models of behaviour to the people we think need to change, but also in *promoting dialogue* between models – our models, their models, other actors' models – and thereby understanding and adjusting the thinking and feeling processes that give subjective support to action.

To illustrate what I mean, I will elaborate the concepts of explanatory model (from my earlier work influenced by anthropology and medical sociology) and conviction narrative (from my current work in economics and decision science).

Explanatory Models

Mr Ison, a manager who played squash in his free time, went to his doctor with a list of worries: a tight, needle-sharp pain in his abdomen, tennis elbow, a complaint that he was full of wind, a worry he might be impotent and a feeling of too much stuff in his throat. After questions and examination, his doctor told him that the pain and probably the wind were caused by his discontinuing too early the tablets he had been given for a stomach ulcer, suggesting also that the impotence might be a side effect of treatment. The doctor advised him to stay on the tablets for another week, to be sure to eat regularly, to take a week off work, and to stop smoking. Mr Ison was also advised to return later for an injection for his tennis elbow.

When we interviewed him a day after he saw his doctor, Mr Ison gave quite a detailed and accurate account of what had taken place (compared to the tape recording of the consultation which the researcher saw only afterwards), He knew what he had been advised about tablets, the tennis elbow injection, staying off work and giving up smoking. However, despite being asked a specific question about eating, he was unaware that he should eat regularly or carefully. Nor did he understand the relevance of eating and diet to his condition.

Why had Mr Ison failed to appreciate the importance of eating? Analysis pinpointed Mr Ison's *explanatory model* of his condition and its treatment – his detailed ideas about what was wrong, how the treatment worked, and how they fitted together inside a causal structure. Mr Ison believed that his ulcer was like 'a boil on the stomach'. According to him it had a centre which was poisonous, caused by gathering up all the poisons in his stomach. To treat the problem, he therefore imagined that the tablets were designed to disperse the poisons and help to dry up the boil. This explanatory model was, of course, markedly divergent from the medical view, and included no conception of the role of stomach acids and of the introduction of food (and alcohol) into the stomach. So Mr Ison had an explanatory model within which what the doctor said about eating and the tablets interfering with the production of acid in his stomach by eating regularly had no meaning for him. Without access to the doctor's explanatory model, he 'forgot' a crucial aspect of what the doctor said to him, undermining the expert advice and treatment offered (Tuckett et al., 1985).

There is a widespread belief in some circles within medical education that patients do not *remember* much of what they are told. By contrast, in our study, we found that nine out of ten patients were able to remember *all* the main points made by their doctors. Moreover, nearly three quarters of the patients accurately interpreted the sense of all the major points made by their doctors.

We also found, however, that this success largely depended on what the doctor said being *consistent with what the patient already thought*. When a patient's explanatory model was divergent, like Mr Ison's, that patient was less likely to remember and interpret correctly points made by their doctor. The consultation almost never made this divergence in explanatory models apparent.

Crucially, this also had consequences for the subsequent commitment of patients to decisions made by the doctor, and therefore to their behaviour. Nearly two thirds of those who began a consultation with ideas convergent the explanatory models of their doctor felt committed to the decisions made. By contrast, nearly three quarters of those who began with divergent explanatory models felt uncommitted or in outright disagreement. The convergence or divergence of prior patient explanatory models is directly linked to both success and failure from a behaviour change perspective.

It is very fortunate that patients are active participants in their medical care – processing, making sense and evaluating their doctors' ideas on the basis of explanatory models of their own. It is only because they can use prior understanding to fill in what a doctor says, and often do so accurately, that quite brief communications, ambiguous or unclear explanations, or even the total absence of communication will often not matter a great deal. Patients correctly adduce what to do and when to come to the doctor because their explanatory models are quite close to those regarded as valid by those caring for them. In fact, like any other social system governed by taken-for-granted beliefs, the entire healthcare system would grind to a halt if explanatory models were not widely shared.

Note that whether or not Mr Ison's beliefs make medical sense is not the point. What matters is the way health beliefs, organised into explanatory models, influence the attention given to and the sense made of new information.[6]

A second case from the same study illustrates this point. Knowledge of Mr Nixon's explanatory model was essential to make any sense of his concerns, to explain anything to him, and therefore to influence his behaviour positively.

---

[6] For those familiar with the field, compare the role played by Bayesian priors.

Mr Nixon visited his doctor to complain of an itching and taut sensation on his leg. He felt it worsened when he moved around. In the consultation, he told his doctor he thought these symptoms might be caused by too much sugar in his diet. His doctor told him that in his opinion he had a minor skin complaint, which could be helped by a moisturising cream.

From the beginning of his interview with me afterwards Mr Nixon indicated, hesitantly, that he thought both treatment and diagnosis were wrong, although he had not liked to say so directly to the doctor. When I saw him I did not know what had happened with his doctor, so I began by asking what he had gone to discuss. In the first few moments he scratched his lower leg around his ankle and mentioned, somewhat as an aside, that he had sugar problems. I, therefore, asked him how he saw the connection between his symptoms and sugar. He told me that he thought he had 'flea-bite-us'. In his model this was some sort of mild heart condition which he believed to be linked to high blood pressure. He told me that too much sugar was not a good idea for heart conditions, mentioning books and television programmes from which he had gleaned information. He also knew that heart conditions worsened on exercise – and this was a specific anxiety for him, as he noticed his symptoms worsened when he moved around. In fact, he added, he had recently watched a programme about the former US president, Richard Nixon. At the time, there were news reports of President Nixon's admission to hospital for phlebitis.

Only at this moment did I realise that the patient's 'flea-bite-us' was probably the medical *phlebitis*. The sophistication and complexity of the underlying thinking became clear: Mr Nixon had an explanatory model of his illness involving a subjectively consistent and plausible combination of observation and logic which mirrored a formal medical model of diagnosis and treatment. Moreover, examining the transcript of the consultation he had with his doctor, I noted that in the opening minute Mr Nixon had hinted at this underlying model explicitly, asking if the doctor thought he ate too much sugar – just as he quickly volunteered to me in the interview his ideas about sugar. The doctor, however, obviously mystified and with the pressure of having to make a diagnosis on his mind, did not ask Mr Nixon to elaborate, but instead jumped to the conclusion that his worry was 'sugar diabetes'. Responding from his subjective position very sensitively, the doctor later said that if Mr Nixon was worried about diabetes he could drop in a urine sample for testing. This, of course, mystified Mr Nixon (Tuckett et al., 1985).

Patients' pre-existing explanatory models, and their convergence with or divergence from the explanatory models used by doctors, influence what they remember, how they make sense of it, how much confidence they have in decisions made, and therefore their subsequent behaviour. Given this, it is obviously important to get information about patients' explanatory models as part of the process of reaching decisions with them. However, in more than a thousand consultations studied, we found few examples of doctors actively using consultations to find out where their patients' ideas, so to speak, were coming from. Moreover, when patients tried, more or less tactfully, to put their ideas out in the open, the result was often an uncomfortable emotional situation and a conversation at cross purposes.

Mr Nixon's doctor knew all Mr Nixon's key observations, but he did not know how they fitted together into an explanatory model. Like many other doctors in our study, he did not try to bring out his patient's ideas further, jumped to conclusions as to what his patient meant, ignored or paid lip service to questions or expressions of doubt, and engaged other activities which inhibited an exchange of ideas. This was despite the fact that half the doctors in our sample – and all the doctors with whom we subsequently worked in an educational phase – were progressive physicians with an espoused interest in modern 'whole person' approaches to medical care.

The lack of inquiry into the patient's explanatory models – the lack of genuine dialogue *between models* – means that where a doctor's and patient's explanatory models are divergent, the encounter often fails to deliver the necessary changes in behaviour.

Conviction Narratives

My ideas about explanatory models developed in a team trying to make sense of doctor-patient communication. Some years later I became concerned with understanding how financial markets work and, in particular, why accepted theories could not explain what happened in them or help to regulate them. The outcome was a new theory, again starting from the idea that reality is subjectively constituted and not given, and that a model shapes the behaviour of the person who *believes* it as much as it does the behaviour of the person it's supposed to be *about*.

Real-world decision-making often takes place in conditions of uncertainty. For example, think about choosing a mate, buying a house, finding someone to manage your money or selecting a career: in each case, you must decide whether or not to put yourself in a dependent relationship – with a person, project or investment – the outcomes of which are deeply uncertain, and can produce significant loss or gain. Or imagine that you have to join others to decide whether or not to build a high-speed rail link, or to engage significant resources today to treat (and so prevent) a new virus in

Africa which *might* one day be like Ebola. Although analysis of data and unbiased sifting of evidence may be helpful, choices of the kind I have in mind cannot be made just with statistics. So how do they get made?

Conviction narrative theory (Chong and Tuckett, 2014) is a new approach to decision-making which seeks to answer that question. The central idea is that to act in such circumstances, when outcomes are consequential and deeply uncertain, people must become *subjectively convinced* about their decision to act, and that they achieve this by developing what we call a conviction narrative. This is a way of making sense of the data, imagining possible expected outcomes, and above all becoming attached to the idea that a particular action will produce a desired outcome, uncertainty notwithstanding. Conviction narratives explain how Steve Jobs built Apple, how other great innovators managed to do their thing – and how others failed completely. Because conviction narratives support the decision to act, they manage the inevitable ambivalence that, in situations of deep uncertainty, might otherwise undermine our and others' willingness to take action.

Consider a specific example from our research: an investment manager, Tristan Cooper, who was trying to decide whether to buy shares in a construction company valued at over two billion Euros. The company was doing some 'very interesting things' which made Cooper believe its future value would be good. At the time, however, the stock was cheap, because one of the company's European subsidiaries had run into difficulty, causing two profit warnings and sale by some investors of their holdings. The crucial question for Cooper was this: would buying the shares cheap bring gains in the future, or would they stay cheap because what had happened was going to continue? To decide Cooper sat down with the CFO 'to try and get a sense of what kind of guy he is'. The CFO, he told us, 'came up with a very decent explanation as to why they had screwed up' in the particular company. 'From a valuation standpoint', Cooper explained, 'if you're a construction company worth 2 billion euro then if you have to write off 60 million, once, it shouldn't matter a lot. Your earnings for the year are going to be destroyed, but you're only taking off this much of your market cap so the stock should only drop 3% or something that day, and then you forget about it'. The share price should recover. His conviction narrative created an unfolding picture of the future in which his investment would pay off. He bought the stock and hoped to benefit.[7]

The concept of a conviction narrative adds a critical ingredient to the explanatory models discussed above: emotion. According to conviction narrative theory, human emotion is not a weakness but a resource, which we use to create reality. On the one hand, emotions associated with excitement act as attractors, allowing us to approach and to commit to projects. On the other hand, other emotions associated with anxiety, create pain and make us want to avoid or repel attachments that seem to create it. It's the organising role played by these emotions that allow us to make decisions where outcomes are uncertain – individual decisions to get married or take a new job, or collective decisions to undertake great projects like creating the NHS or the European Union. Like Cooper, we use a mixture of emotion, knowledge and imagination to create stories about the future, which allow us to *feel* we believe.

So how do conviction narratives develop? How does the prospect of satisfaction trump the prospect of pain? In part, this process draws on the brain's abilities – for example, the ability cognitively to order available facts to simulate a subjectively 'true' picture of their future evolution into an

---

[7] See Tuckett (2011) and http://sbk.li/1162701 for supplementary material and a randomly selected sample of similar accounts.

outcome, which is experienced emotionally. However, it's our view that conviction narratives are created not by individuals in isolation but in *social interaction*. For example, action in financial markets is supported by conviction narratives that develop through discussion, testing, imagining and learning from others in everyday contacts – think how people in markets constantly share rumours and thoughts about the benefits, implications or troubles associated with holding dotcoms, CDOs or sovereign debt, or are wondering about the impacts of leverage, quantitative easing, tapering, etc. Ideas are excitedly or anxiously spread and shared among market participants as they learn from each other and create conviction narratives in so doing.

Unfortunately, these processes can also lead to problems. Individuals can idealise objects of desire (for example a dotcom stock) to the point where they cannot entertain doubts about them; or their desire to feel the same as others can undermine their ability to question shared narratives. In this way conviction narratives can become highly compelling 'phantastic object narratives' – narratives which don't just help us to act in conditions of uncertainty, but which also blind us to evidence on which we could draw (Tuckett, 2011; Tuckett and Taffler, 2008; Tuckett and Taffler, 2012). In the health education field similar enthusiasms may affect ideas about diets, special treatments, or health service provider theories and practices.

Meetings between experts

In this paper, I've looked at models not as things *about* people, but as things people *have*. I've explored the impact these explanatory models can have on behaviour, and their importance in contexts like doctor-patient interactions, where one party is trying to influence the behaviour of the other. And I've argued for the central role played by emotion in the conviction narratives that underpin many of our most important decisions.

What does this mean for people working in the field of behaviour change? If behaviour change is an exercise not only in *applying* models of behaviour, but in also *promoting dialogue* between models, what are the implications?

I find the concept of 'meetings between experts' useful here. Applied to a doctor-patient interaction, this concept emphasises that, before giving expert advice, the doctor must first recognise the 'expertise' of the patient, and elicit their explanatory models and conviction narratives – recognising that both are rooted in emotional states, and that convictions manage both approach and avoidance. The same basic principles can be applied to any situation in which an 'expert' seeks to influence the behaviour of others.

One especially important area where this is relevant is in the application of science to policy. Policy-relevant science – science that influences what policymakers remember, understand and act on – is not an end in itself: it is a system for reaching conclusions in a more transparent way, and constructing arguments which provide confidence against objections and build the conviction necessary for action. Just as those doctors should have taken account of the explanatory models and conviction narratives of Mr Ison and Mr Nixon, so too policy-relevant science must from the outset take account of those whose behaviour it seeks to influence.

17. Models, stories and leaders

David Newkirk

Corporate advisor and educator; formerly CEO, Executive Education, University of Virginia's Darden School of Business and Senior Partner, Booz Allen Hamilton

Leadership is, at its heart, all about changing behaviour. From a leader's perspective, however, the value of models of behaviour lies less in their offering 'theories of change' than in their power as 'instruments of change' – thanks to the influence models can have on the people who embrace and believe them.

In business, leadership is essentially about changing behaviours – of employees, of customers, of suppliers and competitors, and of the broader economy in which the enterprise operates.

At first sight, therefore, one might imagine that successful leaders use models of behaviour primarily to guide their decisions, providing what Yusuf describes in the Dialogue as a 'theory of change'. In this article, however, I'd like to argue that the relationship between leaders and models is rather more complicated.

To understand why, we first need to look at what I'll describe as a 'conventional view' of business, and identify some of its shortcomings. In particular, this 'conventional view' overlooks the fact that businesses are human enterprises – and that the most successful ones respond dynamically to their environment.

In the context of a human enterprise, models aren't just 'theories of change', used merely to guide the leader's decisions. Rather, they are often 'instruments of change' – the means of driving organisational change through their influence on individuals. Indeed, shaping and communicating the 'models' that guide an organisation and its various stakeholders is perhaps a leader's most powerful tool.

Models and the conventional view of business

The business disciplines are shot through with models. In finance, the capital asset pricing model (CAPM) links risk and return, and the Black-Scholes model values options, each model bringing the prescriptive certainty of financial physics. In operations, Jay Forrester and his followers (most notably Peter Senge) developed models of systems dynamics to capture interactions, especially feedback, across supply chains. In marketing, the common view of Homo Oeconomicus treats buyers as rational decision-makers, optimising 'utility' within their own valuation framework. Projected into organisational management, this model of human behaviour leads to a focus on incentives to motivate and align employees. Infection models drawn from public health predict the spread of innovations through various groups, ranging from early adopters through change resisters. At the most abstract level, Michael Porter's 'five-forces' model and Ed Freeman's 'stakeholder theory' describe strategy, competition and cooperation at the industry level.

The pervasiveness of these models can be seen in the curricula of business schools, with their emphasis on quantitative methods and veneration of spreadsheet skills. I started my own career in the mid 70s, building financial models of new diesel engine projects, certain that they reflected the likely flows of income, expense and capital over the decades-long life of the plant.

While many are useful, models in business are subject to all the challenges outlined in the Dialogue. They can oversimplify – for example, in the case of Black-Scholes starting from a more tractable probability distribution rather than a less tractable but possibly more accurate one. They can be context-dependent and difficult to validate. Critically, they can be mistaken for descriptions of existing behaviour, rather than blueprints or, worse, aspirations for future behaviour. Moreover, the implicit, inaccurate view embodied in a model can shape the very data gathered: for example, in the case of Homo Oeconomicus, causing us to see individuals through a reductionist, quantifying lens, rather than in their full complexity as human beings.8

More critically, the conventional view of business (to the extent it addresses the underlying nature of business and management at all) imitates naïve science in its claim to deal with independent phenomena subject to deterministic rules. Many of these business models reflect a false positivism, for example by treating finance as a set of fixed relationships – 'the physics of money' – by talking about 'discovering' market segments and consumer needs, or by choosing 'where to compete'. By focusing attention on the physical and financial assets, they may overlook the people and ignore their agency.

An alternative view: business as a human enterprise

It's my contention that organisations, including businesses, are in their essence human enterprises, and need to be understood in terms of the people involved. (For a fuller discussion of this view and its implications, see Newkirk and Freeman, 2008.)

This view is not new. As Plato describes in Book 2 of The Republic, societies, and within them trade, arose as means for individuals to create greater value by co-operation and specialisation. Adam Smith's 'invisible hand' is the result of commercial interactions through which people exploit differences in their capabilities and demands (and values).

Even today, businesses can be explained in terms of aggregated human behaviour, in addition to the flows of

---

[8] The rise of behaviourism in marketing, finance, operations, organization and economics is painting a richer picture of individuals.

materials and money. The beliefs, interests and actions of the various groups of humans – including customers, employees, suppliers and business partners, regulators and, most critically for this discussion, managers – shape an organisation's actions and ultimately its success.

This is most easily seen in the knowledge and service businesses. When I started out, working in the diesel engine business, it was easy enough to believe that the machine tools were the heart of the process, producing our products and embodying our technology. Later in my career, however, leading a consulting business, our 'product' was the interaction of my partners with their clients. Most recently, at a business school, the faculty 'created value' behind the closed doors of their classrooms. The success of these organisations depended on how these professionals reacted to the situation in which they found themselves. And looking back, it's now clear to me that even in more traditional manufacturing businesses human action is critical to success. Sales people collaborate with customers to craft solutions to their specific challenges. Local managers adapt global strategies to their own market realities. The best innovations grow out of subtle insights into customers as human beings.

With human beings at the centre of business, it is harder to hold a positivist view. Individuals have agency. And, importantly, their response can evolve, with their values and behaviour shaped by their context, experience, and understanding. Their actions both reflect and change the world around them. This is most readily apparent when innovation opens new possibilities: it's not hard for anyone who has lived through the last decade to see that the world of the Internet, apps and social media was created, not discovered, and that it is dependent on, not independent of, human behaviour.

Models as a cause of behaviour

With human behaviour at the heart of business, models play a more influential role, moving from describing a business to changing it.

Sumantra Goshal (2005) describes this as: 'the "Double hermeneutic". Unlike theories in the physical sciences, theories in the social sciences tend to be self-fulfilling... a management theory – if it gains sufficient currency – changes the behaviours of managers who start acting in accordance with the theory'. When embraced by the people they purport to describe, models can thereby influence those very individuals and the organisations they work in.

The Black-Scholes model offers a simple, possibly benign, example. Does it accurately predict the value of financial options because it describes the underlying distribution of possible outcomes? Or does it predict prices because most of the players in the options market use the Black-Scholes model to calculate the options' value?

In a human enterprise, we need to ask not whether a model is right or wrong, useful or useless, but how it may change the behaviour of those who adopt it.

The risk is that a flawed model may lead to counterproductive behaviour. For example, the view that financial incentives are effective, rooted in the *Homo Oeconomics* model of individual behaviour (and regularly shown by research to be false in all but the most routine of tasks – see Pink, 2009), has encouraged managers to use compensation systems (especially bonuses) as a critical signal to employees about desired activities. This focus on financial incentives, however, has caused employees to frame their own success solely in monetary terms, inviting them to maximise their rewards, sometimes with adverse side effects.

Leadership as shaping behavior

Leadership is often contrasted with management. A good manager makes sure the organisation 'does things right', while a leader ideally ensures it 'does the right things' – and in particular that it changes in structure and behaviour as its world changes.

Businesses today are operating in a more dynamic world, with customers and competitors acting quickly. Many are operating across multiple markets, requiring local adaptation. For most, the issue is not exploiting positional assets (resources, equipment, technology) through some predetermined set of actions. Rather it is responding rapidly to opportunities and challenges as they emerge, ideally in a way that is consistent with the organisation's purpose and values.

To give an example, during the height of its success as a partnership, Goldman Sachs was distinguished by its ability to detect emerging market opportunities and to mobilise its resources (largely human) to serve them. Today, success stories such as Whole Foods Markets are built from multiple actions by managers across the system, more so than from single, central decisions. And recent failures, including Tesco's loss of market position, often have at their heart a failure to react to change.

An organisation's response is determined by the behaviour of its people and its key stakeholders: both the sense they make of the world they see and the actions they take. The leader's job is to shape that behaviour.

This is where models bring an opportunity. The 'double hermeneutic' – the fact that theories and models can change the ways managers (and other human beings in the business's environment) behave – makes models among a leader's most effective tools for creating a more valuable and sustainable institution. In the volatile, dispersed and diverse worlds in which most businesses operate, 'models', which leave room for individual action, are often superior to rules. The models might try to capture 'why customers choose us', 'how we create value', 'how our brands work'. These 'models' of the underlying dynamics let the manager respond to the immediate situation in a way that is consistent with the organisation's purpose and principles.

In practice, business 'models' are often best communicated as stories. Great leaders are often described in the shorthand of the stories they tell and the stories they embody. Walt Disney and Steve Jobs continue to influence their organisations through the stories they represent. Human beings are storytellers and, critically, story listeners. We can fill in a partially drawn picture, making it relevant to us and our moment. Organisations can also complete pictures, bringing origin stories to bear in new circumstances. This human response to stories makes them longer-lived and more adaptable than simple rules.

Final observations

The essential role of people in the creation of a business means that there cannot be a single, canonical business model. Every successful organisation has its own distinct purpose and context, its own stories. To the extent that there are 'rules' of accounting or 'models' of market behaviour or 'principles' of strategy, these are more often conventional languages, allowing common description of the organisation, not a prescription or positivist conclusion about its underlying nature.

While the argument of this essay is that models and stories are the most effective way for a leader to create a responsive, adaptable business, this is not a unique feature of commercial entities. Perhaps the argument needs to be made initially for business because, in seeing them through their financial metrics, we often lose sight of the human faces. But I'd argue that all organisations are human enterprises, whose members' actions are shaped by the sense they make of their world and the models they bring to bear in it. And all leaders are responsible for the impact of their stories on their organisation's behaviour.

Suggested further reading

For works cited, see References at the end of the book.

Newkirk, D. and Freeman, R. E. (2008) 'Business as a Human Enterprise: Implications for Education', Social Science Research Network. Available at: http://sbk.li/1172811

This article reviews the current critiques of management scholarship and education and argues that the view of business as a human enterprise resolves a number of challenges, notably giving a fundamental role for ethics in business.

Goshal, S. (2005) 'Bad Management Theories are Destroying Good Managerial Practice', Academy of Management Learning & Education, 4(1), p. 77.

The late Sumantra Goshal argues that our theories of business and management in fact shape managers' behaviour, often for the worse.

Pink, D. (2009), Drive. New York: Riverhead Books.

Dan Pink draws together research on motivation to show that 'if-then' incentives actually reduce performance on all but the most routinised tasks, showing how alternative 'models' of human motivation give rise to radically different, highly effective organizations.

Senge, P.M. (1990) The Fifth Discipline: The Art and Practice of the Learning Organization. New York: Doubleday/Currency.

Senge's book, which applies Jay Forrester's system dynamics tools to organisational behaviour and learning, is among the most approachable descriptions of organisational modelling.

18. Behaviour change through political influence: the case of tobacco control

Deborah Arnott

Chief Executive, ASH (UK)

Population behaviour change often requires political behaviour change and this needs to be guided by a model of the political system. Even a simple model can provide an effective blueprint for action.

Core funding for ASH and its campaigning work is provided by the British Heart Foundation and Cancer Research UK, both of which are also leading members of the Smokefree Action Coalition. The SFAC was set up to fight the successful campaign for comprehensive smoke-free laws and continues to campaign for evidence-based measures to reduce the harm caused by smoking, most recently for standardised packaging of tobacco products.

Leadership is, at its heart, all about changing behaviour. From a leader's perspective, however, the value of models of behaviour lies less in their offering 'theories of change' than in their power as 'instruments of change' – thanks to the influence models can have on the people who embrace and believe them.

Much behaviour change occurs when environments change, and this in turn often calls for political decisions – which is why ASH spends so much time and effort on encouraging politicians to take action. We believe that this is key to unlocking many of the most effective, evidence-based behaviour change techniques to improve public health.

To change the behaviour of politicians, however, we need a model of political influence. We start from the premise that improving the public health is a generally accepted political objective in countries such as the UK. However, this is usually overridden by the more urgent and immediate need to acquire power and to keep it. This leads to a simple model of *political* behaviour change in which, in order to take action, politicians need:

- to **know** what needs to be done
- to feel **confident** that doing so is to their political advantage, and
- to be given the **opportunity** to act.

When it comes to smoking, step one has been achieved in the UK. Politicians generally accept that discouraging smoking is a good idea. But that doesn't mean they feel confident that the public and powerful interest groups will support them if they take action, or that they have the opportunity to take action.

The introduction of the law to prohibit smoking in enclosed public places in England is a good case study of how to address these two further steps to political change.[9] When I started working for ASH in 2003 with the prime objective of getting smoke-free laws in place, the problem we had was not that the then Labour Government did not accept the evidence that secondhand smoke was harmful, but that it did not believe that there was sufficient political support for action. It was essential to mobilise such support and make it politically visible: in the words of a Health Minister's political adviser, 'Show us the votes'.

How do you prove that there are votes in smoke-free laws? In Spring 2004, ASH commissioned MORI to assess the level of support in Great Britain. Four out of five of the 4,000 people polled supported a law to ensure that all workplaces became smoke-free, but opinions varied when people were asked about specific environments, ranging from 96% wanting hospitals smoke-free, to just under half wanting smoking ended in pubs and bars.

Breaking responses down by voting intention, of great interest to politicians, showed that voters, whatever their party allegiance, were much more likely to support smoke-free legislation than non-voters. When asked whether they wanted pubs and bars smoke-free, between 50% and 56% of voters agreed, compared to only 38% of non-voters.

The poll – which asked each respondent a number of different questions – also illustrated the very different answers you get depending on how the question is framed. For example, 90% of Labour voters agreed that all workers had a right to a smoke-free environment, while only 74%

---

[9] ASH worked with many other key health organisations, the Royal College of Physicians, Cancer Research UK, the BMA, the British Heart Foundation, the Chartered Institute of Environmental Health, Asthma UK, the British Lung Foundation, the TUC and many others. ASH doesn't and shouldn't take all the credit. But ASH coordinated the alliance that led the campaign (the Smokefree Action Coalition or SFAC) and was responsible for the strategy and that's what I'm going to describe here.

wanted all enclosed workplaces, including public places, to be smoke-free; and when asked if they wanted pubs and bars to be smoke-free, only 50% answered yes. We explained to the Government that, if smoke-free environments were framed as a yes/no issue of workplace and public health and safety, there was overwhelming public support.

So the key message of the Smokefree Action Coalition (SFAC) – an alliance of health organisations and others led by ASH – was that everyone has a right to a smoke-free workplace, and our objective was for all enclosed workplaces to be smoke-free, including those in the hospitality trade. This last point was particularly important because we knew the hospitality trade was where the highest levels of tobacco smoke existed, both in concentration and proportion of venues. In addition, the majority of workers in the hospitality trade are low-paid and have little choice about where they work.

Opponents of legislation tried to argue that secondhand smoke wasn't harmful, but this was not the argument that had most traction with politicians. The argument with most traction was that legislation would be an example of the 'nanny state', a term of British origin which implies government interfering too much in personal choice. In Britain, politicians are strongly influenced by John Stuart Mill's harm principle – that government has the right to intervene to prevent harm to others – and both supporters and opponents cited this principle in promoting their position. The battleground became whether workers had a right to a smoke-free environment. A sign of our success is that it came to be accepted, quite rightly, that the rights of workers to a smoke-free workplace overrode the right of smokers to smoke where they pleased.

From the start the SFAC and its supporters balanced a proactive and reactive media campaign, which proved highly effective, particularly given the lack of a large public relations budget. It was greatly helped by the fact that, in his 2002 annual report (launched in July 2003), the Chief Medical Officer for England urged Ministers to ban smoking in public places. Media interest escalated as a result, and from then on ASH observed a marked increase in the number of journalists interested in running stories. Indeed they would often ring us up, thirsty for new angles, desperate to find new ways of covering the story. Media interest increased still further after the successful introduction in March 2004 of smoke-free legislation in the Republic of Ireland, the first country in the world to introduce comprehensive smoke-free laws including pubs and bars. The reason the journalists were interested was because the public was interested. People wanted to debate the rights of smokers versus the rights of workers to a safe working environment, and increasingly were interested in the rights of nonsmokers versus the rights of smokers in a country where less than one in four of the population smoked.

So public and media support was demonstrably growing. But there was still one step we needed to achieve. Without parliament being given an *opportunity* to bring in legislation, no laws could be passed. How could we make that happen?

In May 2004, following publication of the Wanless review, the Department of Health began a public health white paper consultation on action to improve people's health. This was just after Ireland had implemented its smoke-free laws, but the then Secretary of State for Health, John Reid, made very clear at the launch of the consultation that he still favoured a voluntary approach. The legislative option had been included in the Wanless review so it had to be discussed as part of the consultation process, but it looked as though Reid would ensure that it was not in the final recommendations. Fortunately for us, he overreached himself. At a public meeting with journalists present he said: 'I just do not think that the worst problem on our sink estates by any means is smoking but that it is an obsession of the middle classes. What enjoyment does a 21-year-old mother of three living in a council sink estate get? The only enjoyment sometimes they have is to have a cigarette.'

This led to a media firestorm, which dominated the news agenda for days, in which Reid came under attack by the media, the public and fellow politicians as much as by the health lobby. In the middle of it ASH launched its MORI poll results showing that 80% of the public supported a law to make all enclosed workplaces smoke-free. John Reid, who had refused to meet us until then, finally agreed to meet. The group that went to see him included all the major medical and public health organisations and health charities, showing that the whole of the health community was as one on this issue. When we met him, it was clear he had been forced to concede that legislation had to be on the agenda. The issue now was what the legislation would contain.

In deciding what form the legislation would take, Reid was guided by the public opinion polls, which showed that the public overwhelmingly wanted smoke-free public places. The only outstanding debate was about pubs and bars, where public support was about 50/50. In contrast, a significant majority of the public supported smoke-free restaurants. On 16 November 2004, the White Paper announcing the legislation was published. Reid proposed smoke-free workplaces and enclosed public places, with exemptions for pubs that didn't serve food (i.e. that were not also restaurants) and for private members' clubs.

Following the general election in May 2005, Patricia Hewitt took over as Health Minister. The SFAC was unable to persuade the new Health Minister to remove the exemptions, despite strong arguments that they would exacerbate health inequalities and would be expensive and difficult to enforce. On 26 October 2005, the Government announced that its Health Improvement and Protection Bill banning smoking in workplaces would include exemptions for pubs that didn't serve food and for private members' clubs. However, this happened only after a public row between Ministers, unprecedented in the Labour Government until that time, which undermined claims that the proposed legislation was logical and coherent.

Polling results also showed clearly how political leadership affected public opinion. In our first poll in Spring 2004, support for smoke-free pubs and bars was lower in Scotland than in England, at only 39% compared to 51%. By the end of 2005, however, while support for smoke-free pubs and bars in England had risen from one 51% to 66%, support in Scotland had risen even more, from 39% to 70%. This can only be accounted for by the political leadership shown in Scotland and lack of leadership shown in England, since active campaigns were being run in both England and Scotland, and the national media cover both countries. On 10 November 2004, following a comprehensive consultation process, Jack McConnell, the Labour Scottish First Minister, announced in the Scottish Parliament that a comprehensive ban on smoking in public places, including pubs and bars, would be introduced by the spring of 2006. This was promoted positively by McConnell to the public as a great prize: 'We in this parliament have a chance to make the most significant step to improve Scotland's public health for a generation'. Significantly, McConnell subsequently nominated smoke-free legislation as likely to prove his single most important political legacy. In contrast, in December 2005, the Department of Health was still promoting partial legislation for England and Wales to exempt pubs and bars which didn't serve food and private members' clubs.

The fact that the SFAC was able to demonstrate such a significant growth in support for smoke-free pubs and bars between Spring 2004 and December 2005, from one half to two thirds of the population in England, played a key role in the success of the campaign to ensure that the final legislation passed by Parliament included all hospitality venues.

The main focus of our political efforts now moved from the Government to Parliament. The House of Commons Health Select Committee, made up of an all-Party group of backbenchers and chaired by Kevin Barron MP, a long-time supporter of tobacco control, decided to hold hearings into the smoke-free provisions of the Health Bill in late 2005. The Committee's hearings were comprehensive. In particular they elicited a memorable statement from the Chief Medical Officer, Sir Liam Donaldson, who revealed that he had considered resigning when the Government decided to ignore the results of its public consultation on the Bill and persist with its proposed exemptions from smoke-free legislation for non-food pubs and bars and licensed members' clubs.

The Chair's political skills ensured that the report of the Committee, published just before Christmas, was signed by all ten members who had attended its proceedings, including Labour, Conservative, Liberal Democrat and Independent MPs. The report stated that the proposed exemption for non-food pubs was 'unfair, unjust, inefficient and unworkable'. It concluded that all workers, including bar staff, deserved protection from the dangers of secondhand smoke and that the exemption would undermine the Government's goal of reducing health inequalities, since drink-only pubs are concentrated in deprived areas.

ASH and the coalition ensured that an amendment to the Bill achieving comprehensive smoke-free legislation was drafted by an independent parliamentary counsel. Kevin Barron then secured the support of all the Select Committee's members for this amendment, which removed the exemptions for non-food pubs and clubs.

On St Valentine's day 2006, at the Report Stage of the Health Bill, the House of Commons voted by a majority of 200 for comprehensive smoke-free legislation. The Prime Minister, Chancellor, Health Secretary, Public Health Minister and many other members of the Government voted for the Select Committee's position and in effect against their own original proposals. Subsequently the Bill passed through its parliamentary process without substantive amendment to become the Health Act, which came into force in July 2007.

Compliance rates for this almost entirely self-enforced legislation have been near 100% from the day the laws came into force. Compare this with the 30mph speed limit introduced over 80 years ago, which is broken by nearly 60% of drivers. It's hard to prove causality, but it is my belief that this is because of the widespread public debate which not only informed opinion but also changed behaviour. This view is supported by evidence of a decline in exposure to secondhand smoke in children in England living in homes where their parents smoked (as measured objectively by continine levels by the Health Survey for England) during the years of the campaign for smoke-free legislation. Exposure fell significantly from 2003 onwards, and most rapidly between 2005 and 2006, which was the most intense period of public and political debate on the issue. Clearly smoking parents were recognising that if it is harmful to smoke in front of your work colleagues, then it is just as harmful to smoke in front of your children, and so were choosing not to do so. The regulations were popular from the start and their popularity has continued to grow since they were implemented, even more so amongst smokers than amongst non-smokers – a good example of behaviour changing attitude, rather than vice versa. Overall support for the laws rose from two thirds at the end of 2005 to eight out of ten by 2009.

The smoke-free laws have led to significant improvements in public health, not just of bar workers but also of the general public. Evidence published in the British Medical Journal shows that in the first year after the implementation of smoke-free legislation there was a statistically significant drop in the number of emergency admissions for heart attacks, resulting in 10,000 fewer bed days for emergency admissions, which saved the NHS £8.4 million.

The lesson of the smoke-free laws has been taken by the public, who don't think that government action to prevent young people taking up smoking and to help smokers quit is unacceptable 'nanny stateism'. In fact the level of support for government action continues to grow. ASH carries out a large poll of public opinion (around 12,000 adults) every spring. Since 2011 the proportion who think the Government is doing too much to limit smoking has declined significantly from nearly one in five to only around one in ten, while the proportion who think the Government needs to do more has risen by more than ten percentage points to over 40% (the majority of the rest – around a third of the total – think government action is about right).

Indeed there is significant public support for smoke-free laws to go further. Our most recent poll found that that 77% of adults, including 64% of smokers, agreed that smoking should be prohibited in cars that are carrying children younger than 18 years of age. Regulations were passed by Parliament in February 2015 and will come into effect in October 2015. This at a time when Parliament as a whole is significantly more opposed to regulation in principle: indeed the Government has a process in place to reduce regulation called the 'red tape challenge'.

Action to reduce smoking prevalence has become widely accepted across the political spectrum as an essential role for government. This is the enduring legacy of the battle for smoke-free legislation and its aftermath. It was a battle that was won in part because we recognised that population behaviour change often requires political behaviour change, and that this needs to be guided by a model of the political system. Even a simple model can provide an effective blueprint for action.

Suggested further reading

For works cited, see References at the end of the book.

Arnott, D., Dockrell, M. Sandford, A. and Willmore, I. (2007) 'Comprehensive smoke-free legislation in England: how advocacy won the day', *Tobacco Control*, 16(6), pp. 423-428, doi: 10.1136/tc.2007.020255.

This provides more of the background to the strategy used by the Smokefree Action Coalition in campaigning for comprehensive smoke-free laws in England.

Mullin, C. (2010) *A View From The Foothills. 1999-2005*. London: Profile.

The diary of Mullin's time as a junior Minister provides a good insight into how government really works. The author is brutally honest, about himself as much as, if not more than, everyone else. His account is useful to anyone trying to influence politicians, with the benefit of also being extremely entertaining. It was David Cameron's book of the year.

19. Modelling as a process of describing and creating change

Rob Farrands

Director, Figure Ground Consulting

Reflecting on experiences as a consultant intervening in interdisciplinary contexts raises questions about the roles played by models – including models of behaviour. On the one hand, models may be the focus of collective and individual commitments, confidently projected out into the world. On the other hand, models may be the very things that open us up to the situational possibilities of otherness and difference.

> *Some of the most interesting stuff happens when we talk across disciplines like this.*
>
> Evie in §1 of the Dialogue

Evie's contribution reminded me of a view on change that has arisen from my experience and shaped my practice, including my approach to models. My practitioner viewpoint can be expressed in two parts:

1. A noticeable feature of practically all change is that it brings together people with different *perspectives*. This feature is exaggerated when those people belong to different groups who have developed models of change to which they are all committed – for example, different disciplines.
2. For there to be a successful interdisciplinary engagement in a change project, those committed to different models need eventually to find, through immersion in the actual *situation*, sufficient common ground to act in concert. In other words rigorous application of a particular model fades under the necessities imposed by the situation.

In short Evie's comment amplified for me a common tension or ambiguity in all change practice: the change agent brings to bear a perspective that tends to construct the situation in a particular way and this meets and engages with the facts of the situation, which may be seen differently by others.

The immediate impact of reading Evie's comment was to transport me right back to my first published article on consulting, when I wrote a description of my experiences of consulting to an interdisciplinary team working on a strategy project. I was led back to that first article and what it had to say about the way a mixed group of geologists, commercial analysts and engineers approached change. That process of reflection then carried me on to think about how I myself developed a consulting model out of that experience, and more generally to how models about change shape the behaviour of consultants, as well as their clients, who are the more obvious subject of the models. In re-engaging with the original case I came to realise just how significant it had been for the subsequent development of my way of consulting and for the lines of inquiry within which it sits. I started to write notes on how things had developed as a consequence of the case, using it as a kind of reflective structure....

What follows is a very personal reflection. It seems to me, though, that if we're serious about interdisciplinarity – if we want to approach conversations about behaviour, change and models with, as Paola puts it, 'an open mind, ready to listen and to be challenged' – then personal reflection on our own models and our investments in them may be a critical step. This essay captures the main points relating to models that arose from my reflection on the old case.

The Brent case

Let's start where I started, with the subject of my first published article. The following account is closely based on that article (Farrands, 2001), which was in turn based on notes made at the time.

I had been assigned to work with a strategy team, looking at how to approach the exhaustion of oil production in the Brent field in the North Sea. My brief was rather vaguely cast as being to support the integration of the technically specialised work being undertaken on subsurface, infrastructure and commercial options. We were assigned to a disused corporate office block awaiting refurbishment in the harbour area of Aberdeen. The team imported computers, each linked to specialised databases – geological, surface engineering, commercial, and so forth. Most apparent, as the team started to work, was their relative isolation from each other. They did not know each other, and their main preoccupation was in exploring discrete technical problems associated with their own specialist models. They had each taken separate offices into which they disappeared to work on the ideas arising from their models – for example the geology team was working on the idea of using the subsea Brent basin for gas storage.

As I spoke with the project team, I noticed that they all recognised the need for an integrated report, but that they had given no serious shared consideration to how this would be achieved. My own feelings were bewildering ones: I felt isolated, and uncertain about how to relate to the team as a whole. I took these feelings as being in some way a reflection of the general situation, and I looked around for what I might do with them.

The building was being renovated, so all the coffee machines had been moved out of our area. However we did have an empty kitchen – together with coffeemaking equipment. I ordered coffee from the building supervisor, and on my way to work the following morning bought milk and bread. Armed with these supplies, I set up the kitchen. This was a large, well-lit room with a stunning view of the comings and goings of the oil supply ships in the old harbour. When I filled the kitchen with the smell of fresh coffee and fresh bread it was not difficult to cajole the team away from their computers to come and eat and drink together.

My milk and bread-buying became a tradition within the team. It became generative of our shared life. We went on to arrange dinners with sponsors and lunchtime visits to harbourside pubs. I was always insistent that these informal gatherings would be places where, among other things, we would talk about what we were doing – so they did not become an escape from what we were collectively engaged in, but were an intrinsic part of the collective enterprise.

I was frankly overwhelmed by my situation, and lacked the confidence to do what I would most probably do now, which is to directly address the dislocated working arrangements, or directly critique the interdisciplinary group's apparent belief that integration could be left to a final stage of writing up the report. Instead I sought to provide the team with *an experience of being together* that was likely to be attractive to them. My own feelings of uncertainty were mobilised to support an unusual approach. Over the six weeks of this assignment, 'I developed a consulting approach that built on my initial intuitive jump into being a kitchen host' (Farrands, 2001). Broadly speaking, this addressed the possibilities for integration as an ongoing process. I sought to build on their shared commitment to a single unified report by addressing their underdeveloped idea of how this would happen. My kitchen experiment developed into a consulting approach where I was 'simultaneously building internal coherence within the team while also developing the team's connection to the broader world' by using the common theme of taking meals together – and inviting as guests various corporate stakeholders relevant to the project. Within this frame I occasionally fitted in pieces of more direct process consulting in support of their team meetings, and, in the second half of the assignment, I wrote up brief summaries of our shared progress, which eventually provided the basis of the written report. These consulting activities were supported from the background by my hosting role. As if picking up on the symbolism, the indirectness and the affect I had been experimenting with on the six week assignment, a couple of days after returning home a bunch of flowers arrived for my wife along with the message: 'Thanks for the loan of your husband'.

Models, commitments and communities

What lessons can be learned from experiences like these? The first point I'd like to draw attention to is the way in which a model can be the focus of a set of communal commitments that holds a profession or discipline together.

The team members in my example were committed to largely incommensurable models of the same place. The subsurface geologists, the economists and the surface engineers dealing with the architecture of pipes and platforms were speaking a different language.

Nor was their commitment a trivial matter. They belonged to discrete communities, each of which was characterised by mutual commitments around specific ways in which to describe the Brent field and identify what was problematic about the current state of the field, and around specific methods to use in exploring possible changes that would be highly consequential for the people dependent on the field for their livelihood. These communally endorsed commitments to ways of seeing, and methods of dealing with, the field had become part of the very identity of the engineers, analysts and geologists working together on the project.

The commitment to a communally endorsed model had a clear pay-off: the ability to see the resemblance between apparently disparate situations – the similar in the dissimilar – which enabled the current problem to be grasped quickly and acted upon. Furthermore, this kind of perception of similarity opened up a whole disciplined set of behavioural responses, also communally endorsed, that could be applied with increasing levels of confidence and competence in varieties of situations.[10]

These models were already *in situ* driving the behaviour of the participants when the consultant charged with 'supporting integration' arrived on the scene. What was unusual in this case was that the models were so explicit, partly because they obviously contrasted with each other. If I had been working with geologists alone, by contrast, awareness of the geological model and its implications might not have been so obvious. This is the situation that normally pertains when a consultant works inside an institution such as a bank or a hospital. Prevailing models are carried implicitly and more or less taken for granted. It takes some experience, some immersion in the situation, for the consultant to see clearly, for example, how deeply the employees of a bank live inside a model of extrinsic (usually financial) motivation as a key aspect of any behavioural strategy.

Models in this sense are not just tools which a consultant such as myself can use to bring about changes in behaviour. They also provide a language for describing and understanding pre-existing communal commitments in the starting situation – for example, those associated with professions, disciplines or organisations. Models express shared perspectives on a situation. A key task for the

---

[10] 'Communities of commitment' is a phrase borrowed from Kuhn (1962/2012). There is a strong family connection between Kuhn's concept of a 'paradigm' and the more generic use made of 'model' and 'perspective': they all describe the subjective place from which the objective world is regarded and made intelligible. Each is likely to be strongly held and to form part of one's identity and sense of self.

consultant is to illuminate and express these pre-existing models – to describe what is already present, beneath the surface. Once expressed, such models will often appear, with hindsight, obvious. Often, however they are *not* obvious to the people still held under their spell.

Models and the paradox of change

Models express a perspective that may fundamentally shape how the change situation is perceived and acted upon. Paradoxically, however, a model may also open practitioners up to the situation, so that it is welcomed and found a home. In other words the model leads the practitioner on to an increasing immersion in the situation. For the practitioner in action, then, a model is ambiguous: is it creating the situation or describing the situation? It's not an ambiguity that ever disappears completely in any formal or global sense: the situation never transcends one's perspective and never completely accords with it either. The model does, however, help initiate a dialectic in which increasing immersion refines one's expressed perspective and leads on to further immersion. The result is a series of practical moves that gradually shift the situation until it is sufficiently resolved to satisfy the client.

To illustrate what I mean, I'd like to briefly describe a case in which a colleague created a model out of immersion in a client's situation and expressed it to found a further piece of work. Here modelling sustains a certain kind of situational continuity.[11] I was working with a co-consultant, Mike Bligh, on a Joint (Anglo/Italian) Venture in Eastern Kazakhstan. Mike and I had previously listened to many stories about the dangerous gas releases that had been the

---

[11] The case is unpublished to date. This account is drawn from the notes in my daybook.

subject of a previous assignment on the field, while working alongside Dupont, the strategic safety consultancy (the field was one of the most highly pressurised and toxic in the world). Like the geologists and economists in the North Sea, the underlying models in play, in particular models of containment, related, not to human behaviour, but to the behaviour of complex physical systems. Mike, however, found a way to use these safety specific experiences and models as we prepared to support the joint venture (JV) senior management team.

We had already noticed that British and Italian managers were closely attached to their home organisations, and were speculating on how this might diminish commitment to the Khazak JV. Mike playfully started mimicking the engineers' language around the forces at work in the field. He proposed a lack of centripetal force. As a result, he proposed, there was a failure of loyalty to the JV. Opposing centrifugal forces were forcing people back to their home offices. The model of containment that had been so explicit in relation to the safety of the field was translated from a concrete model of physical systems into a metaphor for a human, indeterminate situation. We explored this metaphor together and then continued to explore it with the senior team. We made the metaphoric content explicit by proposing a direct comparison between the human and geological systems. We asked if the human system was under similar stresses as the field itself. We asked them to consider how a human system might 'lack containment'. Humour helped defray the politics of loyalty.

The metaphor showed our understanding of the situation by problematising it in a way that had an immediate appeal to the management team of engineers, but also opened our frame up to enquiry. The metaphor completed its journey into being another model – a model of human behaviour now – when we proposed a Lewinian force field analysis (see

Weisbord, 1991) which generated a number of activities to increase the 'centripetal' and/or diminish the 'centrifugal' forces at work in the management of the field.

The reflexive turn

Consultants like Mike and myself are also committed to a definite perspective. We are no more able than our clients to act without acting from a particular point of view. We bring our own communal commitments and metaphors to bear on the situation. We see the similar in the dissimilar, and by doing so open up a disciplined set of behavioural responses, also endorsed by the community of our profession or discipline. In short, we have a model of consulting, which can either hold us under its spell or be explicitly articulated and examined.

For example we might propose that the two cases demonstrate a model of consulting based on immersion and expression. One could flesh out the proposed model by articulating the words and action that support immersion in the client system and the expression of that system. Indeed, this kind of explicit articulation of one's consulting model might form part of a reflection on the consulting approach and underlying beliefs. This would not necessarily take place at a distance, but could take place in the midst of action, as the consultant articulated his/her model as a way of making sense of his/her moment to moment action. Something of this reflective model-articulation is taking place in the Brent case where I engaged with feelings of disconnection and bewilderment to create a model of consultancy based on immersing in the situation and expressing this immersion in action.

We can take this process of reflection further. So far, my discussion of models has emphasised their projective power in the enactment of established theories and concepts in a new situation. Projection is a form of dominating the new situation. It is very agentic, emphasising the skill and knowledge of the human actors, and the way they create the models that enable understanding and action. The examples I've presented, however, indicate that something else is happening that moderates this emphasis on human agency. The account of the Brent case, for example, is full of perceptual detail such as the view over the harbour, the smells from the kitchen and the feelings (such as bewilderment) of the consultant. In the Kazakh case, feelings in the form of playfulness, humour and loyalty are also a significant part of the description in my notes. The human actors have much less control over these perceptions and the feelings associated with them. To be bewildered, for example, is to be touched and moved by a situation rather than to adopt a deliberate stance. It is the exact opposite of a form of agency – more like a dispossession of the self's perspective by the impact of the situation which floods in through the portal opened by the model.

A model projects sense onto an indeterminate situation, but in doing so it also opens up a doorway into the situation through which rush perceptions and feelings that create moods, atmospheres and felt states that are highly consequential for how people behave.

However, what I now notice when I look back on my accounts of these consulting engagements, written at the time or shortly afterwards, is the extent to which these systemic aspects of openness and passivity are clouded (especially in the Brent account) by the consultant narrator's narcissism. The accounts portray all perceptual sensitivity and intelligence as a capacity of the consultant, while the clients are portrayed as projective controllers of the situation. In fact perceptual sensitivity has as much if not more to do with the consultant's passivity than his agency. As just explained he and every other actor is being shaped by the situation whether they are aware of it or not.

The paradoxes of passivity in agency are representative of a larger paradox at the heart of all *experience* of the world, which is that we are both strongly committed to a first-person perspective and also open to the disturbance of our perspective by the situations in which we come to work. It is a mystery how we can be both projectively confident and simultaneously undone, attached so strongly that we are enveloped in the models we create and simultaneously liable to be taken by the unfolding situation.

I can't help wondering if those same paradoxes lie at the heart of the project of interdisciplinarity. The communal commitments which disciplines so confidently project into the world at the same time open up those disciplines to disturbance and change. There is practical sense in sustaining a communal commitment and also in holding it lightly enough to be able to contact the indeterminacy and contingency in the situations one is seeking to help resolve

It may be that a model does its work by satisfying our need to project meaning onto situations as a way of reassuring us that we know what is going on, while in the background the model does its real work, which is to open us up to the possibility of difference and otherness from which a new future has to emerge. After all, the projection of what we have already validated is likely only to reproduce what we already know.[12]

---

[12] In this respect, a model resembles T.S. Eliot's (1993) description of a poem: 'The chief use of the 'meaning' of a poem, in the ordinary sense, may be to satisfy one habit of the reader, to keep his mind diverted and quiet, while the poem does its work upon him: much as the imaginary burglar is always provided with a bit of nice meat for the house-dog'.

Suggested further reading

For works cited, see References at the end of the book.

Flyvbjerg, B. (2001) Making Social Science Matter: Why social inquiry fails and how it can succeed again. Cambridge: Cambridge University Press.

The idea that a model is a door that swings both ways onto a situation can be seen as another attempt to contextualise social inquiries and defray the tendency to accept without challenge the idea that individually or socially we construct our realities. This work provides a fuller discussion of these themes: especially Chapter Two, which represents the work of Hubert and Stuart Dreyfus.

20. Behave yourself: why behavioural modelling needs subjective disclosure

Jonathan Rowson

Director, The Social Brain Centre, RSA

Does the personal biography and subjective experience of those working on behaviour change have any place in a scientific understanding of behaviour? Once we recognise the reflexivity of behaviour – the fact that humans do things differently as a result of knowing why they are doing them or being asked to do them – then we may conclude that they not only have a place, but that we cannot do without them.

On 19 July 2011 *Guardian Comment is Free* published my response to Baroness Neuberger's House of Lords Commission report on behavioural insight in public policy (Rowson, 2011a). The headlines the previous day proclaimed that 'nudge is not enough', but the real story was of peers pulling their punches. The report was keen to imply, but curiously unwilling to say, that Science, the presumed foundation of behavioural insight, doesn't provide a legitimate case for shrinking the State. It felt exciting to be at the forefront of public debate, but there were no paparazzi following me home that evening. Instead, when I scrolled through the assembled comments, I found some pungent counsel from *CorneliusLysergic* posted at 3:20pm: 'Fuck off with your change our behaviour shit. Just fuck off'.

I enjoyed reading the relatively cordial dialogue between 'Evie', 'Yusuf' and 'Paola', and admire both the creative construction and the clarity and tenacity of the inquiry. There are many ways to respond, but I have built my reaction around a gently subversive question: who are these people?

The difficulty Evie and Co. have in pinning down a science of behaviour change is familiar, but what I found particularly intriguing is that by virtue of not being real people there were certain things they couldn't do to attempt to resolve the inevitably thorny philosophical and methodological issues that arose. Sustained explorations of difficult subjects inevitably reach a point where we have to put down our shared tools in the conversational commons and go hunting for fresh resources in the landscapes of our own experience. Yusuf and Co. have no such hinterland, no singular perspective to bring to bear beyond the marionette vernacular of their stated opinion, and I think that matters for anybody who cares about the direction of behaviour change research. 'Hinterland' is a useful concept here because it points to the breadth and depth of knowledge that has value by virtue of being formally outside of scope and beyond the issue in focus. Our hinterlands give us knowledge grounded in distinctive personal experience rather than the relatively permissible arcana of impartial expertise.

Look at where the conversation ended up. Our felt sense of what it is to be human and our implicit conceptions of behaviour, science, evidence and ethics are invariably implicated in whatever position we hold on behaviour change models. What is less obvious is that the provenance of such personal opinions are both biographic and epistemic in nature. By that I mean we have access to forms of knowing and evaluating and justifying from our own lives that we cannot afford to do without, but which we tend to disavow or neglect. We speak of such content as being 'anecdotal', as if anecdotes didn't shape and direct understanding; 'subjective', as if perspective and context wasn't of primary importance; and 'personal', as if there is anything else that is meaningfully universal.

So here's what I want to explore: what if those implicit perspectives on behaviour that stem from such 'epistemic hinterlands' – perspectives on knowledge that arise from formative aspects of subjective experience – turn out to be the *sine qua non* of good behaviour change research? What if the recurring challenges relating to research legitimacy, predictive and explanatory power, and model building, stem from coming too directly and too quickly at behaviour change as an applied tool, neglecting to stop to think what it means *to us*, and why?

I develop this argument below; but, in the interests of consistency, let me first apply my own conclusions and reflect on how I came to this view.

A personal account of epistemic hinterlands

I am currently the Director of 'The Social Brain Centre' at the RSA (Royal Society for the encouragement of Arts, Manufactures and Commerce) in London. We're a small semi-autonomous unit of researchers focusing on the ways in which implicit understandings of human nature shape theories of change and impact in policy and practice. We are nested within a larger organisation that is part global ideas platform, part membership organisation and part policy research institute. I have been working on the theory and practice of behaviour change with public, private and third sectors organisations at this curious nexus of academia, media, practice and policy for about five and a half years.

Neither 'behaviour', nor 'change', nor 'behaviour change' can withstand a canonical definition because they are too porous and contested, so to make sense of this work I had to find my own felt sense of these terms (Rowson, 2011b). Relevant influences on my view of behaviour change, some of which I unpack below, include the physiological know-how involved in being a type-one diabetic since I was six; the exacting cognitive, emotional and volitional process of becoming a chess Grandmaster; searching for an academic home and not finding one; and the spiritual conviction that people can not only change their behaviour, but also their practices, their values, their sense of themselves, and thereby in some ethically meaningful sense transform for the better.

The confluence of these biographical influences explains why I have never *wanted* to disentangle the empirical matter of what we do from the philosophical question of what we are, and the ethical question of what we should be (Rowson, 2013a).

Chess

Chess was my main vehicle of identity formation and development. I can see now that I used chess as a way to signal I was bigger than the perceived constraints of diabetes, and more profoundly as a daily escape from adolescent growing pains, parental separation and the harrowing incursions of family mental illness. The collateral benefit of having chess as a coping mechanism was a deep love for the beauty of ideas, the experience of learning from mistakes, and a felt sense for what it means to grow rather than merely change.

In the second decade of my life, by regularly analysing my games, I spent thousands of hours forensically examining how thoughts and emotions arose automatically and how they shaped decisions and results. Being good at chess, I now realise, is about being an instinctive choice architect, rapidly deciding what needs to be known to choose the next move, and framing complex problems for opponents in ways that maximise the probability of mistakes.

I became a Grandmaster, competed and trained with World Champions, and won the British Championship in three successive years (2004-6). Two of the books I wrote drew on sports psychology and cognitive science to make sense of the curiously difficult challenge of post-plateau improvement in adulthood (Rowson, 2001; Rowson, 2005). Through playing, teaching and writing about chess I became fascinated by the challenge of supplanting bad habits with good ones, and came to view this habituation challenge as a microcosm of the human desire to feel free.

I didn't view it as such then, but in Kahneman's terms my chess career was characterised by putting 'system 2' (the effortful, conscious system) to work on 'system 1' (the fast, automatic system) often enough to know that system 2 was the most important, even if system 1 was more powerful; just as in chess the queen is much more powerful than the king, but the king ultimately matters more. This precious space of inquiry and adjustment, where the part of us that is intentional kindly attends to and gently adjusts the part of us that is habituated, is our wellspring of vitality – our way of staying awake to ourselves. I came to see this encounter of conscious and automatic systems as a deeply valuable middle way, superior in a moral sense to abject surrender to the automatic system or hubristic underestimation of its defining role in our lives.

Wisdom

Chess was always plan B, but there was no plan A, and without any particular sense of direction I enjoyed eight years of intense but unconsummated flirting with a range of academic disciplines and university tribes. Politics, Philosophy and Economics at Oxford became Mind, Brain and Education at Harvard, which led to some research methods training and then a PhD thesis at Bristol under the supervision of Psychologist Professor Guy Claxton in what was substantively a mixture of philosophy and psychology, but was technically 'Education'.

And it was an education, in the literal sense of 'drawing out'. I began my PhD with an abstract and analytical mode of inquiry formed in chess tournaments, Oxford tutorials and Harvard seminars; trained to get to the point and make it as sharp as possible. Whenever I attended research classes and seminars at Bristol I was therefore dumbstruck by the extent to which my cohort – mostly comprising female teachers and therapists – answered academic questions very differently, by sharing stories from their own experiences and practices. I was at first highly uncomfortable and even a little embarrassed by this form of inquiry, but now feel deeply grateful for having had the chance to experience its legitimacy.

My planned methodology was a post-positivist experimental design on the precursors of wisdom in adolescence ('proto-sagacity') and how they would measurably change following classroom interventions. ESRC gave this research plan a score of 90/100 when awarding funding, but at this point I had given little thought to what wisdom meant to me. The more my cohort asked me simple questions like – Why wisdom? Why now? Why you? – the more my sanitised, pseudo-objective approach began to feel hubristic and inauthentic. Something is very wrong here, I thought. In an effort to appear like a serious researcher I was running away from myself.

My doctorate came into shape as a sustained reflection on the process of trying to make sense of what it might mean to become 'wiser', which involved looking at the automatic system from an ethical rather than competitive vantage point (as I had with chess). That process involved some conceptual analysis of definitions, critiquing the meta-theories and methodologies of a range of psychometric models of wisdom and trying to make sense – partly through my own meditation efforts – of what exactly is supposed to transform through spiritual practice. I also created a data stimulation method based on selected vignettes, to tease out some of the features of wise action. The shortest and sweetest illustration is the story of Mahatma Gandhi boarding a train that had just started to pick up speed. One of his sandals fell off in the process, and he instinctively removed the other one and threw it down, so that somebody else would have a pair to wear. That's the kind of behaviour that makes me want to change (Rowson, 2008).

Social Brain

By the time the thesis drew to a close I was an expectant father, and had grown weary of squeezing meaning out of 64 squares, so I started looking for a soft landing in the real world. I joined the RSA as a Senior Researcher in their 'Connected Communities' programme, funded by the Department of Communities and Local Government (Rowson et al., 2010). This work on how social norms spread through social networks in deprived communities made a deep impression, and sat alongside the time-bound Social Brain project, which I took over within a year, after a range of staff changes. After expanding the range of our activity and raising some money I became Director of the Social Brain *Centre*; the change of title signalled an indefinite commitment to the RSA's work on behaviour change.

The elision between brain and behaviour is the kind of casual ontological slippage that complicates the academic/policy interface; but the bigger issue was that my default settings on behaviour change were at odds with the prevailing mood of the time, suffused as it was with *Nudge*, *MindSpace*, and the birth of the Behavioural Insights Team. I felt excited because rethinking human nature was now mainstream, but I watched in disbelief at the speed at which the potentially broad, deep, multi-faceted and interdisciplinary terrain of behaviour change was quickly framed (yes, really) as applied behavioural economics. There are many broader perspectives of course, but in my professional orbit it took only about three years, from roughly 2009-12, for an impressive but relatively limited and limiting intellectual hegemony to emerge.

Nobody ever decreed that all behaviour change is applied behavioural economics, nor did they argue that human nature is merely that which is revealed through experiments about decisions, but in practice it felt like a *fait accompli*. As the rich and multifaceted ontology of *behaviour* was tacitly equated with the relatively hollow epistemology of decision theory within *economics*, 'behaviour change' became technocratic, apolitical, utilitarian and psychometric. It felt like the prevailing view of behaviour was such that it captivated us intellectually without challenging us ethically or spiritually, which I found vexing, and actually quite annoying.

Partly as a reaction to this misplaced hegemony, I found myself interpreting 'behaviour' very broadly indeed. The Social Brain team has worked on the cultural constraints on how police reflect on their decisions (Rowson and Lindley, 2011), fuel-efficient taxi driving (Rowson and Young, 2011), psychological foundations of The Big Society (Rowson et al., 2012), social marketing to reduce child abuse, the experience of risk and trust in informal care relationships, and relatively 'conventional' forms of behavioural insight to improve financial capability and reduce the attainment gap in education (Spencer et al., 2014). Most recently we examined the limitations of behaviour change in the context of climate change (Rowson and Corner, 2015), and took a deep dive into 'spirituality' as the foundation of transformative behaviour change (Rowson, 2014).

Reflexivity highlights why the personal is political

If there is a pattern that connects this work, it's the conviction that reflexivity – circular relationships between causes and effects in thinking agents and most complex social systems – cuts in a deep and distinctive way when it comes to the idea of directing and measuring behaviour change.

The point is that humans do things differently as a result of *knowing* why they are doing them or being asked to do them – sometimes as a form of defiance, but mostly as a form of creative and generative intelligence. Our descriptive and explanatory accounts of how and why people behave as they do become part of the very thing they purport to describe and explain. Our models sit midway between what we believe to be the case and what we think we *should* believe. It is not anti-scientific to be normative when your subject matter oozes normativity in this way.

How we talk about, model and measure behaviour can either emphasise this point as central, or downplay it as peripheral. I see it as central. Reflexivity, I believe, is a feature rather than a bug in human behaviour, which is therefore only ever partially predictable in principle. The ill-fitting, multiply-influenced, volatile, situational and porous nature of human behaviour will always elude or subsume the best models designed to capture it. You might even say we are at our most human when we do not *behave*.

This point is not about gratuitous subversion, and it's of huge societal importance in 2015. Collectively, we are just waking up to the power and ubiquity of defaults, salience, comparative judgments, loss aversion and so forth, many of which have shaped our lives for good or ill for many years, and not all of which are belief-independent i.e. knowing more about their effects on us will change how we respond to them.

The extent to which you face up to the inherent waywardness of reflexivity is an open choice for researchers, and one that matters politically. Although the idea of a new generation of 'behavioural natives' is not unimaginable, it is hard to see the majority of us becoming, for instance, immune to advertisements by detecting their underlying principles, or creating our own technological defaults as second nature. Still, we should be open to the possibility that behavioural models could be more democratic in spirit, and reflect on what behaviour change of the people, for the people, by the people might look and feel like.

Reflexivity alone won't get us there, but it does highlight a form of freedom that is different in substance and spirit from the top-down model of a libertarian paternalist who conventionally seeks to maximise choice and direct it. Instead reflexivity points towards a more lateral model of influence in which informed mentors – not least behaviour change researchers – advise on the general principles that underlie choice and behaviour so that they can be refashioned for purposes that are as autonomous as possible.

At present, this shift of emphasis sounds abstract and utopian, but isn't it closer to how we might want behaviour change to manifest socially and politically? Accepting reflexivity as a central feature of human behaviour makes a more reflexive approach to *research* productive and legitimate. For instance, if you want to measure the impact of mindfulness meditation on stress reduction, you can measure cortisol levels in those who meditate, but your explanatory account will be deficient unless you learn to meditate yourself.

If you are just tweaking contextual inputs to shape discrete actions (here I'm thinking of those witty spillage saving urinal flies in Schipol airport) you can get away with a dispassionate third person ('he', 'she', 'it') account, but that's the easy stuff. If the behaviour you are looking to change is less discrete and more deeply connected to broader cultural, social, economic and political factors the behaviour will generally be experienced and enacted in the first ('I, we') and second ('you') person, in ways that need to be understood for an intervention to be worthwhile.

For instance, some personal behaviours appear to be obvious environmental gains and can be measured as such if the model starts and ends with a target behaviour alone, but with a bit more empathy, imagination and political honesty, such outcomes are often pyrrhic victories. To give a specific example, some apparently positive behaviour changes may actually *increase* national carbon emissions when factors like moral licensing (e.g. 'I fly every week but drive very little') single action bias ('I know I need to do my bit for the environment – so I recycle'), consumption-based emissions ('most of the products in my home were imported from China but their embodied carbon don't effect national emissions targets') and systemic forms of rebound ('I saved £100 on my heating bill, so I'm getting a cheap flight to Spain') are factored in (Rowson, 2013b).

In such complex cases, understanding the particularity of the people and context being studied involves (perhaps even demands) introspective, associative and empathetic forms of inquiry, not a third ('he/she/it') person account of apparent stimulus-response relationships, however sophisticated they might be. We need to know not only what people are doing, but why they are doing it, why they think they are doing it, and how those perspectives are shaped by socio-economic and cultural factors. Only that tangled interplay of influences will begin to make sense of what might follow from an intervention. Reflecting on that goal, how can we authentically and authoritatively make sense of what is called for unless we involve ourselves more fully in the inquiry?

To conclude, the biography and interiority of people working on behaviour change has methodological legitimacy and epistemic warrant, and we should give it greater salience. I believe both behaviour and research about behaviour are best conceived as fundamentally reflexive processes, and that doing so will ultimately help the empirical and theoretical fields of behaviour change converge in the complex cases we care about. Understanding behaviour requires psychological insight, yes, but it also requires skilful introspection, cognitive and emotional empathy and political awareness – factors that are shaped by our lives as a whole. As long as we remain strangers to our epistemic hinterlands, we don't really know what we are trying to do.

Suggested further reading

For works cited, see References at the end of the book.

Soros, G. (2011) The Soros Lectures: At the Central European University. New York: Public Affairs.

In these lectures, particularly the first chapter, 'The Human Uncertainty Principle', Soros reflects on the nature and importance of the idea of reflexivity, which has been central to his philanthropic decisions and his enormous financial success.

Analysis (2013) BBC Radio 4, 18 Nov. Available at: http://sbk.li/1203211

The political philosopher Roberto Unger is interviewed about what it means to be 'a progressive' at LSE and unpacks his notion of reorganising society so that more people can live what he calls 'a larger life' in which they 'die only once'. Proactive human agency is central to this vision, and I think it connects in interesting ways to the notion of behavioural reflexivity.

Kegan, R. and Lahey, L.L. (2009) Immunity to Change: how to overcome It and unlock the potential in yourself and your organization. Boston, MA: Harvard Business School Press.

Kegan's earlier books developed a neo-Piagetian theory of the development of 'mental complexity' across the lifespan, and this co-authored book puts the theory to work in a more targeted and applied way. The most relevant point here is that Kegan argues policymakers have 'an astonishingly naïve sense of how important a factor is the level of mental complexity' because the level of complexity will determine how people respond to any policy intervention. More generally, Kegan's work deserves to be more widely known in the behaviour change community because his perspective on behaviour is deeper and richer than most.

Rowson, J. (2013b) 'A New Agenda on Climate Change: Facing up to Stealth Denial and Winding Down on Fossil Fuels', RSA. Available at: http://sbk.li/1203221

This report was initially about behaviour change in the context of climate change, but a deeper examination of the climate challenge brought home to me the enormous limitations of behaviour change research that is not informed by political consciousness. The report expanded to include a broader picture of individual behaviour in the context of the global political economy.

21. Becoming a force of nature: a new direction for health promotion and disease prevention

Victor J. Strecher

Professor and Director of Innovation and Social Entrepreneurship, University of Michigan School of Public Health

Current models of health-related behaviour have fallen short in adequately addressing a root cause of our resistance to change: ego defensiveness. Recent scientific evidence from research on self-affirmation and purpose in life, combined with technological advances in biometric monitoring, the availability of 'big data', and predictive modelling support a new direction that follows the two great Greek imperatives: living in accordance with one's true self or purpose (Aristotle) and knowing thyself (Socrates).

Why are people so resistant to change? When I think about this question the metaphor of the boiling frog comes to mind: if you put a frog in boiling water it jumps right out, but if you put it in cool water and gradually turn up the heat the frog gets sleepy, rolls over, and boils to death. Most of our public health problems – such as sedentary behaviour, cigarette smoking, or climate change – are slow, incremental 'boiling-frog' problems.

To encourage the frog to jump, we might shout out: 'Frog, this water going to boil! Get out or you'll die!' How would the frog respond? Most likely, the frog would take a defensive posture: 'What do you know? Are you an expert on boiling water? This water isn't so hot. I know other frogs in much hotter water'.

The frog in this metaphor is the 'self' and his defensiveness is a function of the ego – a kind of barrier which protects the self, but which also prevents us from seeing reality. So how do we see ourselves in a more realistic way?

Purpose, energy and self-control

One way to see reality more clearly is to rise above – to transcend – our ego. We can do this by focusing our lives on *purposes that are bigger than ourselves*. Cigarette smokers who are asked to consider core purposeful values important to them also begin to think about love, compassion, and other ego-transcending concepts. As they transcend, they lose their defensiveness to the prospect of quitting smoking (see Crocker et al., 2008).

Recently, we studied the neural activity of 67 sedentary adults (Falk et al., 2015). While in a magnetic resonance imaging scanner (fMRI), half of the participants affirmed their purposeful values – values such as friends and family, independence, money, and religion. The other half did not affirm their purposeful values. Then, still in the scanner, participants received 50 health messages related to the importance of increasing their physical activity. Compared with a control condition, participants affirming their purposeful values had greater activation in a part of the brain related to the self (*transcending their walls?*) in response to the health messages. This activation, in turn, predicted significant increases in objectively monitored physical activity over the following month.

Two thousand years ago the ancient Stoic philosopher Seneca wrote: 'When a man does not know what harbour he is making for, no wind is the right wind'. A harbour, or purpose, in life is a meta-goal that engages focus and greater performance. Energy (or vitality) provides the 'wind in the sails' but even given a destination and wind in the sails, one also needs a rudder, or self-control, to direct behaviour toward the goal.

Which behaviours influence energy and self-control? Numerous studies have demonstrated that both are boosted by improvements in sleep, mindfulness, physical activity, and diet. Useful in themselves, these behaviours could enhance energy and self-control, thereby improving the chances of changing many other behaviours, including substance abuse, stress management, and self-care behaviours.

Constructing models or researching ourselves?

One could readily construct a model or approach to change involving purpose in life, ego transcendence, energy, self-control, and relevant health behaviours. It would be largely consistent with Self-Determination Theory, Acceptance and Commitment Therapy, and Motivational Interviewing, among other approaches. *But how do we actually get the frog to jump?*

I would like to see people become *better researchers of themselves*. It strikes me that many people pay attention to the factors causing their bad and good days. A low ebb morning (low energy and/or self-control) might be attributed to drinking too much alcohol the night before, failing to exercise, or a startling news event. The attributions of causality we make are a part of our nature, and are essential to survival. However, we don't typically notice the influence of multiple days of behaviour and their interactions with other behaviours (e.g. lack of physical activity yesterday combined with three nights of poor sleep) or with environmental and temporal factors (e.g. overeating combined with a snowy winter day after the local football team has lost).[13]

This is where biometric devices, mobile phones, the Web, big data, and advanced forecasting science become relevant. All the data in the examples above could be collected either briefly from the individual, or invisibly from a biometric device, from existing databases, or from social media. Combining these data, couldn't we provide people with the equivalent of a local weather report of their energy and their self-control? Wouldn't this be a more beneficial report of one's health and health behaviours than standard health risk assessments, which really haven't evolved a great deal since the 1970s?

---

[13] A study carried out in the US looking at the impact of the success or failure of a National Football League team on its community showed interesting results. If the team lost, their fans ate on average 9% more saturated fat the next day. But if the team won, fans were found to eat 13% *less* saturated fat (Cornil and Chandon, 2013).

Equipped with a better understanding of the behavioural and environmental influences of energy and self-control, we may also become interested in adjusting these influences. We may seek help from experts; or, as we often do, we may look to others like ourselves who have successfully changed *their own* behaviour. In the world of technology, this is called 'collaborative filtering'. Recommender systems, such as those used by Amazon or Netflix, employ collaborative filtering algorithms to identify others similar to you who have used a product that would be likely to appeal to you. We can, for example, identify others similar to ourselves who have improved their diet, and their strategies could be recommended to us. The tips that work best could receive high ratings, just as Yelp allows us to rate restaurants and other establishments, and become elevated in the recommender system.

From clod of ailments to force of nature

George Bernard Shaw once said that 'the true joy in life' is 'being used for a purpose recognised by yourself as a mighty one. Being a force of nature instead of a feverish, selfish little clod of ailments and grievances complaining that the world will not devote itself to making you happy'. Rather than health promotion and disease prevention interventions focusing on the lowering of risk for disease and death, what if we were to help ourselves become 'forces of nature' with self-transcending purpose?

I'm suggesting that we may be able to generate greater engagement in behaviour change activities if we help individuals – starting with ourselves – align daily living with an enhanced sense of purpose in life. It's not a new idea. Aristotle called this type of alignment 'eudaimonic well-being'.[14]

And it's not only the public that needs to change. We researchers and practitioners need to change how we think about what it means to be healthy. What it means to be human.

Like the frog in boiling water, it's time for all of us to jump.

---

[14] Recent research by Fredrickson et al. (2013) has found that, compared against individuals exhibiting 'hedonic well-being', those with eudaimonic well-being tend to have lower expression of damaging inflammatory genes.

References

Ajzen, I. (1985) 'From intentions to actions: A theory of planned behavior', in Kuhl, J. and Beckmann, J. (eds.) Action control: From cognition to behavior. New York: Springer-Verlag, pp. 11-39.

Ajzen, I. (1991) 'The Theory of Planned Behaviour', Organisational Behaviour and Decision Processes, 50, pp. 179-211.

Ajzen, I. (2011) 'Behavioral interventions: Design and evaluation guided by the theory of planned behavior', in Mark, M.M., Donaldson, S.I. and Campbell, B.C. (eds.). Social psychology for program and policy evaluation. New York: Guilford, pp. 74-100. Available at: http://sbk.li/1213291

Arenas, À., Cabrales, A., Danon, L., Díaz-Guilera, A., Guimerà, R. and Vega-Redondo, F. (2010) 'Optimal Information Transmission in Organizations: Search and Congestion', Review of Economic Design, 14, pp. 75-93.

Ayoub, C., O'Connor, E., Rappolt-Schlictmann, G., Vallotton, C., Raikes, H. and Chazan-Cohen, R. (2009) 'Cognitive skill performance among young children living in poverty: Risk, change, and the promotive effects of Early Head Start', Early Child Research Quarterly, 24(3), pp. 289-305.

Baddeley, M. (2013) 'Herding, social influence and expert opinion', Journal of Economic Methodology, 20(1), pp. 35-44.

Bailer-Jones, D.M. (2009) Scientific Models in Philosophy of Science. Pittsburgh: University of Pittsburgh Press.

Becker, G.S. (1976) The Economic Approach to Human Behavior. Chicago: Chicago University Press.

Bell, C., Johnston, D., Allan, J., Pollard, B. and Johnston, M. (in submission) 'What do Demand-Control and Effort-Reward work stress questionnaires measure? A Discriminant Content Validity study'.

Bettelheim, B. (2010) The Uses of Enchantment, New York: Vintage Books.

Bhat, C.R. and F.S. Koppelman (1999) 'Activity-Based Modelling of Travel Demand', in Handbook of Transportation Science, International Series in Operations Research and Management Science, 23, pp. 35-61.

Biran, A., Schmidt, W.-P., Varadharajan, S.K., Rajaraman, D., Kumar, R., Greenland, K., Gopalan, B. Aunger, R. and Curtis, V. (2014) 'Effect of a behaviour-change intervention on handwashing with soap in India (SuperAmma): a cluster-randomised trial', The Lancet Global Health, 2(3), pp. 145-54.

Blumer, H. (1969) Symbolic Interactionism: Perspective and Method. Engelwood Cliffs, NJ: Prentice Hall.

Bowlby, J. (1988) A secure base: Clinical applications of attachment theory, London: Routledge.

Cacioppo, J.T. and Cacioppo, S. (2013) 'Social Neuroscience', Perspectives on Psychological Science, 8, 667. Available at: http://sbk.li/1213301

Campbell, J. (2008) The Hero With A Thousand Faces. 3rd edn, Novato, CA: New World Library.

Caplin, A. and Schotter, A. (2008) The Foundations of Positive and Normative Economics. Oxford: Oxford University Press.

Cartwright, D. (ed.) (1952) Field theory in social science: Selected theoretical papers by Kurt Lewin. London: Tavistock.

Cassidy, J. (2013) 'The Reinhart and Rogoff controversy: a summing up', The New Yorker, 26 April. Available at: http://sbk.li/1213302

Chong, K. and Tuckett, D. (2014) 'Constructing Conviction through Action and Narrative: How Money Managers Manage Uncertainty and the Consequences for Financial Market Functioning', Socio-Economic Review, pp. 1-26.

Christoforou, E. Fernández Anta, A., Georgiou, C., Mosteiro, M. A. and Sánchez, A. (2013a) 'Crowd Computing as a Co-operation Problem: An Evolutionary Approach', Journal of Statistical Physics, 151, pp. 654-672.

Christoforou, E., Fernández Anta, A., Georgiou, C., Mosteiro, M. A. and Sánchez, A. (2013b) 'Reputation-based Mechanisms for Evolutionary Master-Worker Computing', In Proceedings of OPODIS 2013, Lecture Notes in Computer Science, 8304, pp. 98-113.

Collins, L.M., Murphy, S.A. and Strecher, V. (2007) 'The multiphase optimization strategy (MOST) and the sequential multiple assignment randomized trial (SMART): new methods for more potent eHealth interventions', American Journal of Preventive Medicine, 32(5), S112-S118.

Cornil Y. and Chandon P. (2013) 'From fan to fat? Vicarious losing increases unhealthy eating, but self-affirmation is an effective remedy', Psychological Science, 24(10), pp. 1936-1946.

Costandi, M. (2014) 'Your nose knows death is imminent', The Guardian, 1 October. Available at: http://sbk.li/1213311

Crocker J., Niiya Y. and Michkowski D. (2008) 'Why does writing about important values reduce defensiveness? Self-affirmation and the role of positive other-directed feelings', Psychological Science, 19(7), pp. 740-7.

Cronin, K. A. and Sánchez, A. (2012) 'Social dynamics and co-operation: the case of nonhuman primates and its implications for human behavior', Advances in Complex Systems, 15 (1), 1250066.

Csibra, G. and Gergely, G. (2006) 'Social learning and social cognition: The case for pedagogy' in Johnson, M.H. and Munakata, Y. (eds.) Processes of change in brain and cognitive development. Attention and Performance XXI. Oxford: Oxford University Press, pp. 249-74.

Csibra, G. and Gergely, G. (2009) 'Natural pedagogy', Trends in Cognitive Sciences, 13(4), pp. 148-153.

Csibra, G. and Gergely, G. (2011) 'Natural pedagogy as evolutionary adaptation', Philosophical Transactions of the Royal Society of London, Series B, Biological Sciences, 12(366) (1567) pp. 1149-57.

Damasio, A. (1994) Descartes' Error: Emotion, Reason and the Human Brain. New York: Putnam.

Damasio, A. (2010) Self Comes to Mind: Constructing the Conscious Brain. New York: Pantheon Books.

Darnton, A. and Evans, D. (2013) Influencing Behaviours: A Technical guide to the ISM Tool. The Scottish Government. Available at: http://sbk.li/1213312

Davidson, P, (1996) 'Reality and Economic Theory', Journal of Post-Keynesian Economics, 18(4), pp. 479-508.

Department of Health, and Department for Children, Schools and Families (2009) Teenage Pregnancy and Sexual Health Marketing Strategy. Available at: http://sbk.li/1213321

Department for Transport (2014a) 'TAG Unit M2: Variable Demand Modelling'. Available at: http://sbk.li/1213322

Department for Transport (2014b) 'Land Use/Transport Interaction Models'. Available at: http://sbk.li/1213323

Dolan, P., Hallsworth, M., Halpern, D., King, D. and Vlaev, I. (2010) 'MINDSPACE: Influencing Behaviour through Public Policy', Institute for Government and The Cabinet Office.

Doris, J.M. et al., (2010) The Moral Psychology Handbook. Oxford: Oxford University Press.

Elder-Vass, D. (2010) The Causal Power of Social Structures: Emergence, Structure and Agency, Cambridge: Cambridge University Press.

Eliot, T.S. (1993) The use of Poetry and the Use of Criticism. London: Faber.

Engel, G.L. (1960) A unified concept of health and disease, Perspectives in Biology and Medicine, 3, pp. 459-85.

Engel, G.L. (1981) 'The clinical application of the biopsychosocial model', The Journal of Medicine and Philosophy, 6, pp. 101-1.

Falk E.B., O'Donnell M.B., Cascio C.N., Tinney F., Kang Y., Lieberman M.D., Taylor S.E., An L., Resnicow K. and Strecher V.J. (2015) 'Self-affirmation alters the brain's response to health messages and subsequent behaviour change', Proceedings of the National Academy of Science, 112(7), pp.1977-1982.

Farrands, R. (2001) 'Sustaining Dynamic Tension When Consulting to Complex Systems', British Gestalt Journal, 10(1), pp. 4-12.

Fernald, L.C., Weber, A., Galasso, E. and Ratsifandrihamanana, L. (2011) 'Socioeconomic gradients and child development in a very low income population: Evidence from Madagascar', Developmental Science, 14(4), pp. 832-47.

Finkelstein, A. (2014) Theories and Models of Behaviour Change - part II. Available at: http://sbk.li/1213331

Fishbein, M. and Ajzen, I. (2010) Predicting and changing behavior: The Reasoned Action Approach. New York: Taylor & Francis.

Fonagy, P. and Allison, E. (2014) 'The role of mentalizing and epistemic trust in the therapeutic relationship', Psychotherapy, 51(3), pp. 372-380.

Fonagy, P., Gergely, G., Jurist, E. and Target, M. (2002) Affect regulation, mentalization, and the development of the self, New York: Other Press.

Fonagy, P., Gergely, G. and Target, M. (2007) 'The parent-infant dyad and the construction of the subjective self', Journal of Child Psychology and Psychiatry, 48(3-4), pp. 288-328.

Fonagy, P. and Luyten, P. (in press) 'A multilevel perspective on the development of borderline personality disorder', in Cicchetti, D. (ed.) Development and psychopathology (3rd edn). New York: Wiley.

Fonagy, P., Luyten, P. and Allison, E. (2014) Teaching to learn from experience: Epistemic mistrust at the heart of BPD and its psychosocial treatment, Manuscript in preparation.

Fonagy, P. and Target, M. (2006) 'The mentalization-focused approach to self pathology', Journal of Personality Disorders, 20(6), pp. 544-76.

Foucault, M. (1979) Discipline and punishment: The birth of the prison, Harmondsworth: Penguin.

Fox J. (2005) 'Images of Mind: In Memory of Donald Broadbent and Allen Newell', in Davis, D.N. (ed.) Visions of Mind: Architectures for Cognition and Affect. Hershey, PA: IDEA Group, pp. 125-48).

Fox J. (2014) 'A credo for decision science and engineering', submitted to Decision Support Systems.

Fox, J. and Das S. (2000) Safe and Sound: Artificial Intelligence in Hazardous Applications. Cambridge, MA: AAAI and MIT Press.

Fox J, Beveridge M. and Glasspool D. (2003) 'Understanding intelligent agents: analysis and synthesis', Artificial Intelligence Communications, 16(3).

Fox J, Cooper R. and Glasspool D. (2013) 'A canonical theory of dynamic decision-making', Frontiers in Psychology, 4, p. 150.

Fox, J., Glasspool, D., Patkar, V., Austin, M., Black, L., South, M., Robertson, D. and Vincent, C. (2010) 'Delivering Clinical Decision Support Services: There is Nothing so Practical as a Good Theory', Journal of biomedical informatics, 43(5), pp. 841-53.

Fredrickson B.L., Grewen K.M., Coffey K.A., Algoe S.B., Firestine A.M., Arevalo J.M., Ma J. and Cole S.W. (2013) 'A functional genomic perspective on human well-being', Proceedings of the National Academy of Science, 110(33), pp.13684-13689.

Friedman, M. (ed.) (1953) 'The methodology of positive economics', Essays in Positive Economics. Chicago: Chicago University Press, pp. 3-34.

Gawande, A. (2014) 'Why doctors fail: the future of medicine', The 2014 Reith Lectures, BBC.

Gergely, G. (2013) 'Ostensive communication and cultural learning: The natural pedagogy hypothesis', in Metcalfe, J. and Terrace, H.S. (eds.) Agency and Joint Attention. Oxford: Oxford University Press, pp. 139-151.

Gergely, G. and Watson, J.S. (1996) 'The social biofeedback theory of parental affect-mirroring: The development of emotional self-awareness and self-control in infancy', International Journal of Psycho-Analysis, 77 (Pt 6), pp. 1181-1212.

Giddens, A. (1974) Positivism and Sociology. London: Heinemann.

Giddens A. (1979) Central Problems in Social Theory: Action, Structure and Contradiction in Social Analysis. Berkeley: University of California Press.

Giddens A. (1982) Profiles and Critiques in Social Theory. London: Macmillan.

Gigerenzer, G. and Edwards, A. (2003) 'Simple tools for understanding risks: from innumeracy to insight', British Medical Journal, 327(7417), 741.

Goffman, E. (1969) The Presentation of Self in Everyday Life, Harmondsworth: Penguin Books.

Goodman, G.S., Quas, J. A. and Ogle, C.M. (2010) 'Child maltreatment and memory', Annual Review of Psychology, 61(1), pp. 325-51.

Green-Hennessy, S. and Reis, H.T. (1998) 'Openness in processing social information among attachment types', Personal Relationships, 5(4), pp. 449-66.

Green, J.D. and Campbell, W.K. (2000) 'Attachment and exploration in adults: Chronic and contextual accessibility', Personality and Social Psychology Bulletin, 26, pp. 452-61.

Griffiths, J. (2013) Kith: The Riddle of the Childscape. London: Hamish Hamilton.

Grujić, J., Eke, B., Cabrales, A., Cuesta, J. A. and Sánchez, A. (2012) 'Three is a crowd in iterated prisoner's dilemmas: experimental evidence on reciprocal behavior', Scientific Reports, 2, p. 638.

Guimerà, R., Díaz-Guilera, A., Vega-Redondo, F., Cabrales, A. and Arenas, À. (2002) 'Optimal network topologies for local search with congestion', Physical Review Letters, 89, 248701.

Halkier, B. (2010) Consumption Challenged: food in medialised everyday lives, Farnham: Ashgate.

Hargreaves, T. (2011) 'Practice-ing behaviour change: Applying social practice theory to pro-environmental behaviour change', Journal of Consumer Culture, 11(1) pp. 79-99.

Hattie, J. (2013) Visible learning: A synthesis of over 800 meta-analyses relating to achievement. London: Routledge.

Hausman, D.M. and McPherson, M.C. (2006) Economic Analysis, Moral Philosophy and Public Policy. Cambridge: Cambridge University Press.

Haynes, L., Service, O., Goldacre, B. and Torgerson, D. (2013) 'Test, Learn, Adapt: Developing Public Policy with Randomised Controlled Trials', Cabinet Office.

Hindess, B. (1990) 'Analyzing actors' choices', International Political Science Review, 11(1), pp. 87-97.

HMSO (1963) Traffic in Towns: a study of the long-term problems of traffic in urban areas. London: Her Majesty's Stationery Office.

Hollands, G.J., Shemilt, I., Marteau, T.M., Jebb, S.A., Kelly, M.P., Nakamura, R., Suhrcke, M. and Ogilvie, D. (2013) 'Altering micro-environments to change population health behaviour: towards an evidence base for choice architecture interventions', BMC Public Health,13, 1218.

Hume, D. (1748; 2007) An Enquiry Concerning Human Understanding, Oxford: Oxford University Press.

Irwin, N. (2014), 'Everything You Need to Know about Thomas Piketty vs. The Financial Times', The New York Times, 30 May. Available at: http://sbk.li/1213361

James, W. (1892) Psychology: The Brief Course. New York: Holt, Reinhart & Winston.

Johnson, A.M., Mercer, C.H., Erens, B., Copas, A.J., McManus, S., Wellings, K., Fenton, K.A., Korovessis, C., Macdowall, W., Nanchahal, K., Purdon, S. and Field, J. (2001) 'Sexual behaviour in Britain: partnerships, practices, and HIV risk behaviours', Lancet, 358, pp. 1835-1842.

Johnston, D.W. and Johnston, M. (2013). 'Useful theories should apply to individuals.' British Journal of Health Psychology, 18(3), 469-473.

Johnston, M. (2014) 'What are theories for? To reduce muddle, model processes and guide 'meddling''. Paper presented at UKSBM conference, Nottingham.

Jung, C. (2003) Four Archetypes: Mother, Rebirth, Spirit, Trickster. 3rd edn. London: Routledge.

Kahneman, D. (2011) Thinking, Fast and Slow. New York: Farrar, Strauss & Giroux.

Kahneman, D., Slovic P. and Tversky A. (1982) Judgment under Uncertainty: Heuristics and Biases. Cambridge: Cambridge University Press.

Kant, I. (1781/1787; 2007) The Critique of Pure Reason. Basingstoke: Palgrave/Macmillan.

Keynes, J.M. (1921) A Treatise on Probability. London: Macmillan.

Keynes, J.M. (1924) 'Alfred Marshall, 1842-1924', Economic Journal, 34(135), pp. 311-372 .

Keynes, J.M. (1936) The General Theory of Employment, Interest and Money. London: Macmillan/Royal Economic Society.

Knight, F. H. (1921) Risk, Uncertainty and Profit, Boston: Hart, Schaffner and Marx/Houghton Mifflin.

Kohn L., Corrigan J. and Donaldson M. (eds.) (1999) To Err Is Human: Building a Safer Health System, Institute of Medicine, Washington, D.C.: National Academy Press.

Kuhn, T. (1962/2012) The Structure of Scientific Revolutions. Chicago: Chicago University Press.

Loney, T. and Nagelkerke, N.J. (2014) 'The individualistic fallacy, ecological studies and instrumental variables: a causal interpretation', Emerging Themes in Epidemiology, 11(1), 18.

Lyotard, J.-F. (1984) The Post Modern Condition: A Report on Knowledge. Manchester: Manchester University Press.

McBurney, P. (2012) 'What are models for?', in Cossentino. M., Tuyls, K. and Weiss, G. (eds.) Post-Proceedings of the Ninth European Workshop on Multi-Agent Systems (EUMAS 2011). Berlin: Springer.

Mankiw, N.G. (1989) 'Real Business Cycles: A New Keynesian Perspective', Journal of Economic Perspectives, 3(3), pp. 79-90.

Mead, G.H. (1934) Mind, Self and Society: from the Standpoint of the Social Behaviorist. Chicago: Chicago University Press.

Michie, S., and Prestwich, A. (2010) 'Are interventions theory-based? Development of a theory coding scheme', Health Psychology, 29(1), 1.

Mikulincer, M. (1997) 'Adult attachment style and information processing: Individual differences in curiosity and cognitive closure', Journal of Personality and Social Psychology, 72(5), pp. 1217-1230.

Mikulincer, M. and Arad, D. (1999) 'Attachment working models and cognitive openness in close relationships: A test of chronic and temporary accessibility effects', Journal of Personality and Social Psychology, 77, pp. 710-25.

Molenaar, P.C.M. (2004) 'A manifesto on psychology as an idiographic science: Bringing the person back into scientific psychology, this time forever', Measurement: Interdisciplinary Research and Perspectives, 2(4), pp. 201-18.

Nagel, T. (1978) The Possibility of Altruism. Princeton: Princeton University Press.

Norman, D.A. and Shallice, T. (1976) 'Attention to action: Willed and automatic control of behaviour', in Shapiro, D.L. and Schwartz, G. (eds.) Consciousness and self-regulation: advances in research. New York: Plenum Press.

Omer, M., Kim, H., Sasaki, K. and K. Nishii (2010) 'A tour-based travel demand model using person trip data and its applications to advanced policies', KSCE Journal of Civil Engineering 14(2), pp. 221-30.

Packard, V. (1957) The Hidden Persuaders, London: Longman.

Peters, G.J.Y., Ruiter, R.A. and Kok, G. (2013) 'Threatening communication: a critical re-analysis and a revised meta-analytic test of fear appeal theory', Health Psychology Review, 7(sup1), S8-S31.

Pinker, S. (1998) How the Mind Works, London: Penguin.

Pinto, J.M. et al., (2014) 'Olfactory Dysfunction Predicts 5-Year Mortality in Older Adults', PLOS ONE, 9(9).

Pollock, G. B., Cabrales, A. and Rissing, S. W. (2004) 'On Suicidal punishment among "Acromyrmex Versicolor" Cofoundresses: the Disadvantage in Personal Advantage.', Evolutionary Ecology Research, 6, pp. 891-917.

Pollock, G. B., Cabrales, A., Rissing, S. W. and Binmore, K. G. (2012) 'Suicidal Punishment in the Ant Acromyrmex versicolor.' Evolutionary Ecology Research, 14, pp. 951-71.

Pradeep, B.V. (2011) 'Inspiring Sustainable Living: Unilever's 5 Levers for Change', in 'Expert Insights into Consumer Behaviour and Unilever's 5 Levers for Change'. Unilever Publication. Available at: http://sbk.li/1213391

Propp, V. (1968) Morphology of the Folk Tale. 2nd edn. Texas: University of Texas Press.

Quinn, F., Johnston, M. and Johnston, D.W. (2013) 'Testing an integrated behavioural and biomedical model of disability in N-of-1 studies with chronic pain', Psychology & Health, 28(12), 1391-1406.

Rieder, C. and Cicchetti, D. (1989) 'Organizational perspective on cognitive control functioning and cognitive-affective balance in maltreated children', Developmental Psychology, 25(3), pp. 382-93.

Rojo-Alvarez, J. L., Sánchez-Sánchez, A., Barquero-Pérez, O., Goya-Esteban, R., Everss, E., Mora-Jiménez, I. and García-Alberola, A. (2007) 'Analysis of Physiological Meaning of Detrended Fluctuation Analysis in Heart Rate Variability Using a Lumped Parameter Model', Computers in Cardiology, 34, pp. 25-28.

Rowson, J. (2001) The Seven Deadly Chess Sins. London: Gambit.

Rowson, J. (2005) Chess for Zebras. London: Gambit.

Rowson, J. (2008) From wisdom-related knowledge to wise acts: Refashioning the concept of wisdom to improve our chances of becoming wiser. Unpublished PhD Thesis. Summary available at: http://sbk.li/1213392

Rowson, J. (2011a) 'Nudge is not enough, but we knew that already', Guardian Comment is Free, 19 July. Available at: http://sbk.li/1213393

Rowson, J. (2011b) 'Transforming Behaviour Change', RSA. Available at: http://sbk.li/1213394

Rowson, J. (2013a) 'Changing Behaviour: How deep do you want to go?' The Guardian, 19 November. Available at: http://sbk.li/1213395

Rowson, J. (2014) 'Spiritualise: Revitalising Spirituality to address 21st Century Challenges', RSA. Available at: http://sbk.li/1213401

Rowson, J., Broome, S. and Jones, A. (2010) 'Connected Communities: How Social Networks Power and Sustain the Big Society', RSA. Available at: http://sbk.li/1213402

Rowson, J. and Corner, A. (2015) 'The Seven Dimensions of Climate Change: Introducing a new way to think, talk and act', RSA. Available at: http://sbk.li/1213403

Rowson, J. and Lindley, E. (2011) 'Reflexive Coppers', RSA.

Rowson, J., Mezey, M. and Dellot, B. (2012) 'Beyond the Big Society', RSA. Available at: http://sbk.li/1213404

Rowson, J. and Young, J. (2011) 'Cabbies, Costs and Climate Change', RSA. Available at: http://sbk.li/1213405

Sánchez, A., Serna, R., Catalina, F. and Afonso, C.N. (1992) 'Multifractal patterns formed by laser irradiation in GeAl thin multilayer films', Physical Review, B46 (1), pp. 487-490.

Scheffler, S. (1988) Consequentialism and its Critics. Oxford: Oxford University Press.

Schutz, A. (1953) 'Common sense and scientific interpretation of human action', Philosophy and Phenomenological Research,14, pp. 1-37.

Schutz, A. (1967) The Phenomenology of the Social World. Evanston, Ill: North Western University Press.

Shmueli, G. (2010) 'To Explain or Predict?', Statistical Science, 25(3), pp. 289-310.

Shove, E. (2010) 'Beyond ABC: climate change policy and theories of social change', Environment and Planning A, 42, pp. 1273–1285.

Shove, E., Pantzar, M. and Watson, M. (2012) The Dynamics of Social Practice. London: Sage.

Simon, H. (1957) Models of Man, New York: John Wiley.

Southerton, D., McMeekin, A. and Evans, D. (2011) International Review of Behaviour Change Initiatives. The Scottish Government. Available at: http://sbk.li/1213411

Southerton, D., Warde, A. and Hand, M. (2004) 'The limited autonomy of the consumer' in Southerton, D., Chappells, H. and Van Vliet, B. (eds,) Sustainable Consumption. Cheltenham: Edward Elgar.

Spencer, N., Rowson, J. and Bamfield L. (2014) 'Everyone Starts with an A: Applying behavioural insight to narrow the socioeconomic attainment gap in education', RSA. Available at: http://sbk.li/1213412

Sperber, D., Clement, F., Heintz, C., Mascaro, O., Mercier, H., Origgi, G., et al., (2010) 'Epistemic vigilance', Mind & Language, 25(4), pp. 359-93.

Strack F. and Deutsch R. (2004) 'Reflective and impulsive determinants of social behavior', Personality and Social Psychology Review, 8, pp. 220-47.

Strauss, A., Corbin, J., Fagerhaugh, S., Glaser, B., Maines, D., Suczec, B. and Wiener, C. (1984) Chronic Illness and the Quality of Life. 2nd edn. St Louis: Mosby.

Sutton D. and Fox J. (2003) 'The Syntax and Semantics of the PROforma guideline modelling language', Journal of the American Medical Informatics Association, 10(5) pp. 1264-1279.

Thaler, R.H. (2015), Misbehaving: the making of behavioural economics. London: Penguin

Thomson, J.M. (1969) Motorways in London. London: Duckworth.

Tuckett, D. (2011) Minding the Markets: An Emotional Finance View of Financial Instability. London: Palgrave MacMillan.

Tuckett D. (2014) 'Uncertainty, Conflict and Divided States: Some Psychological Foundations for Macroprudential Policy', Bank of England, 2 April. Available at: http://sbk.li/1213421

Tuckett, D., Boulton, M., Olson, C. and Williams, A. (1985) Meetings Between Experts: An Approach to Sharing Ideas in Medical Consultations. London: Tavistock Publications.

Tuckett, D. and Taffler, R.J. (2008) 'Phantastic Objects and the Financial Market's Sense of Reality: A Psychoanalytic Contribution to the Understanding of Stock Market Instability', International Journal of Psychoanalysis, 89, pp. 389-412.

Tuckett, D. and Taffler, R.J. (2012) Fund management: An Emotional Finance Perspective, New York: Research Foundation of the CFA Institute.

Urry, J. (2007) Mobilities. Cambridge: Polity Press.

Vincent C., Neale G. and Woloshynowych M. (2001) 'Adverse events in British hospitals: preliminary retrospective record review', British Medical Journal, 322, pp. 517.

Warde, A. (2005) 'Consumption and theories of practice', Journal of Consumer Culture, 5(2), pp. 131-53.

Weisbord, M.R. (1991) Productive Workplaces. San Francisco: Jossey-Bass, pp. 70-87.

Welch, D. and Warde, A. (2015) 'Theories of Practice and Sustainable Consumption', in Reisch, L. and Thøgersen, J. (eds.) Handbook of Research on Sustainable Consumption. Cheltenham: Edward Elgar.

Wilson, D.S. (1976) 'Evolution on the level of communities', Science, 192(4246), pp. 1358-1360.

Wilson, D. and Sperber, D. (2012) Meaning and relevance. Cambridge: Cambridge University Press.

Zamir, E. and Medina, B. (2010) Law, Economics and Morality. Oxford: Oxford University Press, 2010, p. 104.

Zunshine, L. (2006) Why We Read Fiction: Theory of Mind and the Novel. Columbus OH: Ohio State University Press.